The World War One Diary and Art of
Doughboy Cpl Harold W Pierce

The World War One Diary and Art of Doughboy Cpl Harold W Pierce

Duty, Terror and Survival

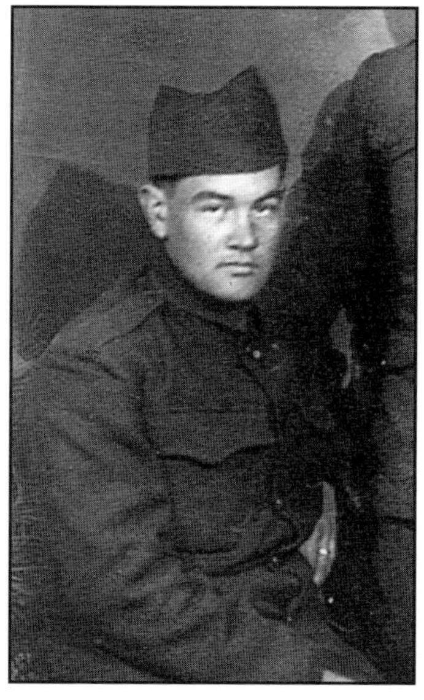

Edited by William J. Welch

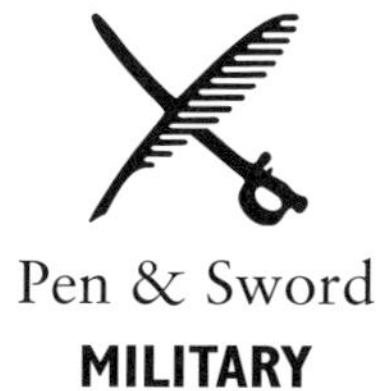

Pen & Sword
MILITARY

First published in Great Britain in 2024 by
Pen & Sword Military
An imprint of Pen & Sword Books Limited
Yorkshire – Philadelphia

Copyright © William J Welch 2024

ISBN 978 1 39905 548 2

The right of William J Welch to be identified as
Editor of this Work has been asserted by him in accordance
with the Copyright, Designs and Patents Act 1988.

A CIP catalogue record for this book is
available from the British Library

Typeset by Mac Style
Printed in the UK by CPI Group (UK) Ltd, Croydon, CR0 4YY.

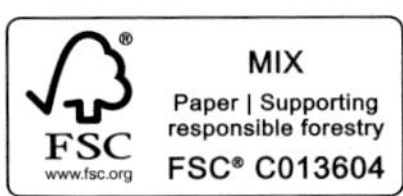

Pen & Sword Books Limited incorporates the imprints of After the Battle,
Atlas, Archaeology, Aviation, Discovery, Family History, Fiction, History,
Maritime, Military, Military Classics, Politics, Select, Transport, True Crime,
Air World, Frontline Publishing, Leo Cooper, Remember When, Seaforth
Publishing, The Praetorian Press, Wharncliffe Local History, Wharncliffe
Transport, Wharncliffe True Crime and White Owl.

For a complete list of Pen & Sword titles please contact

PEN & SWORD BOOKS LIMITED
47 Church Street, Barnsley, South Yorkshire, S70 2AS, England
E-mail: enquiries@pen-and-sword.co.uk
Website: www.pen-and-sword.co.uk
or
PEN AND SWORD BOOKS
1950 Lawrence Rd, Havertown, PA 19083, USA
E-mail: uspen-and-sword@casematepublishers.com
Website: www.penandswordbooks.com

The front cover is from part of a painting by Harold W. Pierce, the author of this diary.
The back cover is also of a painting by Pierce. Each was displayed for decades at the Corry,
Pennsylvania, Archie Thompson Post 264. The post donated the paintings to the Erie County
(Pennsylvania) Historical Society, which approved their use for this volume.
Front and back covers designed by William J. Welch.

Contents

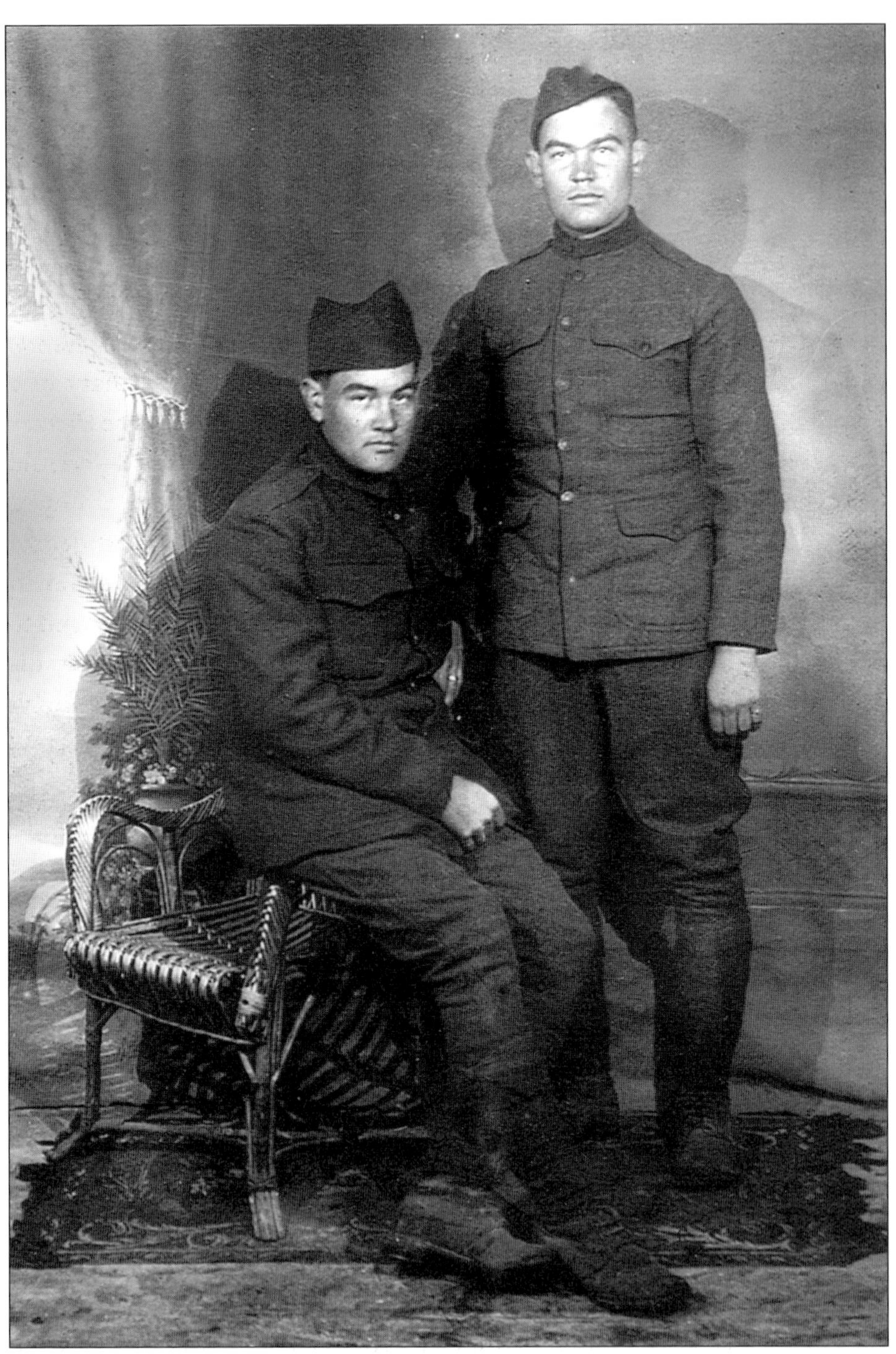

Brothers Harold (sitting) and Hugh Pierce.

Foreword

More than 60 years after World War One, the diary of one of America's 4 million doughboys surfaced in *The Titusville Herald* in Crawford County, Pennsylvania. Published as "Diary of a Doughboy," for two months the serialized entries of Harold Wayne Pierce's journal enthralled readers, who saw him transformed from an 18-year-old boy who dutifully left high school to enlist in the local National Guard unit into a 20-year-old veteran who had gone through the darkest depths of fear and had seen the unspeakable harm that modern weapons could do to a person. They read as he grappled with that terror and still managed to do his duty – sometimes reluctantly. They saw how he was sustained by his faith, thoughts of his mother, the comradeship of his older brother, Hugh L. Pierce, and the other men in his unit. Somehow, he survived many close calls. Very close calls.

Harold Pierce wrote it all down, covering from April 1917 to November 12, 1918, the day after Armistice. Through it all, he carried a small leatherbound journal in his pocket. It was about the same size as the canvas-covered New Testament he also carried. In handwriting so small it was barely legible decades later to his daughter, Brenda Pierce Simpson, he chronicled his experiences. He went on to keep a diary the rest of his life. Brenda has them all.

At some point, Harold Pierce typed up his wartime diary – all 78,000 words – and his younger brother, G. Reid Pierce, submitted it to *The Titusville Herald*. On October 1, 1979, the first installment appeared on page 3, with older brother Hugh L. Pierce mistakenly getting the byline. The newspaper corrected that October 5. Through October, November and until December 29, the *Herald* printed installments most days of the week, likely as space allowed. Reader reaction was enthusiastic. James B. Stevenson, publisher of the *Herald*, wrote then that "this was one of the most popular features we ever published." Copies went like hotcakes, he said.

Reid Pierce also sent copies of the diary to various historical societies and museums, among them the Pennsylvania Military Museum at Boalsburg, Pennsylvania, and the U.S. Army Center for Military History at Carlisle, Pennsylvania. Over the years it caught the eye of researchers and military historians, who cited it in their works. Among them was Edward Lengel, who wrote *To Conquer Hell: The Meuse-Argonne, 1918* and *Thunder and Flames: Americans in the Crucible of Combat, 1917-1918*. Daniel Keifer saw the diary while an intern at the Pennsylvania Military Museum and wrote a paper on it for *Pennsylvania History: A Journal of Mid-Atlantic Studies*. What Lengel, Keifer and others, including myself, found was a journal that expressed the honest thoughts – and emotions – of a young man at war. We don't see him charge a machine gun nest or bayonet a fearsome German soldier. We don't see him flee either. We do see him cope with not only fear but also with forced marches through cold, rainy nights, with intense hunger, the never-ending itch of lice, or "cooties," more hunger, then dysentery, utter exhaustion, frustration with Army ways, admiration for some leaders, and much more. Through it all, he does his duty the best he can. As he says, "Discipline conquers fear." His descriptions of events are clear, detailed and insightful. How did someone who described himself as a bad student and who was so young produce this? The question arises: Did Pierce add to or modify the diary after his initial entries? That might account for the insights that seem so mature for a 19- or 20-year-old. But his daughter Brenda does not think that happened. "My father's intent in sharing his diary was to depict the feelings of a soldier who had actually experienced the horrors of WWI. He studied the Civil War and preferred reading accounts of battles written by actual participants, not historians," she explained to me.

In transcribing the diary, I nearly always stayed true to Pierce's words. Sometimes the punctuation, especially the use of commas, could be vexing. Where absolutely needed, I inserted commas or occasionally took them away. I corrected the spelling of some places and some soldiers. I likely missed some, though. I left untouched his spelling for "sargeant" and "cigarets."

Harold Wayne Pierce was born September 24, 1898, at Butchers Mills, Forest County, the son of Edith Oviatt Pierce and Levi Jackson Pierce. His father was a logging camp contractor and his mother a cook at the camps. Levi's was a job that required moving from place to place. At Edith's insistence, the family moved to Youngsville in Warren County and made that their permanent home. Harold was the third of their four sons. Lewis was born in 1894 and died in 1903; Hugh was born in 1895; G. Reid in 1901. While Harold enlisted in April 1917, Hugh, who worked as a printer for W.F. Clinger in Tidioute, enlisted in the same unit that September, just in time to join A Company at Camp Hancock, Georgia.

Harold Pierce enlisted in A Company of the 16th Pennsylvania Regiment on April 21, 1917. Once at Camp Hancock, the 16th merged with the 8th Pennsylvania to become the 112th Infantry Regiment, 28th Division. During training, Pierce became a scout for the regiment's First Battalion. This may be in part due to his drawing abilities. You'll read of several occasions when he was detailed to draw maps. His daughter said he kept some of them. And we know from the artistic works he produced after the war that he did, indeed, have artistic abilities. Five of his oil paintings and a pen-and-ink drawing are included in this book.

I took advantage of owning a copy of *The Twenty-Eighth Division: Pennsylvania's Guard in the World War, Vol. III* to look up photographs of the men Pierce mentioned in his diary. I couldn't find all of them, but tried to use as many as I could. That book was also useful, along with access to Ancestry.com, to check the spelling of the soldiers' names. I corrected the spelling when I was reasonably certain it was needed.

William J. Welch

Chapter 1

Choice is Made

April 6, 1917. I am a junior in high school, a student but in name only for I have not been a very good one. There has been plenty to distract my attentions from my studies, most of which I hate anyhow. Last summer the Mexican Border trouble and the National Guard was off to the border. It was too much for me to lie my age from seventeen to twenty-one so I did not go. There are plenty of rumors of war with Germany and today it looks like the real thing. I am now eighteen, big for my age and feel like a man, but the enlistment age is still twenty-one. I know I will not get my mother's consent so if I go I will have to lie my age. My problem now is to decide whether I will tell a lie or stay at home and feel like a slacker. My school work is a failure and I have no other trade so I may as well be a soldier.

School is out and I am off in the general direction of home, after having to stay after school as I usually did. A recruiting officer from "A" Company, 16th Pennsylvania Infantry of Corry meets me. He has talked to me of enlisting before and I have put him off. Today, when he asks me again I say, "Well if the U.S. declares war I will enlist." "Well, you're just in time," he answered, "for the U.S. declared war this morning." Expecting the news as I have, still it is a great shock. War at last and I said I wanted to go. The truth is I don't want war and I hate to go to it. I am young and I do not want to sacrifice my life. Eighteen has plenty ahead and little behind. I make excuses to the officer and manage to get away even if it does look as if I am backing down.

April 21. I have thought it over for fifteen days and today I have decided to go. Mother has refused to sign the enlistment papers. My arguments were of no avail. It has been a trying time for both of us. I am certain I should go. But I hate to kill and I hate to be killed. Could I shoot a man or run a long bayonet in him and hear his screams? Could I go where some man could do the same to me? But I feel I must. I have talked it over with relatives and friends and they laughed at me. "They don't want children, they want men," they said. But many boys of my age have enlisted, Martin and Alton Henning, John and Stuart Aberg, Percy Beebe, Jerry McKinney, Herman Mouer, Bill Lyons, Clyde Martin and Haley Munson, all of my age or younger. The last straw was when Ray Wingard and Davey Lett signed up and Davey only sixteen: If Davey, one of my best friends, can do it, I can.

Sgt. Dean Hyde and Martin Henning have me cornered in a hotel with the enlistment papers and I sign them. I am relieved of one worry at least, they have reduced the age limit to eighteen so I do not have to lie my age. My next worry is to tell my mother. I hesitate a day or so, though she suspects, I am sure, but finally I break the news to her. Instead of an outburst she said quietly, "Well alright, if you are determined to go I won't try to stop you."

No one in our home town takes us seriously, pitied a little, scoffed at by older men who have not enlisted, envied perhaps. Some say we should be playing with the other children. A little hero worship by the girls but not as much as I supposed should come to brave soldiers. They can't imagine gawky, bashful schoolkids as fighting men ready to do or die. The Old Civil War Vets are encouraging and remind us that they were our age when they enlisted.

CALLED INTO SERVICE

July 15. The National Guard in Pennsylvania has been marking time since the declaration of war. The time has been spent in recruiting the companies to one hundred and fifty men. We have drilled twice a week at least, attended a few patriotic meetings and listened to a lot of patriotism by people who were not going to war. "Boy Scouts" and "Tin Soldiers" were common utterances in our presence. No one can understand how a bunch of kids just out of short pants can be soldiers.

Now the big day has arrived when we will leave home. About twenty of us boys from Youngsville are to report at the Corry Armory today. The ladies of the town have presented us all with toilet kits. We line up in front of the Odd Fellows Building for a picture in uniform. While the pictures are taken I feel dizzy. Next an embarrassing few minutes when we are pawed over by friends and relatives. A big neighbor woman cries on

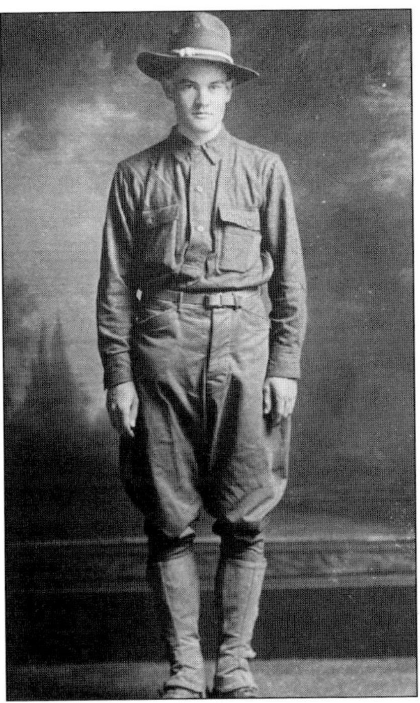

Newly recruited Harold Pierce.

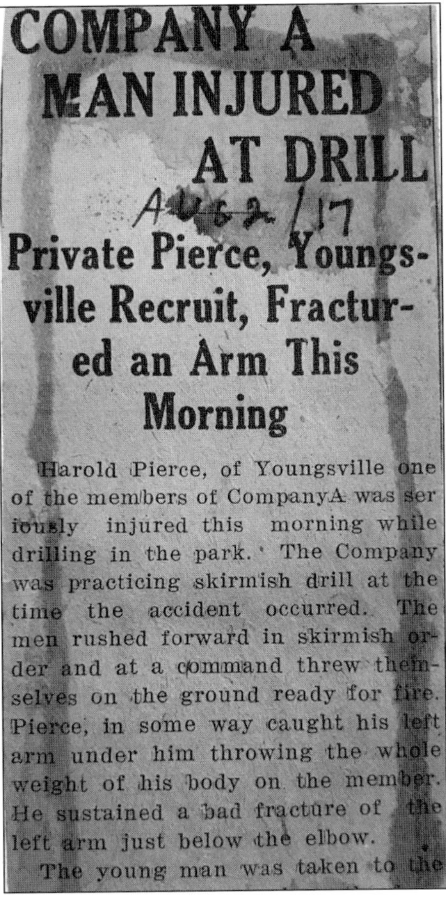

COMPANY A MAN INJURED AT DRILL

Private Pierce, Youngsville Recruit, Fractured an Arm This Morning

Harold Pierce, of Youngsville one of the members of Company A was seriously injured this morning while drilling in the park. The Company was practicing skirmish drill at the time the accident occurred. The men rushed forward in skirmish order and at a command threw themselves on the ground ready for fire. Pierce, in some way caught his left arm under him throwing the whole weight of his body on the member. He sustained a bad fracture of the left arm just below the elbow.

The young man was taken to the

Pierce's injury made headlines in his hometown newspaper, the Corry Journal.

my shirt and I wish she would go away. Mother does not cry, rather she is smiling cheerfully. I notice that most of the crying comes from those whose boys are not going. Our mothers are braver.

We march by twos to the railroad station and fall out. The band does not play "Tenting Tonight" as they did when the boys went to the border. Today they play more stirring music. I bid goodbye to my friends with tears in my eyes. But when I am back with mother she kids me and soon I am grinning again. The train pulls in, a last kiss to mother and a handshake with my brothers and I am aboard. A feeling of lonesomeness comes over me and I can hardly keep back the tears. But it is soon over and we are as cheerful as any kids can be off to war.

Six weeks at the armory at Corry, learning the rudiments of soldiery and anxiously waiting to be sent to a big camp somewhere. Drills, inspections, parades, and physical examinations. The doctor says I am a well set up lad and I pass easily. A few fail and leave sadly. My first wound is a broken wrist, sustained during extended order drill. In early September, my brother Hugh enlists with us.

In early September we leave for Camp Hancock in Georgia. Large crowds are at the station to see us off. Mothers and sweethearts cry again. Not a cheerful prospect. The band plays "Farewell to Thee" as we board the

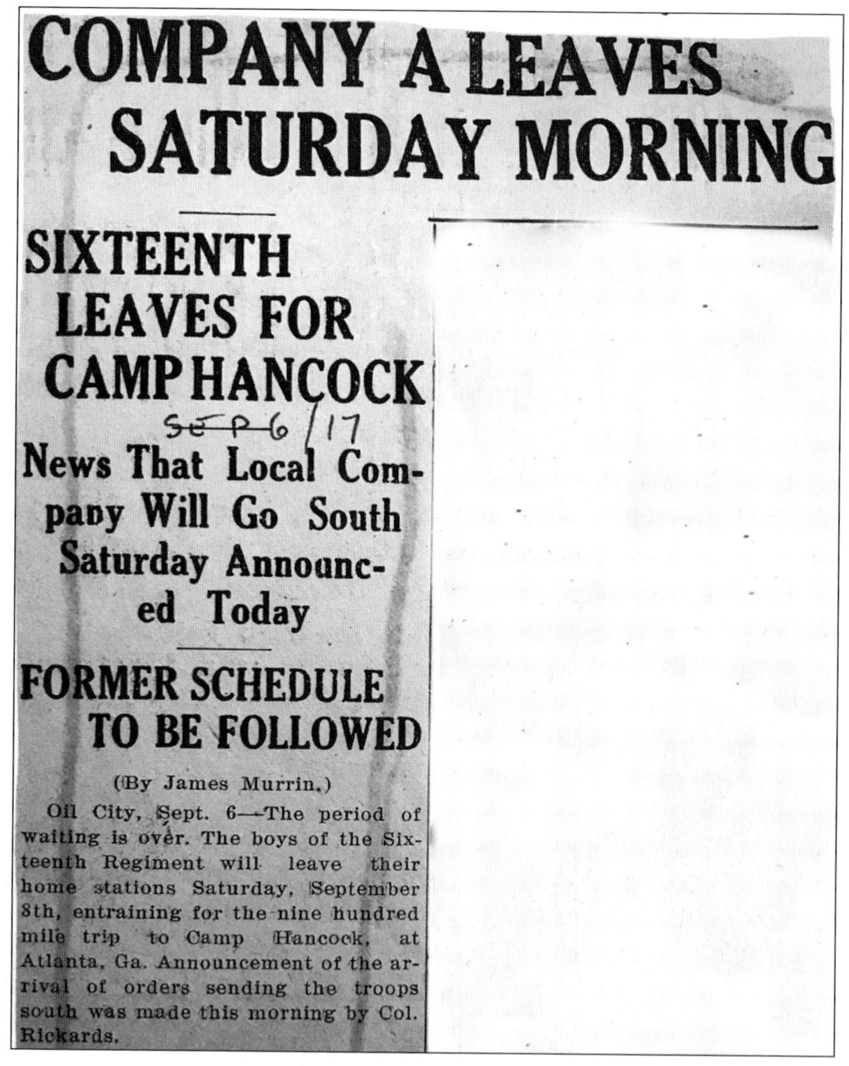

COMPANY A LEAVES SATURDAY MORNING

SIXTEENTH LEAVES FOR CAMP HANCOCK

SEP 6/17

News That Local Company Will Go South Saturday Announced Today

FORMER SCHEDULE TO BE FOLLOWED

(By James Murrin.)

Oil City, Sept. 6—The period of waiting is over. The boys of the Sixteenth Regiment will leave their home stations Saturday, September 8th, entraining for the nine hundred mile trip to Camp Hancock, at Atlanta, Ga. Announcement of the arrival of orders sending the troops south was made this morning by Col. Rickards.

The Corry Journal, the daily paper at Corry, Pennsylvania, which was home to "A" Company, carried many stories reporting on the progress of the local "boys" from the area. (*Courtesy of Corry Area Historical Society*)

train and then there is a flood. Our relatives are not there so my brother and I escape that. I wish some girls would kiss me goodbye. The troop train passes swiftly through Youngsville, but I have a last glimpse of mother and kid brother on the station platform. At Warren the train takes on "I" Company. Kathryn Gallup and Vivian Dunham are there and I am the hero. My uncle is also there to bid us goodbye. We are on the road two days and nights in day coaches and the third night we arrive in Augusta, Georgia. We hike to camp two miles from the station and sleep at night on the mess hall floors and on the sands outside. The next day we start making our camp.

GEORGIA

Eight months of hard, stiff training makes men of boys. We drill eight hours a day and the rest of the time spent in necessary work. We sleep sound, in bed before ten o'clock, too tired to wait for Taps. The southern sands are blistering hot in September and biting cold in winter. We have little fuel for the Sibley stoves and they are issued weeks after we have suffered more with the cold than we ever did up North. The camp food is good and is better as the camp grows older. Again, drills, long hikes, maneuvers, parades, bayonet exercises, calisthenics to harden us and make us good man killers and good bullet stoppers.

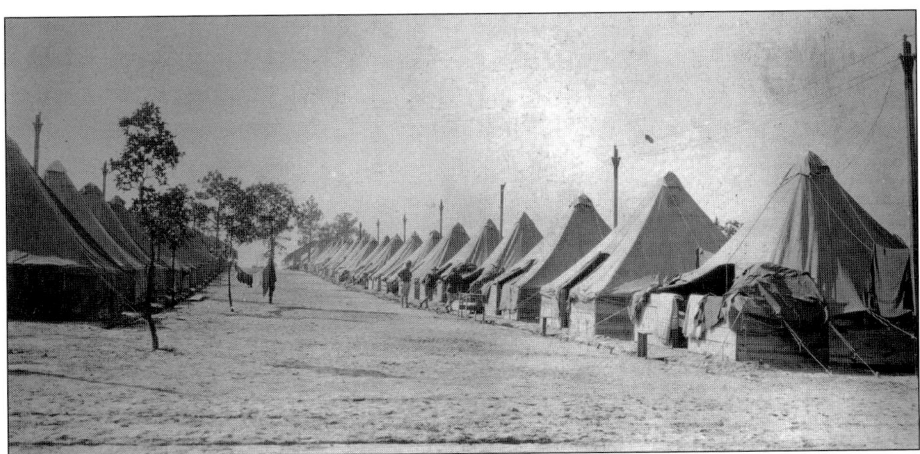

A street of tents at Camp Hancock, Georgia, during the time the 28th Division trained there. This photo was taken by Pvt. Henry Vogt of Company G. (*Courtesy of Elaine Ruggiero*)

Early in the fall the old 16th and 8th Pennsylvania Regiments combine. "A" of the 16th and "A" of the 8th from York form the new war strength company of two hundred and fifty men. Our new designation is "A" Company, 112th Infantry, 56th Brigade, 28th Division. The entire division has been reorganized also. The 109th and 110th Infantries are the 55th Brigade, the 111th and 112th Infantry Regiments, the 56th Brigade. The 107th, 108th and 109th Machine Gun Battalions, with other smaller units, all making up the 28th Division from the Old Pennsylvania National Guard.

My wrist heals early and a few weeks later in the fall I spend two weeks in the Base Hospital with Chronic Appendicitis. Soon after my release from the hospital I am attached to the 1st Battalion Headquarters. Our training is under Lieut. Fenno, Regimental Intelligence Officer, Lieut. Akerly, 2nd Battalion Scout Officer, and Lieut. Abel, 3rd Battalion Scout Officer. Sgt. O'Connor, Cpl. Mars and Cpl. Mayer are our first non-commissioned officers but later I was made a corporal together with many other sargeants and corporals. Burt Oudett and I are the first Scouts from "A" Company.

Our training is the regular training of an infantryman plus day and night patrols, map-making and reading, estimating distances, signaling, landscape sketching, observation, messages and many other subjects.

In April 1918 the 28th Division, having completed training, moved to Camp Upton, Long Island, preparatory to going across. We wait there five days to be fully fitted according to War Department ideas, which meant being weighted down with every possible device they could pile or hook onto a man. The two hundred and twenty rounds of ammunition and the rifle and bayonet would be enough without the helmet, pack with two blankets, shelter half, tent poles and pins, extra shoes, extra socks, extra shirt, mess pan, knives, forks and spoons, underwear, canteen and then personal belongings. Now in front they give us a gas mask. I cannot see how a man can move, much less fight in all the junk we have.

May 6. Entrain for New York, and in New York we take a ferry down the river.

It is a great trip, for most of the Pennsylvania men from my section have never been in New York before. We embark on the Aquitania, one of the largest vessels afloat. The bunks are in tiers in the different staterooms.

With all the men assigned to a room packed in there is no room for anyone unless the men are all in their bunks. We go to bed at night expecting to be far at sea by morning and the Great Adventure just beginning.

AT SEA

May 7. Awoke expecting to be seasick or at least to feel the motion of the boat on the water. I think this boat must ride smooth and peek out of porthole to get my first glimpse of the mighty ocean but there is the same New York we saw last night. But early in the forenoon the boat swings away from the dock, with us ordered below decks and all we could see of the bay and town was a few glimpses through the portholes. I did see the Statue of Liberty and then we were headed for the mighty ocean, the big fight in France or wherever we were going. It is a big undertaking, the ocean is dangerous, lurking with submarines and beyond the ocean, if safely cross, lies nothing but death or horrible wounds for most of us. Yet we are cheerful.

The trip over was uneventful except for lifeboat drills, band concerts, entertainments and arguments with the English cooks. This boat has no escort but is armed with six long naval guns with English gunners. The only sub scare was when the gunners dropped a target and began firing and of course everyone thought it was a submarine.

Three days from England we were met by six destroyers who escorted us the rest of the trip. In the submarine zone, scouts were detailed on the submarine watch. We were on duty from the first hint of daybreak till after dark, working reliefs of a half hour. The second day of our watch was stormy and the boat rolled. My stomach had also been doing a little rolling. At five-thirty it was my turn to go and eat. On the next deck below, I made the rail just in time and vomited the easiest I ever did in my life. Then I felt O.K. and went down and ate a hot supper of fish and biscuits.

ENGLAND

May 14. Land is sighted and we learn that it is the shores of England. We dock and walk down the gangplank about one thirty and then learn that we are in Liverpool. On the dock we wait for hours. At last a dinky little engine ran up a long string of little cars. We load into these cars, a squad to a compartment and then lay bets that the little engine won't pull all these cars. But the thing started so quick and went so fast we worried for fear it would wreck. We passed through Crewe and Rugby, towns I had read about in English history. Most of the night we spent in that compartment.

May 15. Before daylight the train halts and we unload and march away in the dim light to some old stone buildings overlooking the sea in Folkestone. The barracks are old stone hotels evidently. We sleep for an hour or so on the hard stone floors and then are up looking around. We are on a cliff above a beach, overlooking the ocean, a beautiful spot. Breakfast was English oatmeal, very tasty but not enough of it.

English soldiers visit us, mostly older men that talked continuously of the Boer war and the late war. Some showed their scars and immediately launched into tales of their prowess in battle. We believed all they said till they began laying it on too thick. Maybe they were old veterans but I had the idea that real veterans had little to say about the war.

We had hopes of remaining indefinitely, but all hopes were dashed when we had the order to roll packs. About two p.m. we lined up, scarcely able to stand under those packs. As it was, standing at attention we had to lean forward like a pack peddler or the pack would throw us.

A Canadian band lead us to the railroad station playing "Over There." Their music is slower than ours and it took a long time to accustom our feet to their step. When we did it was much easier than the fast step the Americans used. English and Scotch soldiers eyed us curiously and made fun of our packs. Loaded down as we were no one could have licked even an Englishman and besides I would rather fight the ones responsible for this pack.

The Troop Train gave us relief from the packs and we spent the afternoon in a pleasant ride through beautiful English farming country. We reached Dover, England and marched through the narrowest and crookedest streets in the world at the base of the chalk cliffs, cheered and ragged by some of the worst looking people I ever saw. We billeted in an old factory with a nice wooden floor for a bed.

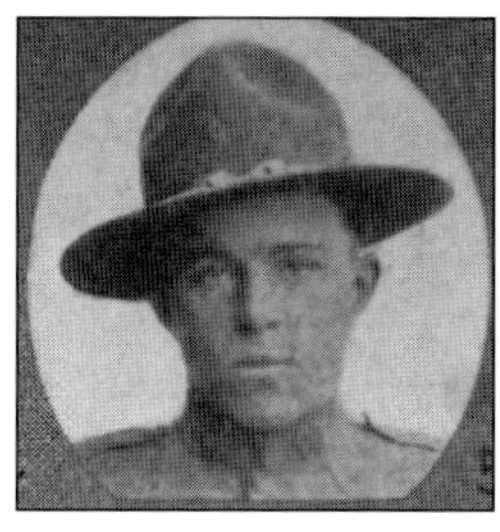

Sgt. Percy LaPaze.

Supper was English rations, bread, jam and tea. An English sargeant started ordering us around but Sgt. LaPaze soon put a stop to that. He told the Englishmen that we had licked England twice and he guessed we could do it again. No wonder he wanted to fight after eating their rations.

My brother and I walk to the top of the cliffs of Dover and there found the most beautiful scenery in strange contrast to the city below the cliffs. English soldiers and W.A.A.C.s were scattered around the scenery in various places and attitudes, affording plenty of chances to gossip and apparently not caring a lot. A gentlemanly old English sea Captain explained the work of the English cruiser Vindictive in its raids on Ostend and Zeebrugge on the Belgian Coast. He pointed out a new type Monitor in the harbor with two fifteen-inch guns, used for close work along the coast. There were many types of warships in the harbor.

May 16. Early in the morning we hike to the docks and embark on a small channel steamer. All were required to wear life preservers. They were also wet, which started the rumor that on the last trip this boat was torpedoed by a submarine. But after a long time someone reasoned that if the boat was torpedoed how did it happen to be taking us across instead of resting on the bottom of the English Channel. The trip across was choppy, only a few hours, and we sighted the shores of France. At last on French soil.

CALAIS

My first thoughts of France are not much. It is a terribly hot day and the sun beats down on us unmercifully, toting those packs to a rest camp two miles away. Then more hours of waiting and assigned to tents. Sixteen men to a round conical tent, smaller even than our eight-man squad tents. The floors are about two feet underground to afford some protection against air bombs. By all sleeping feet first to the pole we can sleep inside but all must turn at the same time.

Sanitary conditions were terrible with swarms of flies everywhere. The latrines were large containers in the middle of the camp, which were filled and spilled over. Chinese coolies were supposed to empty them but never seemed to. We cannot help a feeling of disgust and hope we are not going to stay long.

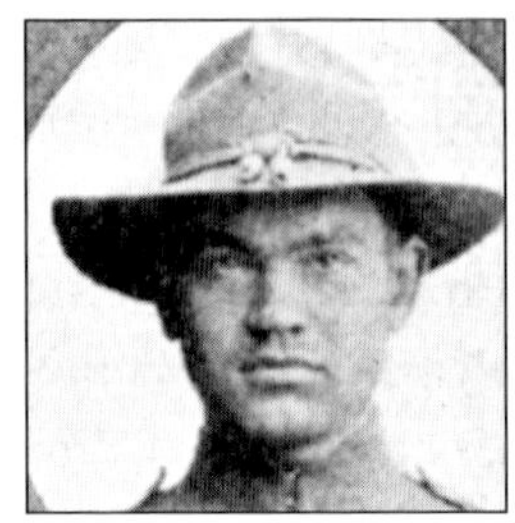
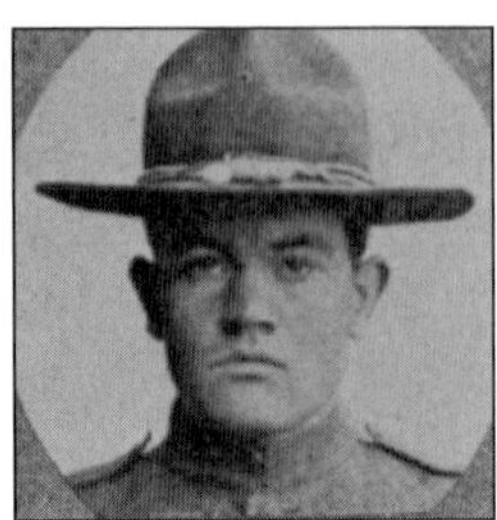

Pvt. Hugh Pierce.   Cpl. Harold Pierce.

Late in the afternoon we are issued red slips of paper to be turned in for a meal. This was to show the American government we had actually received the meal so that England could collect the money for our rations. We lined up and waited for hours. In my line the mess ran out and we had to wait till they cooked another. When we did receive it, it was the worst looking goo I ever tried to eat, mostly fat, greasy half cooked meat with greasy potatoes. I thought our company cooks were bad but they never could cook anything as bad as that. During the cooking of the meal the English cooks were entertained by, "Well, we licked you twice, I guess we could do it again." At night I tried to sleep inside the tent but it was no go. Freeman and I sleep on the sandy ground outside where we can have a little comfort. A day of disorder and turmoil, hungry, dirty and disgusted with France, England and everything else and only our first day.

May 17. English soldiers are on guard outside to keep us in. Naturally the Americans want out and the arguments with our allies are worse than before. The English of course had to be reminded again that our forefathers licked them twice and we guessed we could do it again. They must think we are a poor lot. Most of the arguments were our fault. One should expect peace and harmony with our allies but it seems as if the first we want to fight are the English.

May 18. We turn in a lot of extra equipment, which we are glad to get rid of. Anything to make that pack lighter yet they are still heavy enough to discourage a mule. We made one good swap today, our heavy Eddystone rifle for the light English rifle. We lose several pounds both in the gun and the ammunition.

At night Freeman and I sleep outside the tent again. Our rifles are stacked in regulation stacks outside each tent. A man comes crawling on hands and knees and stops by our stack. He has been in Calais city and vin blanc and conyac has taken its toll. Through the blur he makes out the stack of rifles and decides that must be his tent. He tries to crawl through an opening but his shoulders stop him. Puzzled, he backs out and looks at it like a puppy who can't get in a rat hole. Another hole is too small for him, so he tries another and another, circling the stack continually with no success. A friend of his grabs him and he tries to stand erect, saluting and yes-sirring at every word. The friend kicks him away from the stack but he is soon back. He gazes at us in a dumb puzzled way, wondering how that tent shrunk so much.

After the drunken man had left, the camp settles down and quiet reigned and we dozed off. Awakened by a blast from the forts near us. Through the air we hear a low zooming noise, rising and falling on the air, as German planes fly over to bomb Calais. Searchlights played long streaks of light across the sky and anti-aircraft guns open up. The guns on the fort near us flash and crackle. High in the air flashes on fire as the anti-aircraft burst like sky rockets. We all crowd into the tents and lie on the floor, hoping for a little protection in these holes. Possibly the Germans have heard we just landed and are starting us off right. The racket keeps up as the planes fly over the city. Then a different noise, a rumbling sound in the town, not the crack of guns, but bombs exploding in the city. More planes circle and drop their loads of destruction. Apparently we are going to be passed up tonight and we breathe easier as the zooming noise dies down and the planes leave for Germany again. The gun fire slackens and dies, the searchlights stop searching the skies, quiet settles down and our first air raid is over. I lie on my back in the tent thinking queer, unquiet thoughts. Lying in a hole expecting a big bird to fly over and drop a charge of high explosive on you is not nice.

WITH THE ENGLISH

May 19. About eight a.m. we fall in with heavy marching order and hike through Calais to a railroad station. We don't know where we're going but we're on our way and any place is better than that rest camp. We have not gotten our land legs yet entirely and though the hike is only two miles, with pack and all I am tired out when we arrive. There, a clean looking YMCA outfit gave us a good lunch or we would not have eaten this morning.

A number of English soldiers were at the railroad station, all wounded veterans just recovered and returning to the front. From their speech and actions they don't want to go back. These men were different than the ones we had argued with before. They were quiet reserved men and much easier to agree with. We did not remind them that our forefathers had licked England twice, rather we assumed the air of respect a veteran is entitled to from a recruit. I began to feel more respect for the English people and ashamed of our actions, for truthfully some of our men had been quarrelsome. I felt more respect for them as ambulances driven by tired looking English girls drove by loaded down with other wounded soldiers for the base hospitals in Calais.

A train of small box cars labeled 40 Hommes and 8 Chevaux backed into the station. And a Homme is a man and a Chevaux is a horse. After the forty are inside there is little chance for observation even if the side doors are all open. It is a warm, sunny, beautiful day. The train wanders slowly through a peaceful countryside with no signs of war except occasionally a few English soldiers. We pass through the city of St. Omer and on to a small town called Lumbres. Near Lumbres we see three airplanes, so high they are mere specks. Little white puffs of smoke appear silently beside them. I have been told the English anti-aircraft shells are white smoke and the Germans black so these planes must be German. We expect these planes to wheel and bomb us but evidently that is not their mission for they continue on their way.

We detrain near Lumbres in the afternoon and there the regiment splits and marches away to billets in several small towns in the vicinity. "A" Company, after an hour's march, is in Waterdahl, a village of only a few houses. Some are billeted in the barn but my platoon pitches pup tents in the orchard and in this summer weather the orchard is the best. It is much better and cleaner than the rest camp at Calais although there is little rest at either place.

May 20 to June 8. We trained at Waterdahl. There it was drills and hikes, bayonet practice and lectures under British and Scotch instructors. We find some of them very likeable men although they are not much impressed with us. According to them our discipline is rotten. They cannot understand why our officers are so friendly to the men. Once the battalion was inspected by an English staff officer and he said, "Very, very unsatisfactory." Others said it would take the entire British army to carry back the casualties after the American army went to the front. These remarks the Americans take good naturedly for we don't have such a high regard for British ideas of discipline.

We spent two days on an English rifle range firing the Enfields. The British tried to show us how to fire a rifle. It's a wonder some of the instructors were not shot for all the arguments we had with them. Yet, with it all, the English said it was the best exhibition of rifle shooting they ever saw.

Our rations were English supervised by the Scotch. Corn willie, bread, hardtack like concrete, cheese, jam, butter, Machonichies[1] ration, boiled beef and slum mostly. All but the slum and beef was issued at night to a squad and the squad leader divided each man his share. A man could easily eat his entire day's ration in one meal. The hard tack is like stone and soon all the fillings in my teeth are gone. The Machonichies ration is a Scotchman's idea of canned slum and meager as the Scotch would have it. We are hungry from the first day to the last.

One night the Jerries raid St. Omer. Though the city is several miles away we can hear the planes in the air, the flash and rumble of the anti-aircraft and the bombs. One plane swoops low over our orchard but drops no bombs. Sometimes at night we can hear the rumble of the guns and see the heat lightning on the front. It is distant but ominous, a growling, dread, discouraging sound.

The Tommies inform us that the war is not going well for the Allies. The Germans have been pushing the English back since March and now they have the French on the run beyond the Marne. Nobody knows where the next blow will be struck but when it does come it will be a hard one. They think we won't be much help against a trained German army.

The English are a discouraged lot. Not a few have asked us sullenly what we ever entered the war for anyhow. Germany had them licked

---

1. Machonichies was a stew of various vegetables and beef with a thin broth. Slum was a stew of beef, onions and tomatoes. Corn willie was a hash of beef and potatoes.

and if we had stayed out the Allies would have made peace by now and they would all be home. One man said it would not be any worse with the Germans in command. I met an English lad who jumped off an English Troop train and the train pulled out before he could get back on. His punishment would be spread-eagled, which meant being tied to a wheel with arms and legs stretched out and remain there all day. After that I decided we had a fairly good army after all.

June 8. We know that we are moving but of course we don't know where and it makes little difference, but likely to some new training area. We have had a year's training but still feel like recruits especially since the unfavorable thing the English say about us. We expect to spend months more in training before we go to the lines and I hope they put that off a long time. The Tommies' idea of the front is not encouraging. But tonight at Waterdahl the war seems far removed, except for that heat lightning and a few dull thuds from the line still many miles away.

June 9. We roll packs, receive a bacon sandwich for lunch, and fall in. The whole regiment is in line, marching by platoons with a goodly distance between them and connecting files between the different units. With the heavy woolen underwear, woolen shirt, woolen trousers and puttees, heavy blouse and a sixty-pound pack, rifle, tin hat, raincoat, two hundred rounds of ammunition, extra shoes, socks, tent poles and pins and a lot of other junk a kind government hung on me. The heat is fearful. But uncomfortable as I am, I am much better off than Percy Beebe, who has all this junk to carry and a big red carbuncle on his neck. I sympathize with him yet I can scarcely restrain a smile at his woebegone look. He tries to keep up but after several miles, loses ground and has to be carried in a truck.

The day wears on and the weariness grows worse. Legs are tired and the shoulders ache from that heavy pack. We move with that automatic movement of tired marching men. The sweat pours off my forehead and a steady stream runs off my nose. I crave water but experience has shown that it is not good to drink the lukewarm water in my canteen on a hike. Better wait till we stop tonight. The ranks that were gay in the morning are silent now. A short halt at noon to eat the bacon sandwich, lingering over each bite to get the most from each morsel. Then all afternoon in the dust and heat again. At last about dusk we halt in a small town. A long wait for billets and at least a meal. Eighteen kilometers since morning makes an appetite that can even eat English hardtack. But tired as we were it did not prevent someone from stealing some Frenchman's wine. There was an investigation but all were innocent and the wine was not returned.

June 10. The hike is resumed early in the morning. Another day on the road: trudging from morning till night. Passed through a town called Fruges, an American Army Headquarters. Saw a woman blowing a fish horn at a railroad station to warn of the approach of a train. We repeated the bacon sandwich when we rested at noon. We boiled under the packs and our heavy clothing. Late afternoon found us tired, hungry and footsore when we finally turned into a green field and halt and pitch pup tents.

We have foot inspection but it won't matter how many blisters we have, nothing will be done about it and we will still hike tomorrow, blisters or not. Maybe the officers will get a little encouragement when they see we have bigger blisters than they. The grass is cool and soft on the bare feet and we relax, glad to be rid of that pack. We sleep on the ground rolled in blankets and asleep not long after dark. We have hiked further today than yesterday.

June 11. The hike is easier today, starting later and resting often, and now at 2:00 p.m. we move into a large open field bordered by a winding stream under large cool willow trees. An ideal place to camp. We pitch pup tents near the stream and prepare for the night. The cooks prepare a good supper.

ON TO PARIS

June 12. Our packs still contain all the junk the government has given us. We are still good soldiers and afraid we will be court-martialed, sent to jail, beheaded or something worse if we throw any of it away. So we try to keep it all for regulations' sake. "Smiles" Moore's arms are paralyzed from the pack. For a cure he can carry it some more.

We spend the day in resting. It is good to lie on the soft green grass and watch the white clouds in the sky. A bath in the stream is a matter of splashes for the water is very cold but it does remove some of the filth. After the bath the heavy woolen underwear feel good even if it is summer.

Canadian cavalrymen join us. According to them we are likely headed for the Marne where the Jerries are chasing the French back. The outlook is bad but the Canucks are confident we will win. They were not as discouraged as some English infantrymen we had met. But then they were cavalrymen and may not have taken it on the chin as much as the infantry. They said Americans had already been in the fighting on the Marne and did very well. We could talk with these fellows more freely, they understood Americans and said they wished they could fight with us.

At dark another order to roll packs. We hike in the darkness to the railroad yards, halt and lie down and wait for our train.

June 13. Our train of box cars arrives about midnight and by one a.m. we are on the move. Between jerks and bumps, I try to sleep on the hard floor listening to the clicking of the wheels on the joints.

Daylight finds us still bumping along. The matter of food becomes pressing, we don't have any. At noon we do get a little corn willie and hardtack. At Chars we halt and unload for a few minutes. A French relief outfit of some kind had prepared tea for us, but they spiked it with rum. I tried to drink it, even though I am a total abstainer, but when I saw old topers (drinkers) making faces and throwing it away I gave it up. I was discreet enough to throw it away when the French relief workers were turned.

Later in the day we are nearing a large city, Paris. We crowd the doorways as the train travels slowly through the outskirts. An American Red Cross train is on a siding and wounded Marines, fresh from Chateau Thierry and the Marne, yell to us to go up and give Jerry "hell." Troop trains of French soldiers also pass us. Something big may be underway. We hope to stop in Paris and see the town but they did not bring us over to show us Paris but to fight. The train winds slow, jerking and bumping, around the city and all we see is a few outlying streets, kids yelling for cigarets, and the Eiffel Tower in the distance. Darkness comes and we still move slowly on. At ten p.m. the train stops at a small siding and we unload and limber cramped muscles.

The night is clear and cool. Over the city the searchlights are searching, for Jerry is raiding tonight and little pinpoints of light appear near the stars as anti-aircraft shells burst. Today we have seen shell holes where other raiders had dropped their bombs. The raid seems to last a long time tonight. Of course we are in no danger here so we dote on the station platform.

Later we hike about three miles but one of the hardest hikes yet. Muscles are still cramped from the train ride. At last we halt and I sit down and fall asleep. I dream I am at home and very hungry. The relatives are all there, the table is all set and we are ready to eat. Mother comes through the doorway from the kitchen with a large chicken. Just then in my dream I hear a horn blowing "Fall in, fall in." Where have I heard that noise before? Mother, the table loaded with food and the chicken fade away and I come to lying on the cold ground with no prospects of food and the bugle still blowing "fall in." I have never been more disgusted in my life and can hardly pick up my pack and rifle and all the junk they gave me to tote around. But it is only a few steps more and the company marches into a great farmyard with a big shed piled full of hay. We drop packs and onto the hay and I am soon asleep to dream of that dinner and get a chance to eat it.

VICINITY OF PARIS

June 14. I awaken early in the morning but turned over for another sleep. The hay is soft and sweet and as fine a bed as a man could want. At 10 a.m. I am up and searching for equipment that slid away during the night. Then breakfast of oatmeal, which broke our fast after yesterday's light rations. About noon we form again and hike a few easy kilos to Roissy. Billets are assigned and we split into platoons. My billet is in a loft but very clean. French cavalry horses are below and a few French cavalrymen are billeted with us.

Our first thought was food. I buy a loaf of delicious French bread at the bakers, then try for some candy. A little shop sells candy and around it is a crowd of American soldiers. The French girls are frantic. Bing Johnson is in the back of the crowd and can't edge forward. Finally he yells, "I speak French, let me up there." The crowd in front opens up but Bing's French sounded to me like "Gimme two bars of chocolate." The candy is better than nothing but made mostly of sugar, chocolate and water.

June 15. Pay Day. The first since we came to France and a double pay for we were not paid in America last month. Things begin to move. As for me I am a teetotaler and do not drink a drop. Today a person passing would say we were all a bunch of drunks. But it is only a few of the entire company that are doing all the drinking and making all the noise. In America liquor was hard for a soldier to get and drunken soldiers infrequent. Georgia was a dry state though there was bootlegging. In France it is different. The estaminets are wide open and plenty of liquor. The American soldier does not repress himself in anything and when he drinks, he drinks. Let it be understood that the majority are not drunk today. Many, like me, have not tested liquor, some have a little and are feeling good and some are disgustingly drunk. There are fights, arguments and misunderstandings. The prostitutes make money tonight though to a drunken soldier any woman may be a prostitute. Decent women are insulted on the streets, although some soldiers think a French woman can't be insulted. They vomit on the streets and fall in their vomit. Men who when sober are clean and gentlemanly now are dirty drunken beasts and a disgrace to the American uniform. Personally, I agree with the majority that they are a disgusting sight. In America we did not have these exhibitions, though occasionally a man did get well oiled.

The crap games are long and loud tonight and before morning the pays have changed hands and most men are as broke as the day before. More fights, arguments and misunderstandings. Soreheads, who are poor losers, are mad at the winners and the winners hog all their winnings.

The carousel lasts long into the night and the sober men who are the majority are annoyed, insulted and kept awake by the drunks. Men wishing to avoid trouble move to places where they will be sure of not having someone vomiting on him in his sleep. If one man in a dozen is drunk, he makes enough noise that an outsider thinks everyone is drunk. Many are boys who cannot stand much. I am glad when the day is over.

June 16. Drill all day, headache or not. A little more order today. Some are sick and vow never again but that does not mean much. I have to make a map of the town. Lieut. Swartz is a bug for maps and I usually get the detail. During my map making I saw through a window a beautiful French woman. I map a lot there but all chances of romance are quashed when

Lieut. Swartz comes in the room also. Beautiful and nice women would never notice a corporal with a lieutenant around. And lieutenants have ways of getting rid of corporals also.

June 19. We are just going to sleep at night when the anti-aircraft battery near town lets go. Jerry is raiding Paris again. The guns blast and reverberate, the flashes light up the scene and the searchlights search the sky for the raiders. Overhead but unseen we hear plainly a droning sound, now rising and falling in the peculiar hum of the German motors. Occasionally the searchlights spot a ship and then the archies burst near the ship till it is able to elude the light. The planes are over us in a few minutes, quiet again and we relax, then a little later a dull rumbling noise in the direction of Paris. There tonight, men, women and children are in danger, perhaps being killed by the raiders. Air raids always seem to me like a sneaking way of making war. It's bad enough to kill a man but child murder is going too far.

June 20. Our companies leave Roissy and hike to Louvres and are billeted in that town. Our rations have improved. Now it is potatoes, cabbage and carrots and beef. Occasionally they change and then we have beef, carrots, cabbage and potatoes but the change is so subtle one can hardly notice it. Corn willie and goldfish are never absent very far. A Y.M.C.A. canteen opened up and at certain times we can buy a bar of chocolate, a package of cookies and a pack of cigarets. Several German prisoners are in town. Their main occupation is hauling away the manure from the large piles in every French farmyard.

I spend some time around the railroad station. The mademoiselles, stenographers and clerks in Paris are usually waiting for a train. About all I can do is look but that is a pleasure for they are remarkably easy to look at. I resolve to spend more learning to speak French, not only to help our allies win the war either.

June 22. I help draw another map of the country surrounding Louvres. We talk to two German prisoners working in a field. One is an arrogant Prussian and for him "Deutschland uber alles und alles ist Deutsch." I feel like taking a punch at the swell headed fellow. But the other is more reasonable and tells us to pay no attention to him. The big head says the

Heinies will soon be here. Right now the news from the front is so bad this Boche can be optimistic. I gather from the rumors that the French are faring badly and they may be pushed back further. Also that we are emergency troops to be used to defend Paris.

June 23. Early in the morning we roll packs and hike outside Louvres. Long lines of camions (trucks), driven by Indo-Chinese soldiers, are waiting. It is a beautiful Sunday, warm and sunny. We ride north through small towns and villages near Paris, probably headed for the Marne and Chateau-Thierry. Both have been in the news very much lately and though we know little facts we know the French have been pushed back to the Marne. American marines and regulars have been in the fighting there and the French are apprehensive of another big drive on Paris.

All along our route the French population welcomes us. Sunday, everyone dressed in their best, church and a holiday. We are cheered heartily by everyone. Pretty girls are on the sidewalks in every town, waving at us and causing commotions in soldiers hearts and considerable vile talk by the "rough boys." We pass through the cities of Meaux and Coulomiers, two towns that will be in the path of the German advance on Paris if we cannot hold them at the Marne. The population is naturally glad to welcome so many stalwart young Americans to stay between them and the advancing hordes of the Boche.

At Coulomiers we pass through a small park. Several women are there smiling and cheering our troops. Three of the prettiest are standing along and as we pass we yell at them and they smile and wave at us. A French soldier walks up to one, grabs her skirts and pulls them up, revealing a perfect pair of feminine legs. Only a glimpse and plenty left to the imagination but legs like these would be great in any language. She blushes and is embarrassed as the others kid her and laugh. As for our truck load, we hope some other French soldier will oblige. We pass this town and the beautiful women give place to open country and peasant girls. The girls' legs fresh in our minds, remind us of other women back home, good and bad, but sweet and feminine. We are young and wish we could spend more time with them. But the truck whisks us away. The men around me are good fellows but they don't fill the place of women in a young man's life. For many today is the last glimpse of well dressed, pretty girls, and for all it will be months before we do see them again, except those in hospitals.

In contrast to those pretty towns and pretty women are the refugees who are leaving the Marne region, abandoning their farms to the Boche, with all they can pile on their wagons. A pitiful lot, old men and women with children, a few cattle, pigs and goats, dejected and forlorn.

Late in the afternoon the truck train stops and we unload and pitch pup tents in an orchard and lie down to rest. At night strange thoughts pass through my mind: war and its horrors, legs, cheering crowds, legs, refugees, more legs and the legs win. I hear a rumbling noise that diverts my mind from its pleasant wanderings. We are much closer to the front now as those flashes on the horizon show. So we must take our place in that hell. It is much pleasanter to think of women.

Chapter 2

To the Marne

Editor's note

Thirteen months after mobilization, the 28th Division arrived in France on May 16 and underwent further training by British combat veterans well back from the front. The German Army had begun a major offensive in March, hoping to decide the war before the American Army could have a meaningful impact. From March to May, the Germans made deep advances into the French lines and now threatened Paris. The Americans were needed now to help stop the Germans.

At Belleau Wood, the 2nd Division, including its brigade of Marines, stopped the Germans in a battle that lasted 26 days in June. At nearby Château-Thierry, the 3rd Division helped stop the Germans at the Marne River, earning that division the nickname that sticks to this day: "Rock of the Marne." Alongside the 3rd Division were the 28th and the 32nd divisions.

The 28th went under French Sixth Army orders on June 22. The 28th Division's 55th Brigade went to the line on June 28 because it had completed its training. Its 109th and 110th regiments saw the brunt of the division's combat in the weeks that followed. The 56th Brigade, which included the 111th and 112th regiments, deployed July 1. A week later, the 112th, including Pierce's First Battalion, had dug in a short distance south of the Marne, largely in a reserve role in case the Germans penetrated even farther into Allied territory.

On July 15, the Germans made one more try. The French, already planning their own attack, also struck. The 109th Regiment attacked as part of the French-ordered effort. The 112th Regiment did not take part in the attack, but the Germans had the regiment in their sights, keeping it under frequent and often intense artillery fire until July 17. French orders sent the 112th marching to Courboin, and a few days later, to Charly. By

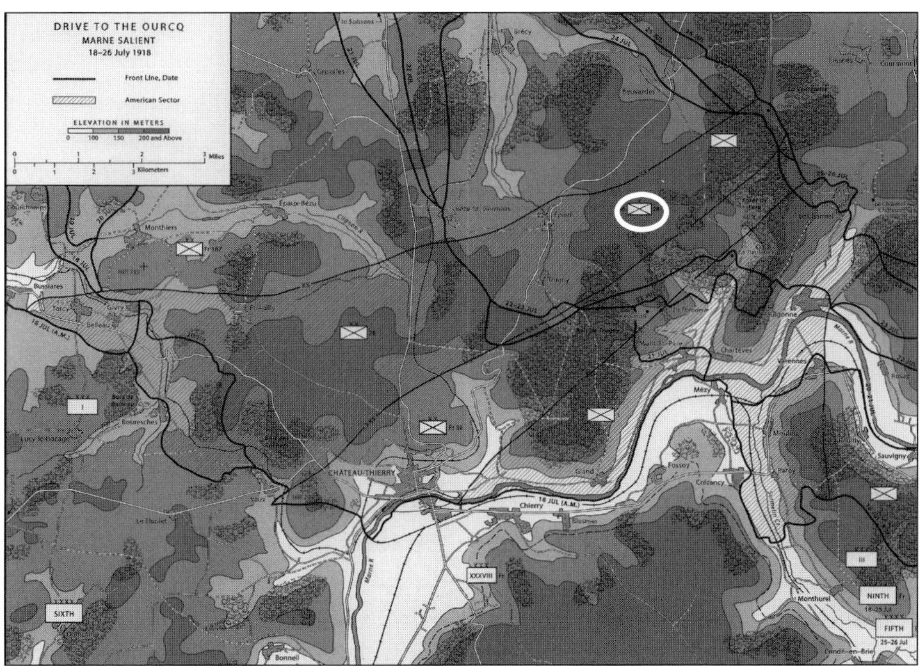

The Marne front from 18–26 July. (*Center for Military History*)

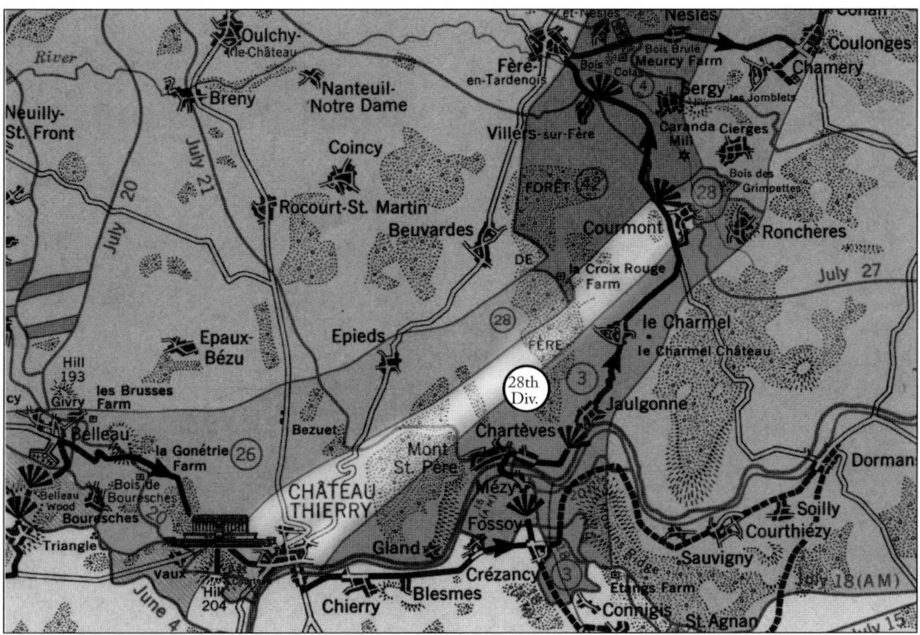

The path of the 28th Division. (*American Battlefield Monuments Commission*)

now the Germans were falling back and set up a defensive line along the Ourq River. For the 55th Brigade it meant more marching and fighting. For the 56th Brigade it was one march after another – often in the dark and rain – in largely supporting roles for much of the rest of July and into the first days of August as the Allies moved forward. But at Epieds on July 25, the 112th engaged the enemy, pushing them back.

Those days in July would earn the 28th Division two campaign ribbons: Champagne-Marne for the defensive effort and Aisne-Marne for the follow-up offensive. Two more ribbons were coming.

Chapter 3

Nearing the Marne

June 24 to June 26. Our field cookers could not follow with the trucks so our rations are issued and we cook ourselves. Steaks fried on a stick and potatoes baked in the coals are better than the tough ones we get at the field cookers anyhow. Drills, a maneuver and instructions in throwing live bombs. Another cold bath in a stream. Cooties are appearing on some men. Turn in a blanket and the overcoat to lighten our load. The last band concert of the 112th Infantry Band. The rumbling noise breaks into the music, a heavy rough baser note, reminder of the music we shall soon dance to. The heat lightning plays stronger on the horizon at night. Occasionally an airplane in the distance and black puffs of smoke in the sky mingle with the white puffs of anti-aircraft.

June 29 to July 3. We strike our tents, roll packs and start to hike North again. I feel an emptiness at the stomach for we are marching now in the direction of that rumbling noise and the flashes at night. As we proceed, the noise of the guns is louder and sharper and more anti-aircraft shells burst in the distance. We are not in danger yet except for air raids but the

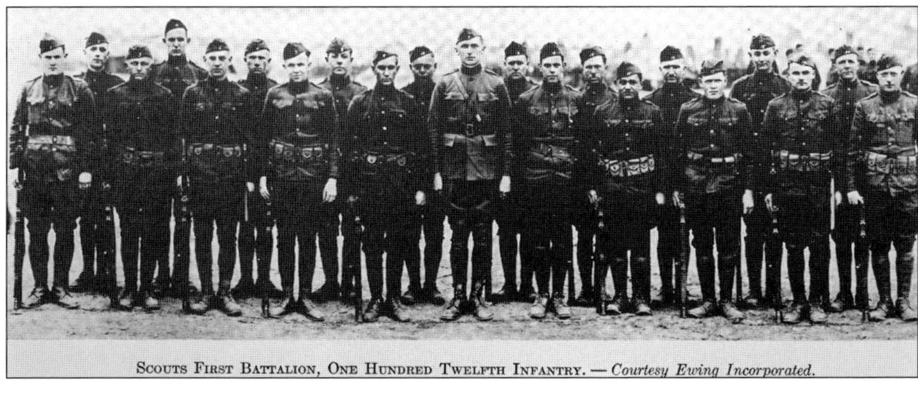

The First Battalion's scouts, including Corporal Harold Pierce at the far left. (*The Twenty-eighth Division: Pennsylvania Guard in the World War*)

time is coming soon. We hike about seven miles, then stop at a beautiful chateau, the estate of Alexander Dumas, a beautiful location with a pleasant patch of woods. Fountains spray into ponds with white swans swimming. Large flower beds are sprinkled around the lawn and under the trees. The platoons split up again and we pitch pup tents in cool shady places. Near my tent are the ruins of an old castle wall, with watch towers on the corners with the figures 1563 and a moat surrounding it all. In these woods war seems far away; rather it is the picture of a quaint peaceful farmland.

A few men have been detailed from our companies and have gone to the front. In an attack on Hill 204 our regiment had three killed and several wounded. The 103rd Engineers are along the Marne somewhere constructing trenches for the defense. Men from the 26th Division, the New England National Guard, arrive. They have been on the Toul Sector in trenches and have just been transferred to the Marne. The 3rd Division of Regulars are in the vicinity. The American Army is soon going to be tried. On the night of July 3rd, we go to sleep with plans of a big dinner tomorrow, the Glorious Fourth of July, a holiday, perhaps a parade. The floor of my tent feels good tonight and I will have a good rest.

July 4. "To arms, To arms, To arms." At 2 a.m. the shrill piercing, chilling scream of the bugle. There is no call so dread, so fearful, so thrilling and so dangerous. It carries all the elements of a fire alarm and more. Before orders are received we are striking tents and rolling packs, groping for each article in the darkness, and rolling them by sense of touch for long practice has made us adept at that. Whistles blow, officers and non-coms bark at us to hurry and fall in. We fall in and report the squads present, then wait. What has happened, has the Germans' long expected push started? Something big is up. We move our company out of the woods to the road and wait while another battalion tramps dustily by. By three a.m. the entire regiment of nearly four thousand men is on the move toward the front.

A few low orders, and silently the column moves off. We believe the Germans are starting their new drive and we are being shoved in some spot in the lines. Probably they are already started and the French are already falling back. But no, the sky is not

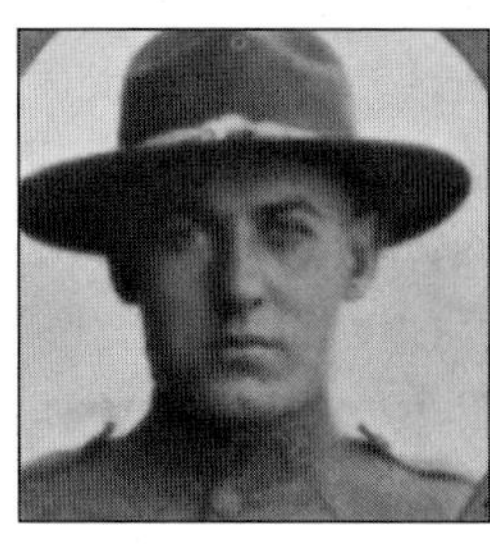

Cpl. Burt Oudett.

lighted by flashes and there is no rumbling. Perhaps it is an expected push. My thoughts are serious now, the big time has arrived for which we have trained so long and how will we stand it? We have no breakfast and the hike is long and fast with no rests. It lasts till noon and then we halt on top of a hill and remain at the edge of a patch of woods. Ahead is a line of shallow trenches, probably the third line. We are near the front at last but it seems no different than any other land I have seen. There is no sign of war or carnage and not even a gun goes off. Some are doubtful that this is the front. Burt Oudett explains carefully that this is not the front, this is just the biggest artillery range in the world.

We have our first meal of the day about two p.m. as the kitchens have followed us this time. Then we remain on the alert expecting something, but nothing happens, so in late afternoon our battalion forms again and we return about three miles and bivouac in a woods called the Grande Foret. Evidently the big occurrence did not take place today for it has been very peaceful; even the distant booming is less. The kitchens arrive, supper is prepared and eaten, we roll into our blankets on the ground and drop off to sleep too tired to care. So passed the Fourth of July.

THE MARNE

July 5. About four a.m. first call sounds through the woods and we are up and roll packs in the dark. The field cookers serve a hurried breakfast and we prepare in our minds to go closer to the front. But instead, we start to the rear over the route we had traveled yesterday morning. This morning's is not as hurried, yet we have covered plenty of miles by one o'clock when we are back at the estate of Alexander Dumas. The companies march to their same camping ground, pitch tents and prepare to stay. There are many comments as to why we made this march but no one has a satisfactory answer.

Many men sleep in the afternoon. Tired though I am by the two days' march I decide to wash my clothes, take a bath in the stream and I will go to bed early tonight for a good rest. The washing finished, I sit around waiting for summer.

But other orders came to be ready to move. I cuss myself for not sleeping and resolve after this not to miss a chance to sleep. We remain under cover in the woods and then at dusk emerge into the open. Our battalion halts at an intersection while another battalion crunches by in the semi-darkness, then we follow them off and we are on our way again. I am already tired from the eight hours' hike this morning. It is just dark with a pale, cold moon showing. There is no gaiety, no high spirits, nothing but a steady rise and fall of tired feet, up and down endlessly it seems. The mind soon knows nothing but to stay behind the man ahead, one foot to place ahead of the other, up and down, over and over again, backs bent to the pack, ahead is the road and the front. A few flashes of gunfire and the rumbling again but it soon ends.

Near midnight we leave the road and enter the woods. Someone has figured a short cut by the map. Under the trees and brush it is pitch dark. I take hold of the man's pack ahead of me and the man behind takes hold of mine to keep contact. The ground is rough and uneven. The man ahead stops frequently and I bump my face into his rifle or pack, then the man behind bumps me. The man ahead pulls away and jerks me and I must jerk the man behind. Over logs, holes, ditches and all the obstructions of a dark woods we go, bumping, jamming and cursing. Branches run into our faces, snag on the equipment or trip our feet. Ahead and behind me the woods are filled with angry, tired men, running into each other, tripping, slipping and falling but all trying to hang onto each other and keep the line going and spare themselves as much damage as possible. There is no path to follow and the only thing to do is to hang on. A mile of this and we are all in a fighting mood.

Relief at last when we finally slide down a bank onto a road through the forest close by a small lake. Colonel Rickards is there with other officers mounted on horses. "Close up. Close up." A man near me yells, "Aw, go to hell" in a loud voice. The officer spurs alongside and angrily asks the futile questions. "Who said that?" No answer. No one would tell if they knew, and coming through that woods was enough to make a man tell an officer to go to hell.

July 6. Midnight and we are still hiking. Dimly and without consciousness the feet rise and fall, behind the man ahead. Up and down, up and down, up and down, without end the feet go plodding along. The pack bears down, the straps cut and swinging pieces of equipment bump the moving legs. We shift the rifle from shoulder to shoulder and stick our thumbs under the pack straps to ease the weight. The feet and entire body aches until exhaustion like an anesthetic eases the aches and from then on the body is like an automaton, a machine running endlessly on.

Davey Yasclovitch (spelled Yossolivitz in draft records), a little Jew in my squad, has been walking for hours on his toes for his heels are blistered so bad he cannot put them down. Oudett and Hoke have quit their arguments. O'Connor struggles on under a heavy pack with loads of extra writing paper. Angel has ceased to make fun of Tony Albino. Little Tony keeps up and does not complain and carries the extra heavy bag of Chau-Chaut[1] ammunition we all are supposed to divide up. There never was a better soldier than Tony.

The hours drag wearily on. Men fall over in their tracks or drop exhausted in the ditches and are sound asleep as they hit the ground. Angel drops out, then O'Connor loses his strength and spirit and drops. The road is wavy now, it goes up and down and tilts sideways. The men are all drunk apparently. At times I believe I am sleep walking. Davey and Tony still hang on with me more asleep than awake. Hoke and Oudett are missing, I cannot blame them. This thing has been going on for ages, we will continue on forever, we are doomed to keep walking for the rest of time, there is no rest, no stopping, no help, nothing but to keep one tired foot passing the other, follow the man ahead and step over him when he falls. My mind is dulled and I walk like in a dream.

Near daybreak, with half the company dropped, Captain Bretz gives the command, "Column right" and we turn and enter a field, form company front, and stand dizzily swaying. "Fall out." My fingers slip off the pack and pack, rifle and I drop together with a thud and I am asleep before I hit the ground.

Awakening is similar to coming out of ether. I am half conscious and sleepily aware of something, then sleep again. At four p.m. I am awake enough to try and move my aching legs and body. The hot July sun is beating down full in my face and I am covered with sweat. Yossolivitz is beside me still asleep and he looks as if dead. I watch his breast for signs of life but at first see none. I examine him more closely and there is just a

---

1. The Chau-Chaut was a light machine gun manufactured by the French and used by both armies. It had a tendency to jam and was not well regarded by American troops.

perceptible movement of the chest. I wonder how he can sleep with that sun glaring into his eyes but I had been doing the same thing for the last twelve hours.

In the twenty-four hours from four a.m. July 5 till four a.m. July 6th we have hiked sixteen hours, and at two and a half miles per hour that makes forty miles. Then nearly a twenty-mile hike on the 4th and we have covered nearly sixty miles since two a.m. July 4th.

Near sundown we have another meal although I am not very hungry. Last night about this time I had a meal but the hike between that time has not made me hungry. We sit around till dark when we roll up in our blankets and sleep on the ground again, another night of tired sleep.

July 7. The aches and stiffness are about gone. This town is back of the Marne river and Chateau-Thierry is a few miles ahead. In the evening a regiment of American Field Artillery of the Fourth Regular Division pass through town equipped with the French seventy-fives, their famous guns that are the best light artillery pieces in the world today. On this sector so far are the 3rd and 4th Regulars and the 26th and 28th Divisions of the National Guard.

July 8. Fleisher and I are detailed to make maps of the reserve trenches we are to occupy over the hill. On the way up we pass a French observation balloon. After we are past there is a swishing, whistling noise and a shrapnel shell bursts near the balloon. It is the first shell I have had go over me, although shells burst near regimental headquarters, and rather than scaring us was quite interesting. We wait, expecting more, and half hoping they will hit so we can see the blaze, but no more come. Ahead, Fleisher and I start maps of half dug trenches. We work all day without excitement. A few miles over the hill in our front is Chateau-Thierry and the Marne and to our left is Chezy-sur-Marne. We pass close to French batteries in the woods and valleys.

Late in the afternoon we finish our map and start back. At a farmhouse on top of the hill a group of French soldiers are gathered talking and gesticulating wildly. We visit them and my brother Hugh is the attraction. He has just eaten with them and has made such a good impression that we are invited. The meal was delicious, juicy roast beef with gravy, potatoes and vegetables and as fine a meal as a person could get at home. We "merci" them plenty as we leave.

We meet our battalion coming up to occupy the trenches, Major Smathers leading. I have to go back for my pack and belongings. Battalion Headquarters was established in a valley at the edge of a patch of woods. The companies moved on into positions in the trenches without disturbance.

July 9. Quiet and orderly. All the Scouts are now with Battalion Headquarters. Hugh is also with Battalion as Lieut. Coburn is now Battalion Gas Officer. He dug a dugout immediately for himself but I was satisfied to pitch a pup tent.

July 10. I helped with the rest of the Scouts making maps of the sector. To our right are elements of the 3rd Division, then the 112th holds the line. Directly ahead are French batteries and the Marne a few miles in front. Our trenches are in shell range but so far there has been no shelling. Bartlett is caught stealing turnips, a vile offense.

July 11. Rain. Ahead of us a few German shells fell near the French batteries but little damage was done. It is new to see the bursts at least a mile away. We are all curious and a shell burst is quite a sight.

At night I am with several Scouts and climb the hill to our left to observe. It is quiet for the most part. Miles ahead at regular intervals the Germans shoot red, blue or white rockets into the air, probably a method of signaling. Later a Boche airplane hums slowly over and drops a parachute flare. The flare drops slowly down lighting the terrain all around us as light as day, especially near the French batteries. He is likely trying to learn of any new night movements of troops. We sit quietly in the grass till the flare burns up.

July 12. Worked on maps and helped Burt Oudett build an observation post in a tree, back of our first line trench. Jerry drops several shells on the hill about a mile ahead. An old horse is grazing there apparently unmindful of the shells. At last one burst near him, he seemed to jump a little, then buckled and laid down. Nothing much, just the passing of a poor old horse but the first living thing I have seen killed.

July 13. Either our rations are short all the time or we have terrible appetites but anyhow we cannot get enough to eat. So in the evening, Burt Oudett, Kightlinger, my brother and I start for Chezy-sur-Marne where we may be able to find food in the deserted houses. We pass the French batteries firing on the Germans across the Marne. It is the first time I am near a cannon when it goes off and the crack nearly splits the ear drums at first. The cannoneers wave to us as we pass.

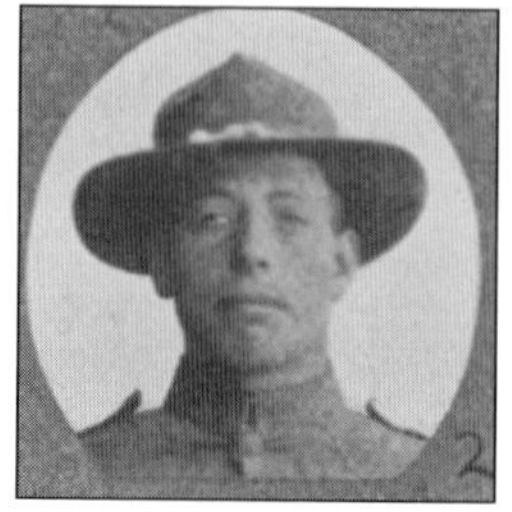

Cpl. Roy Kightlinger.

Chezy-sur-Marne although close to the front is not damaged much yet. We pass by large beautiful homes that have lately been abandoned by their owners in the path of the armies. Our mission is food, so we enter some of the houses. We find some beans and rice, which we take along with some pans. The houses were all wide open and had apparently been ransacked by French or American soldiers. The furniture was in good condition but some dresser drawers had been opened and the contents left on the floor. One house belonged to a naturalist for the walls were covered with stuffed alligators, snakes, turtles and birds. There were also some ancient spears and swords. I found two of these old spears in the yard where some soldier had wantonly thrown them and returned them to the house. Outside we found some currants in the garden. All we were after was something to eat and to cook in, so after we had our beans, rice and currants we left. All the destruction in Chezy so far has been caused by the allied soldiers.

The artillery has been firing more today. The French think another big drive is imminent. Tomorrow is Bastille Day, the French National Holiday. Many are expecting the drive tomorrow as the French are all expected to be drunk for the celebration.

July 14. I make a fire and cook the rice and bake some beans. Pete Migliore, the cook, allows me a little bacon. Some French soldiers offer me some good advice about a cooking fire. I had thought I knew plenty having been a Boy Scout, but I find that these old world soldiers have also gone through the mill. It takes about six hours for the beans and rice but in the end I have a pan of delicious baked beans and rice. Kightlinger and I eat half the pan and at last we are filled. For the first time since I came to France I can eat no more.

A few shells come over but none closer than a mile away. The French artillery are on the alert whether because they are a little shaky or because of Bastille day. They have an extra ration of champagne and some are drunk. I saw several today, hilarious and happy and some too drunk to stand up and vomiting. If the Dutch would attack they would not be in very good condition to stand it.

In the evening the French and American artillery open up. They put over the heaviest artillery fire I have seen yet. Guns on every hill for miles are blasting away. We do not know the cause but something is up. Of course we are only the men in the ranks and usually ignorant of what is going on. Yet we feel that before long something is going to happen on the Marne. The fire lasts for about two hours then dies down. Our positions are too far away to be much disturbed by the gunfire though.

July 15. I have bad dreams in which lightning is flashing and there is a great roaring sound. I waken gradually and the lightning is real and the roar genuine. At first I am dazed by the noise and flashes, then as my senses clear I know I am surrounded by a German barrage. A continuous series of explosions so fast that they cannot be counted are ahead of me on the trenches. New to the front and careless I have neglected to dig a dugout. I need one bad so I run for my brother's hole hoping he still has room. It was built for two but I am the last of six that jump in. Hugh is glad to have me in. We sit with our heads just below the ground and our knees to our chins.

The air is filled with the screeching of shells and blasting explosions sending spent pieces of steel, dirt and stones around us. Heavier shells, sounding like freight trains, pass over our heads back into the back areas to roads and villages behind us. Occasionally a shell comes closer and we cower in the hole. Gradually we decide that the worst of the fire is ahead on the trenches and that we are comparatively safe now but at any minute the fire may shift. The horizon ahead is filled with the heat lightning of German guns, a steady flickering light that maintains a glow as steady as that of a huge fire.

My beans begin to work. I had eaten too many of them and now I am paying the price. I am sick with fear and indigestion. My head falls over I am so sick and for a time I do not worry about the shells. I sit there doubled up with my head on my knees praying for it to end soon. The other five heartily wish I was out of that hole.

Hour after hour drag painfully by, the sky still maintains its steady glow, the shells screech and the explosions keep up their steady roar on the trenches where my regiment is being baptized with the worst and heaviest concentration the Germans ever put over. In our hole we see that so far, none have burst close to us so we relax and try to sleep. But now and then a shell skips over the trench system and bursts closer, sending its whining steel messengers around our hole and causing us to cower apprehensively in the hole. Alternately we relax and then tension grows. Men in my regiment are being killed and wounded ahead of me. Our own guns are silent, the fire having driven them to their holes also. The big German push so long expected on the Marne is on.

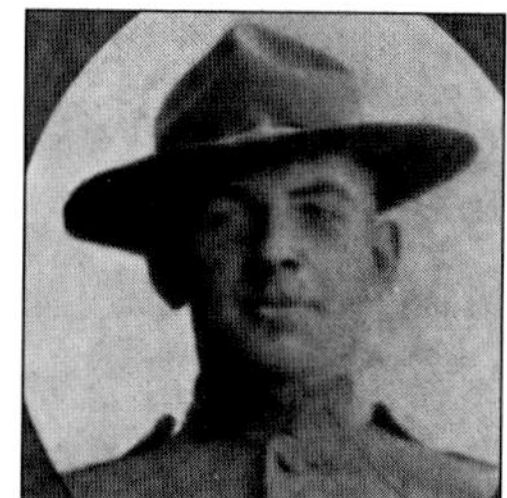

Pvt. Jerome Crist.

About three thirty a.m. two Scouts, Crist and Davis, are sent to each observation post to tell them to watch for a Star Rocket from the direction of the front. This means that the front line has been overrun by the Boche and that now we hold the front. I am glad I am not chosen to go. It may be the end of those men as the chances of getting through that fire are not good. But Crist and Davis cross the fields and somehow get through O.K.

Little observing can be done as a man must spend too much time under cover ducking shells. The 3rd Division are ahead and by morning we know that they must have held as no Star Rocket is seen. Towards morning the fire slackens and by daylight the worst is over although he is still sending over enough to make it uncomfortable. Then we come out of the holes and look around, always close to the hole so if they do shift onto us we can soon be underground again. Ahead French infantrymen have burst through our lines yelling, "Le Boche, le Boche, allez, allez." Our men don't see anything to "allez" from, except shells, so they elect to stay. A dressing station is established near us and wounded and gassed brought in.

I go to breakfast at "A" Company kitchen, eaten as shells still search the sector plenty. We have prunes. A French artilleryman, caught by the barrage on the road, is carried by on a stretcher with the top of his head blown off and his brains dripping out. He is unconscious and cannot live long. The prunes are very dry. A man from "C" Company walks by with his arm bloody, then another man from "C" hobbles by with his big toe shot off. The black blood on his toe and my prunes look alike. I force a few prunes down but only to try and make my buddies think those things did not affect men. Several men are killed, wounded and gassed, mostly in "C" and "E" Companies but "A" has only three slightly wounded. Breakfast hurriedly eaten I hurry back to Battalion Headquarters. The Frenchman has died and has been rolled to the side. The wounded and gassed Americans are being cared for and ambulances soon arrive to take them away. The dead are still in the trenches. Close to a hundred men in our battalion are casualties and still mounting.

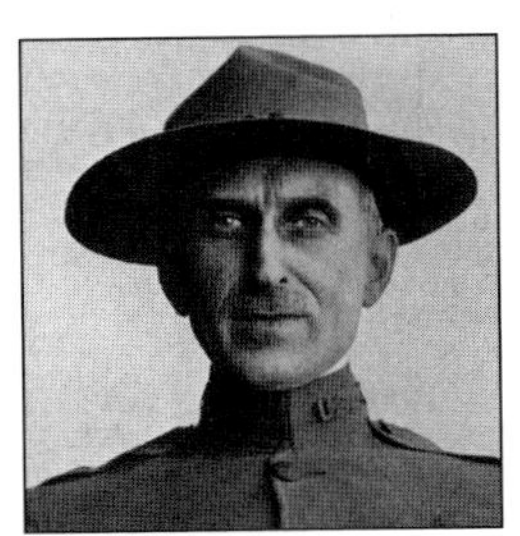

Major Charles Smathers.

We start a big dugout for the Scouts. The runners also are digging in. The Pioneer platoon commence a large dugout for Major Smathers and his staff but they make a serious error for the entrance faces the Germans. But we have learned the first lesson of war and that is to dig in wherever we stop. Shells fall all day on our sector and we work ready to take cover if the warning screech of a shell sounds too close. The work is a relief from the strain of sitting and waiting.

In the afternoon I am detailed to take a message to the observation posts. I cross the fields on a run as shells burst on the other side and start up the hill. Further up the hill I smell gas and adjusted my nose and mouthpiece of my mask. I feel terribly sick again and I am sure I am gassed, but it may be those beans again. I rest a moment, shells burst below me again, and sick or not I must run into the woods. I become confused in my directions and imagine I am lost. Just then the long, sad, mournful notes of "Taps" come to me from the valley where they are burying the dead of the regiment. "Taps" is beautiful at night but over dead men on a battlefield it is terrifying. This is my first battle and it is no wonder I am afraid. I have a helpless, hopeless feeling, and I pray to God and pull myself together. A few yards more and I see a French battery pulling their guns out of the woods to a safer place. The sight of men, even strangers, is cheering and a little farther and I find Strauss and O'Day at the Observation Post. With them to talk to I have more courage. They had spent the night in a latrine while shells burst all around them and riddled their packs. They came back to headquarters with me.

We still do not know what has happened ahead. Rumors are thick. First that the Germans have crossed the Marne and will soon be on us and then that they have been stopped. At times we are looking for them to come over the hill but as the day ends and none comes we feel sure that they could not have come far. Our trenches are dug deeper, more dugouts also, so if they do come we will be ready. As evening comes, their shell fire, which has been continuously searching the back areas all day, slackens. Our own artillery, silent all night while we were getting the punishing, is firing now. We do know that a big battle has been fought and by the end of the day we have every reason to believe that our side won. We still hold the reserve lines, there has been no mass movement of retreating to our lines so most of the front is intact. I sleep at night in the new dugout, a fitful sleep as the line is still very noisy, waking when the fire concentrates on our sector as it does often and sleeping during the quiet periods. My part of the line has only been in the edge of things but what a hot edge.

July 16. Fritz did not forget us. We remain in the same place and dig deeper dugouts and trenches. German shells hit our sector. The regiment is on the alert all day still expecting the Boche to come over the hill head. We still do not have any definite word although the little information filtering back is that they did cross the Marne in several places but so far they have been able to do little. But at most places they were repulsed with great loss.

July 17. Still in reserve in the trenches but the fire has slackened and today it is quieter. It looks as if our line in front has held and the big German attack has broken down. It starts to rain. At night the observation posts are called in and tomorrow we are moving.

July 18. Before daylight we are on the move. We move to the rear through Essesses, then to the right of our old positions. Batteries of American Field Artillery are chugging away as we pass. The hike lasts several miles and then we stop in a woods and camp. A Y.M.C.A. canteen is in a small town a mile away and I buy some chocolate. Men from the 3rd Division Infantry are there and a sorry looking outfit they are. At our camp one of their outfits halt to rest, tired, dirty and filthy. They are a battalion of the 30th or 38th Infantry, which had met the heaviest German attack on the Marne River and had chased them back. On their front the smallest gain had been made by the Germans, not over a mile. It was their defense that saved the day. This outfit, about sixty men, is all that is left of a battalion. Two trucks drive up and take them away. On the 28th Division front, different companies had been sandwiched with the French but the French left them without warning when the attack came. They had fought well but had to retreat after losing a great many men in killed and captured. It is rumored that two companies each of the 109th and 110th Regiments were annihilated. My brother and I dig a hole and line it with wheat straw from a wheat field nearby. It makes a soft comfortable bed and we sleep sound at night.

July 19. We remain in the woods all day and improve our dugout. A few men return from an inspection of the front and say that the dead are still unburied and the stench is awful. During the night I am awakened by an explosion and hear pieces of steel hitting our trees. A German plane is above us and he has dropped one bomb but no one was hurt although it was close. We cower in our holes, expecting more, but the Jerry plane leaves and does not return.

July 20. In the evening we fall in and march a mile or two to where long lines of trucks are waiting. We ride till about ten p.m. when we cross the Marne at Charly. At Charly we unload and hike to the heights above the town. It is a beautiful moonlight and the Marne River gleams serenely in the distance. Hidden are the ghastly, wrecked and bloated corpses and other horrors. The scene is one of peace and beauty not at all suggestive of the awfulness of the last few days and the terrors of the next few days. I feast my eyes on the beauty as I see it tonight, then when we halt, lie down beside the road and sleep. A light rain falls later that wakens me for a few minutes.

July 21. Late in the morning we eat a light breakfast prepared by the field cookers. Later a Commissary Truck drove up and sold cigarets and candy. And then the hike is resumed through the woods. We descend a long hill and see the signs of a terrific battle. We enter what was left of the town of Vaux, which had been captured by American Regulars prior to the big battle of the 15th. The American artillery had leveled every house in town and there was no living thing in town but a gassed goat, which follows us, a wheezing, coughing skeleton that cannot live long. Beside the road are crosses above the graves of Americans killed in battle.

We pass this desolated town and hike to Essomes. This is a larger town and although it is deserted has not been leveled as bad as Vaux. Burt Oudett picks up an old saxophone but only makes noises like the gassed goat. A fleet of planes pass over our heads and we take cover in the houses when the cry "under cover" comes down the line. But we see the red, white and blue circles underneath and know they are French. Road signs point to Chateau-Thierry and we assume we are to attack there.

Through this town and we see the city of Chateau-Thierry a few miles further. Americans pass and say the Boche have left the town and are retreating, then others say they still hold the town. But no fire is directed against us so we believe they must have left.

Our regiment marches into town. It is not as badly damaged as I had expected. Troops, already there, say the Germans left that morning. One American yells, "We have them on the run boys, the cavalry can't even find them." Just then I hear the scream of a seventy-seven coming over to town and exploding in the river, so they can't have gone far. More shells follow, all from one gun, which cannot be far away as we can hear its reports. We twist and squirm through Chateau-Thierry, over wrecked streets, as houses are wrecked by the shelling. Two men are killed in the regiment and several wounded as we pass through the town. It must be a sacrifice gun the infantry passed up. Through to the edge of town and we halt, before we start up the hill, so the companies ahead can form a single file for protection against artillery. General Weigel, our Brigade Commander, has his headquarters on a hill to our left. The gun drops a few shells near them and we expect them to fire at us on the road. Now we hike in the ditch a file on each side of the road. There is an odor of decaying flesh from dead Germans. On all sides are signs of the German retreat, pieces of equipment, clothes, and a helmet with flesh still sticking to it. We cannot understand what made the Germans retreat so suddenly; a few days ago they hit us with all they had.

A mile or so beyond Chateau-Thierry, a French lancer marches two German prisoners ahead of his horse. They are both strong, husky young fellows capable of fighting hard and it reminds me of stories of the old men and young kids supposed to be in the German army. These two look dangerous. When they pass between our files they raise their noses in the air and look down disdainfully at us with an arrogant look on their handsome faces. Several men are for taking a poke at them for their insolence. We hike about two miles beyond the city and bivouac for the night on a hillside protected from German fire by its steepness. The Germans have surely left suddenly and traveled far today as there is no sound of firing at night. Nothing to eat all day and nothing tonight either so we go to sleep hungry.

ADVANCE BEYOND THE MARNE

July 22. When I waken I have slid out of my blankets and down the hill about fifty feet. My bed and equipment are above me but I find them O.K. for there are no thieves in this army. Lieut. Swartz and I are sent with a detail of ten men to look for German stragglers. We spread out in a skirmish line and scout ahead for about two miles and see no signs of friend or foe and return hungrier than ever. During our absence the companies have been fed and I am out of luck again. No other prospect of food today and none yesterday. But my brother has saved half his breakfast for me, small though it was. I am thankful for even that. A YMCA man walks up with a pack of chocolate and cigarets. I just buy a small piece of chocolate for a half franc when an officer disperses the line as it is too good a target for artillery. Small though the chocolate is I give half to my brother for did he not save half his breakfast for me?

In the evening the regiment moves on to the top of the hill and conceals in the woods. It rains and we sit covered with raincoats. Occasionally batteries of seventy-fives fire in the valley below, salvos and single shots. At regular times in the distance a German shell whistles through the air and bursts on some distant target. I sit beside a German foxhole with a helmet near covered with flesh and blood. We remain squatted on the ground, tired and uncomfortable, the rain drips off the trees onto our helmets and slickers. The hours drag on and the night is blacker and blacker. Midnight, most are asleep on the wet ground and still no word.

July 23. About three a.m. word is passed along the line to assemble and we line up again in the blackness and wet. Slowly we start to move ahead a few steps at a time. We slip and slide onto a road but how contact is kept is a mystery. A long wait and we start to hike over the mud road, sliding and slipping in the darkness. The field artillery begins to fire and the flashes give us a little light. We move a few yards then stop and wait, then a few yards more, stop again and so on till daylight. The guns fire harder and behind the seventy-fives now the howitzers join in. A few German shells pass shrieking over our heads and burst behind us. One makes a direct hit on one of our field kitchens.

We enter a small village just as daylight has made things a little plainer. Trees have fresh cuts in their bark, fresh branches strew the ground and new shell holes are everywhere. The noise keeps up although we are ahead of the artillery. Surely we are going to attack now. We halt in the town again and rest beside the road as it grows lighter. A strangling mule is tied to a tree and at each blast the terrified animal strains at its tie strap and jerks till the strap nearly cuts his neck off. Kightlinger and I try to cut the strap and save a life even if it is only a mule but the poor beast kicks us away. After getting this close to the front I don't want to be injured by a mule. Some of the boys walk over to a house and return horrified. Inside the building dead boys from the 26th Division are piled on top of each other.

A platoon of the 26th Division march rapidly into town led by a Second Lieutenant. Just boys, like us, dirty, filthy and exhausted. "What outfit," they ask excitedly. "112th Infantry, 28th Division," we answer. Joy and hope revives them. "Oh, you're going to relieve us, you're going to relieve us. Thank God," they cry as they see the relief an infantryman is always looking for at the front. One mumbles, "Thank God, Thank God" to himself as he passes. There is no doubt of their relief in the knowledge that we are to take their places in the front and no question but what they have been through enough already to satisfy every one of them.

Their actions are not encouraging. I have a queer weak feeling in the pit of my stomach. Such looking men as they were with that gleam of fear and horror in their eyes. We will soon look the same way; maybe I do already. I am frankly afraid. I hate to go where these boys have been and do what they were doing. We are sure now that we are going to relieve the 26th and by the way these fellows act the place they have been is not nice.

Our command moves on through the village and up a small rise. Daylight now and we can see for miles in all directions. A battery of seventy-fives of the 26th fire over our heads as we pass. These little field pieces are a wicked thing, they snap and crackle viciously and the burst wracks the ear drums. They are firing rapidly, several shots to the minute. The artillerymen are in a merry mood. "Give em hell doughboys, we're right behind you." BANG. "Here's one for Jerry." BANG. "Here's another." BANG. "And here's another one." BANG. The gunners are following the role of artillery men for many years, trying to encourage the doughboys going up to close grips with the enemy. I notice the difference between the artillery and the infantry but then the infantry take it on the nose much harder than anyone else.

About a mile ahead and to our right the Germans are shelling a patch of woods. Above the smoke, tree trunks, branches, rocks and dirt and erupting seemingly in a continuous up and down movement as the shells churn the ground. Doughboys of the 26th leave the woods on a rapid walk and retire in good order to a safe distance and wait. Shells drop closer to them and again they retire out of danger. We believe it is the outfit we will relieve. The men up there would be tickled to death to have us come up and tell them to run along, we would handle the situation from now on.

But instead the head of our column turns to the left and away from the front. I feel intensely relieved; evidently we are not going to relieve that outfit in the woods. I breathe easier as we hike down a small hill and I am sure we are leaving the front. In the valley are batteries of 155 howitzers, still firing, not able to fire as fast as the 75s, but a louder roar that is not as hard on the ear drums as the crack of the lighter guns. Men from these batteries ask us where we're going. They know we are new to the front. Some ask how many handkerchiefs we have in our packs. After passing them a lot of unnecessary equipment is tossed to the side of the road. Our packs were too heavy anyhow.

We hike in the direction of Chateau-Thierry about two kilos, turn to our right and march several miles. Yesterday morning we had a small meal and by now we are plenty hungry. Still we hike till noon. By then men are turning over old empty corn willie cans beside the road. At one place we find a pile of rain-soaked French hardtack that some try and eat. Orders to eat our Iron Rations at the noon halt. What a foolish order: only a few including me still have them. I open the can and eat a handful and divide with a few others while the rest look hungrily on. Those that ate theirs in camp keep quiet.

The hike is resumed after the noonday halt but soon ends in a large woods, lately the scene of heavy fighting. It is the Bois de Belleau, where the 2nd Division fought so well. We rest concealed under the trees and underbrush. Back of the woods in the direction of the Marne is the wheat field the Marines crossed. It must have been suicide to try and cross that.

I change my underwear and find I have a large supply of cooties whose existence I have suspected for several hours. My dirty underwear, socks, extra shoes, extra shirt, tent pegs and poles, condiment can and bacon I can throw away. No one is going to ask me again how many handkerchiefs I have in my pack. Now I have the clothes on my back and the pack is much lighter.

During the afternoon, cheering and shouting. Must be news of a great victory. I rush over to the shouting, but it is something better. The field kitchens are coming. "A" Company kitchen sets up beside five rotting German bodies. But disregarding the odor we stick around and watch the cooks work. It is the first cooked meal I have had in three days and only three light meals in that time.

After the meal we fall in and hike a mile farther to a small town. There, evidently other orders were received for we turned around and started back in the direction of Chateau-Thierry. After dark we halt in another woods. Maybe someone knows where we are going or what we are going to do but every man in the regiment doubts it. For days now we have been walking up and down behind the front, sometimes close and sometimes far away. And for what purpose? We do know that Jerry has retreated many miles in a terrible hurry and we don't know where to find him or why he did it so quick. We bivouac in the woods tonight. The night is quiet, no gun fire, I hope Jerry goes a long before stopping.

July 24. Before daybreak, the bugle sounds and we are on the move again, back towards Chateau-Thierry again, then turn and start north again. The Boche are retreating fast, men of the 26th inform us. Asked again how many handkerchiefs we had in our packs and Burt Oudett nearly threw his away. The artillery is gone from their positions of the day before and moved up for Jerry has taken a big jump. They are fighting only rear guard actions, a few machine guns to delay the advance of the allied armies. At last, months of losing battles, the French and Americans have won and Jerry is doing the running now. All morning the army is on the move. The day is clear and warm and on the hilltops the vision is good and we can see all these movements for miles around us. In every direction, on every road, French and American troops, infantry, artillery, cavalry, engineers and other troops are moving northward. Today we are moving as the old armies moved in the old wars. Ahead of our regiment and 2nd Battalion is deployed as the advance guard. Flank guards are skirmishing in the fields on each side of us. Every type of vehicle is on the road, trucks, ambulances, field kitchens, field pieces and caissons. Motorcycles dash in and out of the traffic. The infantry keep to the ditch to allow the heavier traffic to pass and must keep eyes open or be run over. There are more signs of a hurried German retreat everywhere. "Verboten" appears on the sign boards. We hike on without dinner as usual, but we had had a little breakfast.

In late afternoon the traffic thins out and the infantry has the entire road though we proceed more slowly to allow the advance guard to clear away. If we were experienced veterans we would know we are getting closer contact with the enemy, although except for a distant burst of machine gun fire, it is quiet.

We pass through "verboten" ridden Epieds, just taken from the Germans only today and the last live German has just left. Just a few hours ago our men had charged across the wheat fields and the grass plots to capture the town. The Boche machine guns had exacted their toll for the passing. Burying details are in the wheat fields wrapping the dead in wheat sheaves before burying them. One young boy is still lying on his face in the ditch and others in the field beside the road. It is hard to realize that these boys are actually dead and not sleeping. And that a few hours ago they were alive like us and charging across that field.

Beyond the town and wheat fields a few German shells burst on a hillside. We pass dead horses beside a large shell hole and the road enters a woods. It is about five p.m. and we have hiked all day, though not fast. The column enters the woods off the road, halts to rest and eat. The field kitchens arrive and start supper. I eat with "D" Company. We have half-cooked lima beans without a speck of salt, bread and coffee like iodine. Hungry as I am I can hardly chew on the half-cooked beans. My brother and I later start a small fire, cook some tea I still have from my iron rations and that is some better.

Around dusk the entire battalion falls in at the edge of the woods facing north with Major Smathers in command. A battery of seventy-fives have just set up in the woods facing the Boche line. In front of us is an open field a kilometer wide with a patch of woods on the other side. A mule team hauling a supply wagon is crossing the field toward us. An artilleryman walks out into the field and starts setting up a little light. I wonder what he is doing that for, then a whistling noise, the artilleryman flattens to the ground fast and a shell bursts beside him. He is up again and runs toward us, the mule team bolts and runs away, the driver frantically trying to stop them. Another whistling noise, closer and I duck to my knees this time and another shell bursts closer to us and the pieces whistle over us. A man from the Signal Corps standing near me did not duck, and he grabs his face and his hand comes away bloody and with blood running down his uniform he walks away. Another man is down groaning with pieces of shell in his legs. Another shell whistles toward us but by this time the entire battalion is on the ground and its burst whistles harmlessly over the prostrate men. Jerry raises the range on each shell and the next shot falls without harm in the woods and then travels farther.

We are all very quiet; I for one do not like to talk as I am scared so bad my voice will shake. It is the first time since I came to the front that I have had men wounded within a few feet of me, although by now I have seen many dead and wounded. I know that when I hear that whistling noise again I will drop as that artilleryman did.

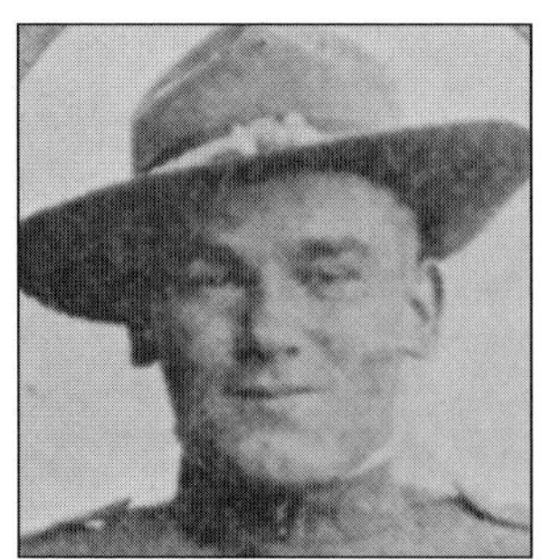

Cpl. Clyde Martin.

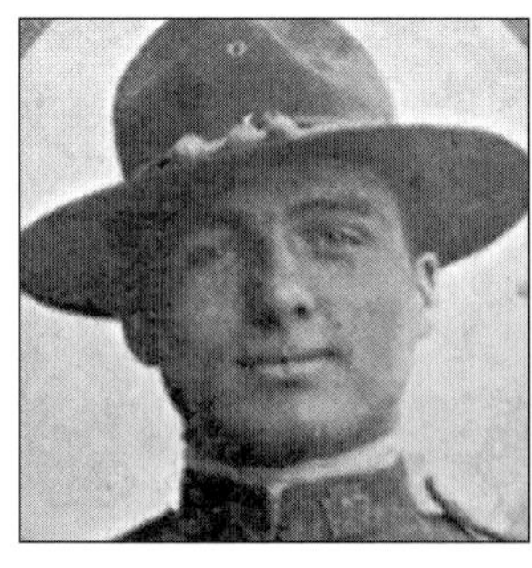

Cpl. Ray Wingard.

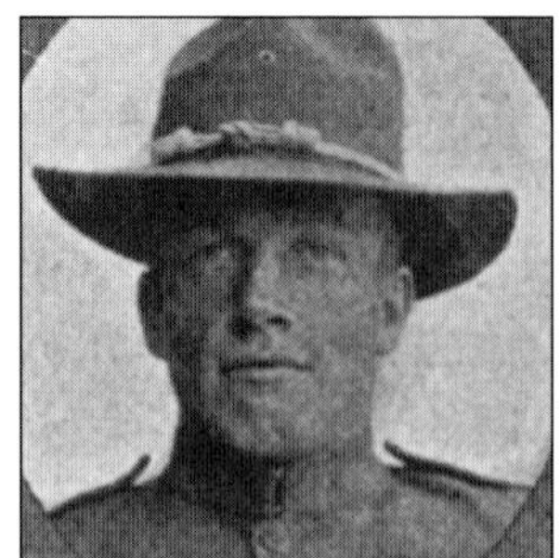

Pvt. Percy Beebe.

Still plenty light and we start to move forward across the open field. It seems a risky thing to do, cross that open field in daylight making an excellent target for German gunners if they can see us. However, we arrive safely at the other patch of woods and halt there. I see men from "A" Company, Clyde Martin, Ray Wingard and Percy Beebe, who were cut and scratched a little but otherwise no one hurt. We stayed in these woods as darkness settled down. The Boche must have seen us go in for we were not there long till we hear his shells coming over in salvos of threes. The men lie on their stomachs and take advantage of every little depression. The woods fill with smoke from the exploding shells. I watch my chance and between shots run over to a little ditch near the woods and drop flat and there unless he drops one right on me I am safe. A few other men follow me into the ditch.

The smoke of the shells hangs close to the ground and at each burst the concussions send it eddying and swirling over the men still in the woods. The woods are enveloped entirely and pieces of sticks, stones and iron drop near me. It lasts fifteen minutes, then a lull, but the men still keep to the holes and depressions. The smoke drifts slowly, the sky clears, the men emerge cautiously like people after a storm. Quiet continues and the search for dead and wounded begins. But not a single man has been hit, which is remarkable for the shells were coming close, trees and branches falling and danger on all sides.

A battery of seventy-fives is to the right of the woods, drawn up under a line of tall trees, their snouts just over a lane embankment. Another battery's front is in the edge of the woods we are in. Now and then they fire a shot but otherwise it remains quiet. About nine p.m. we form again and start forward. The artillerymen say a sympathetic "good luck doughboy" as we pass their batteries and on into the open field ahead. The sky is cloudy but the moon peeps through occasionally making the field bright. We walk ahead in silence except for the soft tread of marching feet on the grass. Commands that are given are low and subdued. A stretcher mounted on wheels is pushed past with a seriously wounded man on it. We know that we are on the very front line now, although for days the front has not been very clearly defined, it has moved back so fast. At last we are going in to attack and I have that queer, weak feeling again wondering what I will do in the attack.

The field we are crossing is about a mile wide. Half way across and the Germans drop a salvo of shells ahead of us. Another salvo bursts but we march on to it. We are closer now and he mixes a little gas with the next salvo. We halt and adjust gas masks to our faces; looks like the officers are intending to lead us right into that fire. Masks on, we move on again as four more shells burst two hundred yards ahead and covering the entire field on a line. I can see no sense in walking right into that but though my mind is set to run my feet keep going on. Discipline conquers fear, otherwise we would all be on the run. Bursts come again as Boche gunners seek to deter us from crossing that field. Yet this is the last burst they fire in the field; the head of the column passes into the smoke and gas, emerges in the clear air on the other side and on into the woods at the other side of the field. The battalion takes refuge in the woods, lies down behind numerous woodpiles, and watch the smoke slowly drifting away in the moonlight. It seems that the German artillery know our whereabouts for we are only there about fifteen minutes when Jerry starts to shell again. The shells drop ahead and the pieces snap and click into our woodpiles. We lay on our stomach and wait, yet as long as we have the woodpiles in front we are safe unless he raises the range fifty yards. Orders are shouted to retire to the fields and wait till the shelling is over. Between shell bursts the men obey, running swiftly out of range and assembling again in the open nearby and all lie down on the ground and watch the show. A woodpile upends suddenly, scattering its sticks.

The field is more comfortable and we sit on the grass and wait when the shelling stops. Overhead a German airplane has been circling since we started and we can hear the hum of his motor dimly. Probably he has been directing the artillery fire for it seems that everywhere we go the artillery follows us. Yet with all their fire no one has been hit.

Near midnight, after a conference of officers, Major Smathers leads us back across the field again, probably another mistake. I secretly hope we are going out altogether. The Boche artillery allows us to go back safely although we are expecting that airplane to be on the job again. If it is light enough for him to see something that looks like a snake crawling we will get it again. We have been extremely lucky tonight, shelled plenty and no one hit. The gunners are asleep as we pass again through their batteries, but some stir sleepily, look at us and fall back to sleep. We halt in the woods and fall out. I make for the ditch, unsling my pack and lie down for a little sleep. Miles away a gas alarm sounds, it comes closer travelling on through several regiments of infantry and artillery, the alarms growing louder till it reaches us, then passes on and dies into the distance. A gas shell bursts miles away; probably someone sounded the alarm and passed it on. The gunners and doughboys come to life, adjust masks but it is a false one. We are still new troops; later on those gas alarms will not scare us so. It becomes quiet again, I doze on the ground and wish I was back home.

July 25. About three a.m. a bustle and stir begins. Officers awaken the non-coms, the non-coms awaken the privates by kicking them on the feet or ribs. First orders to drop our blanket rolls and carry combat packs. We pile the rolls in piles, which some will never be able to identify, although I can tell mine by the method of rolling I use. The companies fall in and report and we move forward across the field again. The moon has gone, and the airplane. Morning fog and chill is in the air. The field is crossed safely and we halt on the other side. Daylight comes slowly through the fog. We move forward again, a shell whistles through the fog and bursts in front of us, sending a shower of dirt and a heavy black smoke obscures our path. Officers order us to adjust gas masks as it may be a gas shell. Masks on, we proceed again till we see a French veteran walking through the smoke with no mask on. He smiles at us recruits; he has known the difference between gas and smoke for years.

We go down a small hill, past a small lake with woods on all sides. Now we are in the Foret de Fere, a beautiful sight. Fog is coming off the lake. A duck flies away warning his mates. Past the lake, we halt on a road that follows the water. Officers tell us that a part of the 111th under Colonel Shannon are surrounded and we are to attack to relieve them. Looking at those quiet, damp, leafy woods that seems impossible. They look like any other woods at home and not a sign of danger. Our gang should be starting on a hunting trip in this place.

"C" and "D" companies deploy and form the first wave. "A" and "B" the second. I remain at Battalion Headquarters till ordered to accompany a flank patrol. I pass with other Scouts near a small soldier of the 26th Division guarding rations for his company. Several men decide to grab him and steal the food. The soldier suspects our intentions, smiles wanly and says, "No fellows, this is for my buddies and they have not eaten for several days." We leave him alone; we ate last night.

The order is given to advance. My ideas of an attack are a complete flop. Over the Top I had always thought meant jumping out of a trench and running wildly toward the enemy with excitement everywhere. All this is a lot of tired men walking through the wet dewey woods. The lines try hard to keep together but in the thick woods this is impossible.

I am on the left flank of the battalion on a patrol to protect the flank from surprise. Lieut. Coburn in command, Sgts. Denning and Leinbach, Dellinger, Casner and I, and five men from the companies. Scouts are also with each company to act as guides and keep them on the right direction with the compass.

Our patrol arrives at a road through the woods. Lieut. Coburn, Sgts. Leinbach and Denning cross ahead of us and then yell for us to cross one at a time. All my Scout training is that they should all cross at the same time so I line them up and we all jump across together. Coburn and Leinbach had already disappeared in the woods and Sgt. Denning had no idea where to go to follow them. So we decide to keep abreast of the companies. Our book learning says our patrol has gone far enough so we should be on hands and knees according to Denning's ideas. Denning drops down on all fours and crawls. The rest of us can't see any reason for crawling so we walk behind him. At last we all sit down to allow Denning to crawl on a little distance; soon he will be crawling on his stomach anyhow, for the book said so. I can see a few men from the companies to our right and they have also stopped. If this is a war, it is a funny one, I want to go to sleep. Denning has crawled off into the woods; where I don't know and don't care. If

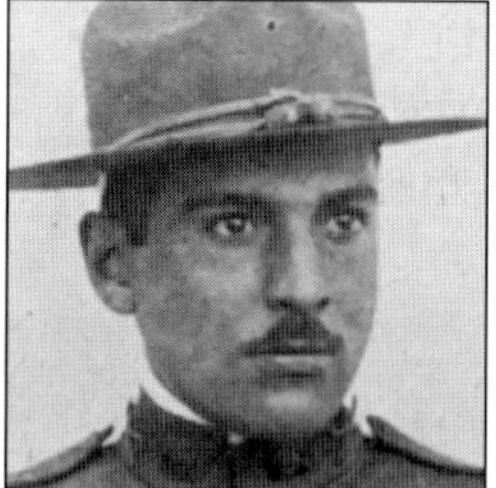
Lt. Camden Coburn.

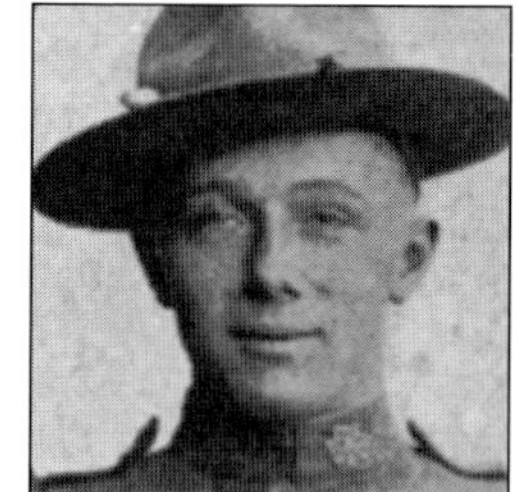
Sgt. Earl Leinbach.

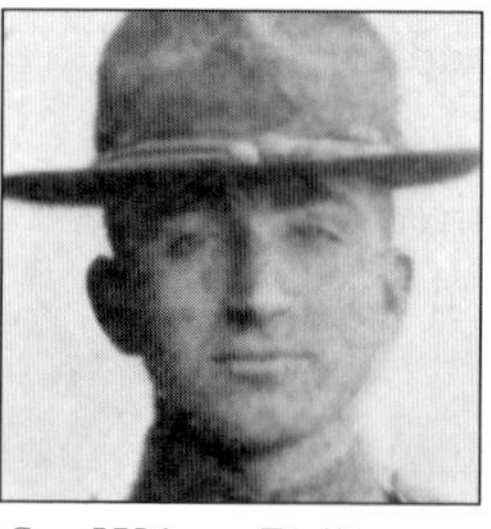
Sgt. Wilmer Dellinger.

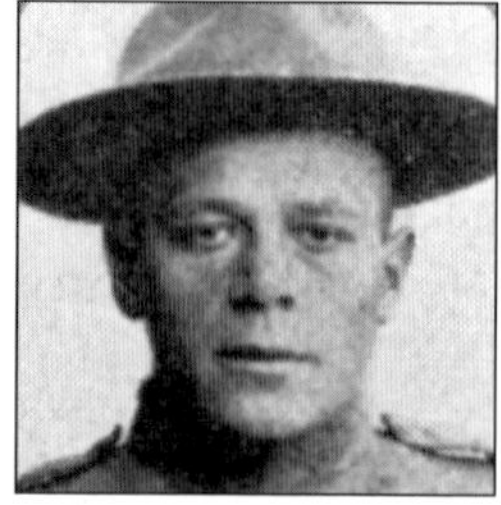
Sgt. Paul Denning.

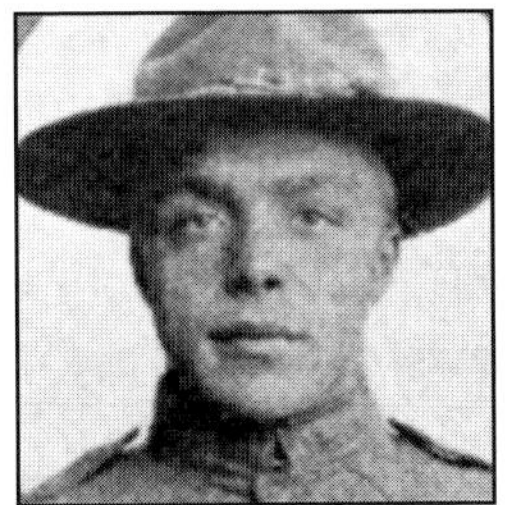
Sgt. Laurance Casner.

they shoot me right now I will just lay down and go to sleep.

The men on our right move forward, so to keep contact we move forward also. The lieutenant and two sergeants have left us so I am in charge of the patrol that is left. Suddenly shells come over and burst to our right. Dellinger, Casner and I move over to our right to get in closer contact with the companies and find out what they are doing if possible. Some of the men say they don't know. I hear a shell coming close and dive into a foxhole with the other two on top of me and escape the shell that bursts close. The hole is full of sneezing gas, which I stir up and inhale. I sneeze and sneeze and sneeze. I try to put on my mask but only sneezed it off. More shells burst close, both high explosive and gas, and confine us to that hole. In that hole we are lying in is powdery mess like iron filings that is causing the trouble. Between sneezes we three decide to run for clearer air. We run through the woods regardless of direction unmindful of the shell bursts that are filling the woods around us with smoke. At last fresher air. We stop, ahead is hot and feverish and I feel dizzy, but in the clear air I sneeze less.

German shells bursting behind us and we believe we are badly gassed. Jerry is shelling the woods, not knowing where we are but dropping them indiscriminately in hopes of hitting someone. We start on the path we are on but soon are confused. We hear guns firing and we decide that is our artillery and we go in that direction. But then guns fire behind us and we decide they are our own so we turn back. Then it seems that guns are firing all around us and we cannot decide which is German or American. My head clears enough to realize we are lost. I don't have any idea how long we had wandered since that sneezing or how far we have gone. As my head clears more I remember that I have been carrying a prismatic compass all over France and we had been travelling north so if we go south we will likely meet our lines. So we go south and soon meet some men from the 26th Division. They divide a box of hardtack with us. Perhaps I am not gassed and only need to eat. They tell us to follow a road and we will be in the 112th sector.

We walk a half mile. Ahead I see two men carrying a stretcher. One of them looks familiar. Dellinger and Casner talk to me but I do not notice them. I keep watching this familiar figure, then start running toward him for I have recognized my brother. We are both glad to know the other is alright. He is helping carry a man badly gassed. Major Smathers had also been gassed and collapsed and Hugh had helped carry him out. He did not know for sure what has become of the companies in the woods but there has been heavy casualties from the shelling and machine guns and the men are pretty well scattered. But "A" Company has again fared well and so far have no casualties due, he thinks, to the excellent judgment of Captain Graff. Another half mile and we find the place beside the lake where we had entered the woods.

Hugh leaves with the gassed man; Casner decides he is gassed bad enough to go to a hospital but Dellinger and I decide to go back and rejoin the outfit if we can find them. We enter the woods again and go in the direction we had followed in the early morning. A few shells come close and we lay in a ditch till they are finished. One shell fells a small tree nearby. A little further we meet a group of men from "D" Company who say we better stay with them. The battalion has been scattered by shell fire into small groups like them and no one knows what to do.

Dellinger and I lie down on the ground. Even with the noise I drop off to sleep. I waken suddenly with a start. We must have been in the center of heavy shelling while we slept, for there are many new holes near us and tree branches nearly cover us. The men from "D" Company must have left us when the shelling started but we slept through it all.

We walk back toward the road undecided what to do. It seems as if we cannot find anyone. Again we rest in a ditch and doze. Then we see men running towards us, Lieut. Flynn of "D" Company leading, across our ditch. A few machine gun bullets are helping them along. It must be bad the way they are running so we run also. They are too fast for us or we are too weak so we slow down to a walk. Again we arrive back at the road by the lake.

Captain Miller of "B" Company is there having taken charge of the Battalion when Major Smathers was gassed. Captain Henderson of "D" is dead. A shell made a direct hit on him and blew him to bits and all they found was his pipe. They think about twenty men have been killed and over a hundred wounded in the four companies but still "A" has escaped. Half of the men are still scattered in small groups not knowing what to do. Some platoons of "C" and "D" kept going ahead and no one knows where they are or what happened to them. A badly mixed up mess. Captain Miller orders Dellinger and I to stay with him. Men drift back from the woods with hard stories. We all lay down beside the road and in the edge of the woods taking advantage of what cover we can find.

The Germans kept up a continuous fire all the time, shifting the shots all over the forest. Some dropped in the lake making a beautiful splash. I wish I could appreciate the beauty of that splash more; at some other time perhaps.

Our field cookers arrive and issue canned corn and tomatoes and bread. We eat it cold from the can, dividing with each other so that all have both. It strengthens me a little even if it does taste raw from the can. The kitchens had innocently driven over the hill and before they knew it had been fired on by the Germans. The attack of the field kitchens will always be a joke in the regiment.

There are still men in the woods, both wounded and unhurt. Captain Miller orders patrols of Scouts sent ahead to order these men back to the road, bring in wounded and report the general situation ahead. Dellinger, Crist and I leave to the front and other patrols are sent to the left and right. We walk ahead a half mile, look over the ground in our sector but find no one so we start back. I am ahead, Crist next, then Dellinger.

Suddenly and for no reason at all I stop by a big beech tree and turn and look at the other two for a moment, then turned and started down the path again. I hear a horrible, rushing noise, a terrifying, howling, screeching thing, that is on to us, we are down, a blast of air and concussion rocks us and passes us, stones and dirt fall from the sky. It had burst about twenty yards in front, directly in the center of the path and exactly where we three would have been if I had not stopped by that big beech tree. I feel that God had stopped us. "Boys," I said, "my mother must be praying for us." "Mine must be too," says Crist. Both voices are shaky with fear and emotion but thankful to be saved. We detour the hole and stay away from the path till we are back on the road and report to Captain Miller. The other patrols return and report wounded men and details are sent for them. I lie in the ditch again and wait, wondering what stopped me by that beech tree and thanking God that he did stop me.

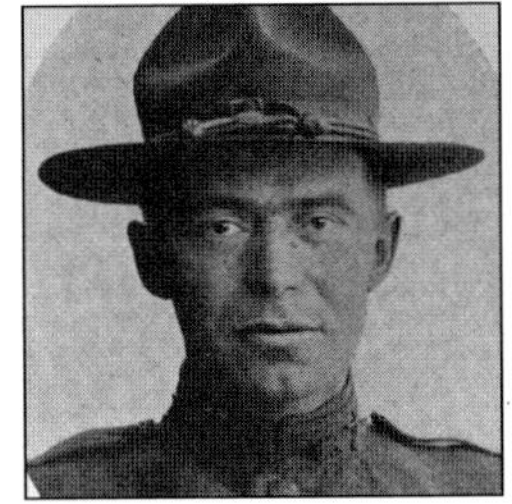

Capt. Harry F. Miller.

High in the air three or four planes are fighting. They maneuver for a long time, swooping and firing at each other, and faintly we hear their machine guns. The machine guns on the ground get in the fight when the Boche ships are close. Suddenly an American plane falters, a moment suspended stationary in air, slips, turns straight for the ground, twisting and turning, falling like a leaf, and end over end, faster, a stream of smoke starts that bursts into flame and when the ship is near the ground is a blazing furnace. The man in it is doomed, there is no help for him. We cannot see it hit the ground for it is miles away and I am glad I cannot be close to it. The others go to it harder than ever. We watch fascinated, hoping an American plane will even the score, but the Boche are too shrewd and finally all leave the scene and fly away.

Bing Johnson and Ed Bowers report that they have slipped through the encircling Boche and had been in contact with Colonel Shannon of the 111th.

About four p.m., Jerry let loose another high explosive attack along our road. The edge of the woods and the lake churn violently. One shell hits a tree trunk about thirty feet from the ground shattering the tree trunk into splinters and shavings. A man near me jumps, stares dumbly around, grabs his head and holds it a minute, rolls over, blood streams down his face, then he recovers a little and he and his buddy run off to a dressing station. A sergeant walks calmly down the road with his arm severed almost entirely off, the hole opening and closing as he walks. Crist and I start for the water carts to fill our canteens. A man white as chalk, but strangely familiar, is carried past on a stretcher with a large hole above his knee. He is past before I recognize Walter Duncan. The burst coming high in the air had caused plenty of damage.

I am sick and disgusted with this war business. Nothing but terror, horror and misery all day and not even a chance to shoot. There is not even a thrill as I had expected. So far, all it seems to be is waiting till someone plants an explosive near enough to kill you. Our attack has been a failure to all appearances, nothing but confusion and disorder all day long, with some going here and some going there and no one knowing what to do. I am not experienced enough to know that this is the inevitable way of war all the time, that there is no order in war at any time and cannot be for how can order come from chaos. But we learn later that the attack did have the desired effect for it caused the Germans surrounding the 111th to leave.

Captain Miller informs the men that we will remain at the road and that the Rainbow Division will relieve us soon. The news is welcome. Now I understand why those boys of the 26th a few days ago were so happy when they thought we were going to relieve them. They come in about dusk, the Alabama Boys, a fine looking bunch of men, as they duck swiftly across the road and on into the woods where they will remain for the night. As they leap-frog us I cannot help but think of what would have happened if this regiment from Alabama had met this regiment from Pennsylvania in the Sixties. I feel a little emotion as they pass to carry on the work of the Pennsylvania and the New England soldiers. As they enter the woods stretcher bearers carry out badly wounded men of our outfit. The incoming men look cleaner and fresher than we who have been in several days. I hope we soon get out.

That last burst of fire must have been the last as no more came over and the Germans must have retreated for Rainbow men said later they did not see a Dutchman in miles. When the Alabama boys are all in line we make ready to leave. It seems now that they cannot walk fast enough and the line drags slowly out. In the twilight we pick up our packs where we left them the night before then turn farther back. As the front recedes I relax more and more till I am practically asleep on my feet. My eyes will stay open just enough to see the man ahead. For nearly a week now we have been hiking and fighting, plenty of mental strain till now we are exhausted.

We are hiking along a country lane now. Half asleep I hear a man yell, "Readieeee – Fire", then a terrific blast and blaze of light that rocks me to my gizzard. My head seems to swell and the world has become a world of red dancing lights. I cannot see for the red lights or hear for the roarings in my head but I know that we have walked in front of a big gun just as it went off. It had been just off the side of the road in the bushes and half asleep I never suspected its existence. I stumble on, trying to follow a dim dark form I see in the red world. Gradually the lights subside but the head roarings continue. My eyes feel the same as if I had looked at the Sun too long. At last a halt and I stand beside a tree after the others had fallen asleep, trying to get my mind to work. My brother finds me against the tree, and makes me lay down and go to sleep although the red lights still dance and the roar still continues.

July 26. When I waken it is raining. I can see better in daylight but my hearing is bad. Hugh has a meal he found somewhere, then he and I pitch pup tents but later in the day moved to another part of the woods. For five days we have hiked with only one small meal a day and now we have three meals. Men assemble and talk over yesterday's fight and hear the news of those that have gone West and those wounded and missing. Estimates are that the battalion lost about one hundred and twenty men. Stragglers unaccounted for drift in during the day. "A" is most fortunate, none injured yesterday and still three slightly wounded on the Marne.

Chapter 4

Fismes

Editor's note

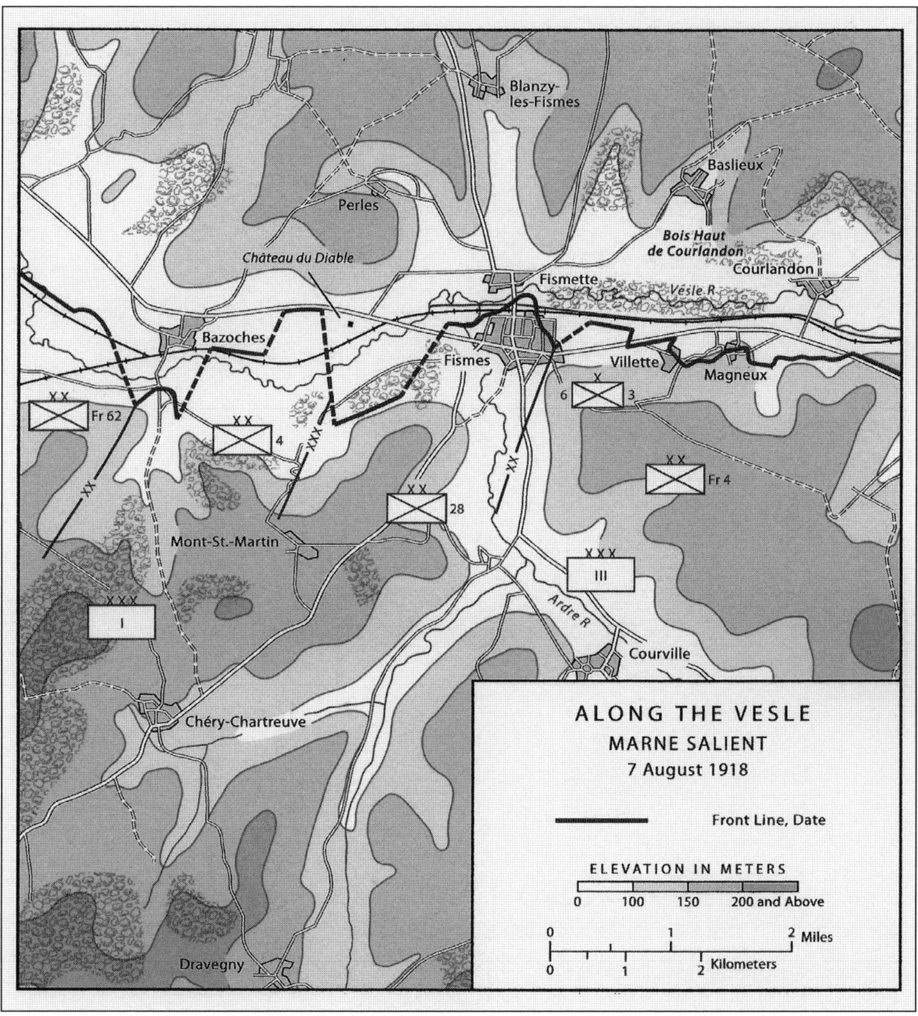

This map from *Center for Military History* shows the Vesle River front in August–September 1918 during operations at Fismes and Fismette.

The American divisions under overall French command continued in the final days of July to push hard on the German Army, whose offensive capabilities were spent. The 56th Brigade with its 111th and 112th regiments continued forward, but mainly behind the frontline action. The Germans remained a formidable opponent, even if on the defensive. The 55th Brigade met stiff resistance as it pushed the Germans back to the Ourq River and then beyond. On August 3, the 56th Brigade moved up, again marching in heavy rain at night, ultimately reaching Chery-Chartreuve by August 6. The next day, August 7, the regiment arrived at Fismes on the south bank of the Vesle River, which was more like a creek.

The original French orders were to take Fismes and then cross the Vesle to its suburb of Fismette and beyond. The French wanted the Germans back about two miles, enough so that more forces could cross the Vesle if needed for additional – though still unplanned – offensive action. By August 6, however, the French had called off the overall offensive. Still, the attack on Fismes and Fismette went ahead on August 7 and the 112th succeeded in establishing a small foothold on the north side of the Vesle.

The division spent the rest of August at or near Fismes and Fismette struggling to hold on to this small bridgehead. The Germans were determined to push the Americans back across the small river. The fighting was vicious, often in house-to-house and room-to-room fighting, as each side tried to gain the upper hand in

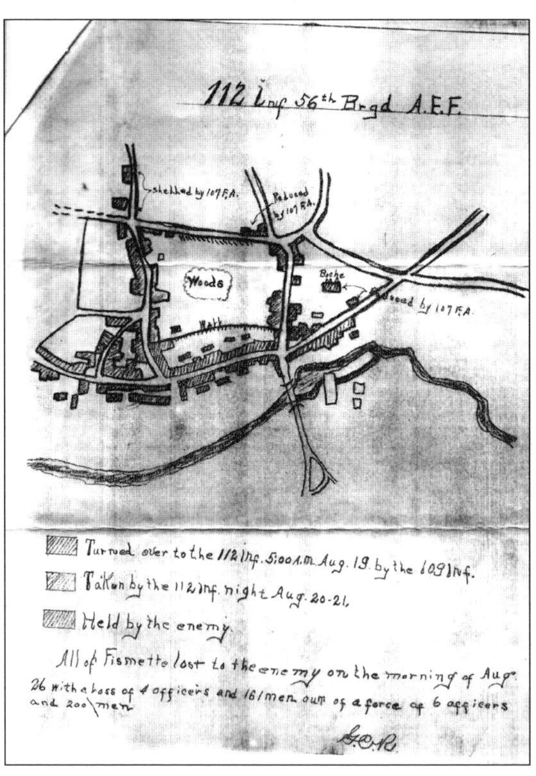

A hand-drawn map of Fismette. (*National Archives*)

Fismette and along the Vesle. The division's regiments rotated their time at this front without trenches. Any man moving near the Vesle faced possible death from enemy artillery, machine guns and snipers; soldiers fought from behind roadside walls, sunken roads, shell holes, railroad embankments and the rubble of blasted buildings. Pierce's diary reports it from the ground level. Most fearsome for the doughboys were the artillery barrages raining down one shattering explosion after another.

American generals wanted to pull back from Fismette. French Major General Jean Degoutte insisted the Americans hold onto the bridgehead. In the early morning hours August 27, a powerful German attack by an estimated 1,000 storm troops hit Fismette just after Companies G and H relieved other units. Both companies lost most of their men as either killed or captured. The American generals were furious and became more

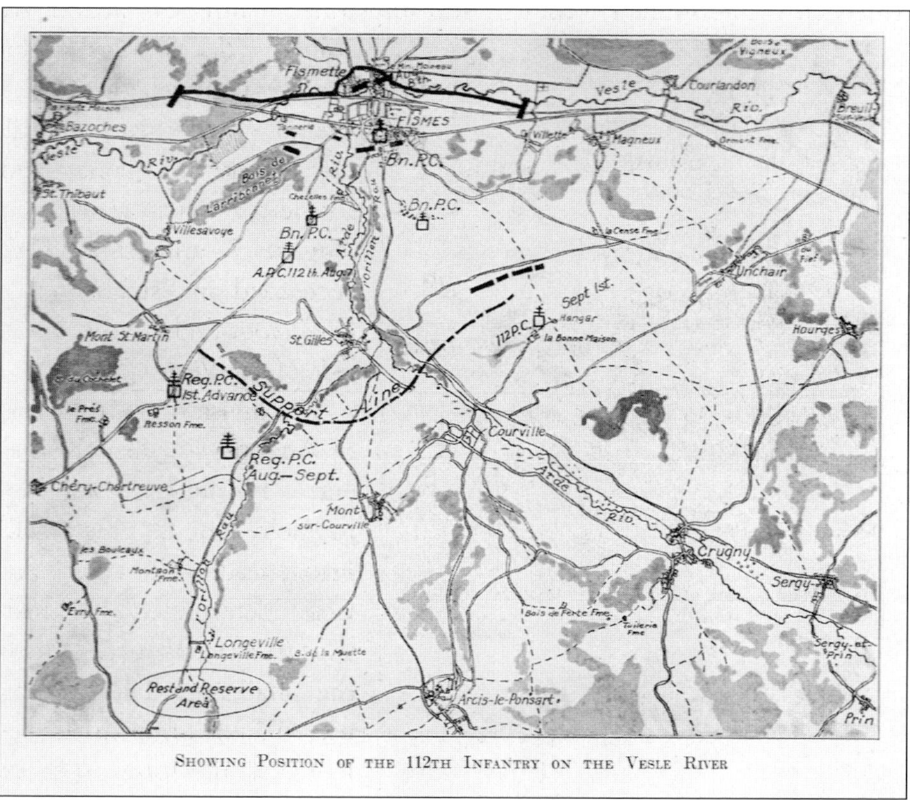

This map from *The Twenty-Eighth Division: Pennsylvania Guard in the World War* shows positions held by the 112th Regiment during operations at Fismes and Fismette.

determined than ever that the French would no longer command American troops. They got their way – the rest of the major actions involving Americans in that part of France went under American command and control.

Not long after the American setback, the German Army in the entire sector retreated before a new Allied advance. The 28th Division joined in that advance but then was pulled off the front in September to stage near Verdun for the big offensive General Pershing and his staff were planning at the Meuse-Argonne sector. While no longer at the front, the men of Keystone Division endured hard marching through cold rain and wind. They thought their arrival in the Verdun sector meant better days ahead.

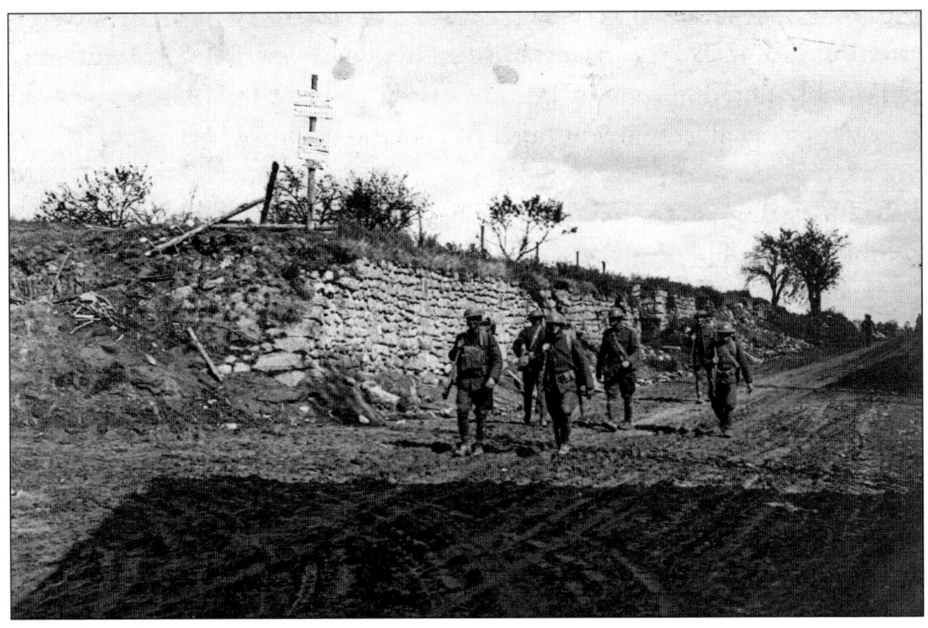

Doughboys advance on Fismes in August 1918.

Chapter 5

On to the Vesle

July 29. We move into another forest closer to the front. A small town is shelled as we pass through. There has been heavy fighting on the Ourcq near Sergy, Cierges and Seringes where the Germans stopped and tried to take the offensive from the Americans. The 109th and 110th are on the front and have had very heavy casualties. Today as we went forward, stretcher bearers were carrying badly wounded men back. The weather is unbearably hot, and men in the lines have stripped to shirts, some even throwing away all equipment but a rifle, bayonet and gas mask.

July 30. In the same woods in reserve. The 55th Brigade had a hard time on the Ourcq. The Prussian Guard tried to attack and there was hand to hand fighting but the Jerries could not stand the bayonet. We hear today they were trying to use tanks.

August 1. Kelly, a runner from "B" Company, and I sneak off to the front to see what is going on. Still hot. Men from the 32nd Division have even thrown away their leggings. They are really going in there to fight. But the line has quieted a little and Jerry is on the run again it seems. The 32nd is pushing ahead. We visit the grave of Lt. Colonel Fetzer of the 110th and six men killed with him by a shell that struck their headquarters. The 110th are said to have lost over one-third of their men in this battle. Signal Corps men in a hole beside the road want us to be careful. We remain with them and they point out infantry crossing an open field a mile ahead in combat groups. We hear bursts of machine gun fire and occasionally there is a whispering in the air as a spent bullet passes. We are close enough. It is much more interesting to watch a battle than to be in one.

August 2. Mother always writes cheerful letters. I write as often as I can, which is not often. I also read the New Testament often. I carry it over my heart in my shirt pocket with my trench mirror and letters. Someone said a bullet will not go through a New Testament. I am certain it will stop shrapnel. A man shoots himself in the foot, "accidently". The front ahead has quieted down; Jerry is running again. He lost the Battle of the Ourcq.

August 3. Orders to move again at dusk. We start for the front. This front has moved back rapidly after the licking Jerry received on the Ourcq. The Battle of the Ourcq is finished in another brilliant American victory. We are to follow the enemy till he stops for another go. A Red Cross truck beside the road hands out cans of tobacco as we pass. Although I do not smoke I take what I can get for my friends.

We pass through Sergy and Caumont where the 55th Brigade fought so well. For about two miles the odor of rotting, dead bodies is stifling. Few of the victims of this brilliant victory are buried and though it is dark and cannot see them they must be thick. It is depressing for we know that in a few days some of us will be the same. I hate to think of my body a horrible thing to look at and people holding their noses as they pass, but then it is the end of us all. We have won another victory but who can feel any elation when they smell the horrid stench of the battlefield. Back home people will brag of the fighting qualities of the American soldier but smelling his dead body is another thing.

The sky becomes overcast and a drizzling rain sets in. Truck trains of the 4th Division crowd us off the road and we must walk in the ditches or be run over as it is all the driver can do to see the road without lights, much less watch for walking doughboys.

August 4. Still on the move as midnight runs on to morning. The rain which started softly is coming harder. Our raincoats are on but we are wet both from the rain outside and the sweat inside. The cooties, stirred by the heat, are moving faster. I itch, but under that pack and all I cannot scratch. All I can do is wiggle my body inside like a cow scratching itself on a post. No wonder I itch; it is weeks since I had a bath.

About two a.m. we halt and rest beside the road. Then for about two miles, the column moves by jerks, a few yards ahead, halt and wait, a few more yards, stop again, and so on for about two hours. This is disgusting for at each halt we do not have time to rest. It rains harder, then lightning and thunder, the water pours from the skies and running in streams ankle deep down the road. At last we halt by a little mine town called Chamery. Above the thunder, we hear the scream of a German shell, adding its burst to the thunder on the crossroads at Chamery.

Captain Miller calls me and sends me off through the night and the storm to try and find the road we are supposed to take. I tramp over wet roads and fields but could find no road of his description. We are supposed to go on beyond Chamery but the storm has made that impossible. When I return without results Captain Miller has already ordered the men into the houses to sleep. By lightning flashes I find a house with a roof, crawl through a hole in the wall and lay down on a pile of rocks and debris and go to sleep in my wet clothes and shoes.

I waken about nine a.m., the storm is over and the sun shining bright. Burt Oudett has a fire going in the old fireplace and I dry my clothes. "A" Company sets up their field kitchen near Chamery and about eleven we have doughballs. Quentin Roosevelt's grave is near, left the same as it was when the Germans buried him when he fell in his plane a few weeks ago.

After dinner we start again and pass through Coulonges and Dravegny. As we pass a 32nd Division Headquarters, a man yells again, "We have them on the run boys, the cavalry can't even find them." I hear a shell coming again, closer and closer and I am ready to drop but it bursts in a house beside the road, throwing sticks, stones and dust into the air. I wish they would quit telling us, "The cavalry can't even find them"; the same thing happened in Chateau-Mary. It looks as if the cavalry did not look very far. We walk on expecting more shells but this is the only one. Beyond Dravegny we turned to the left across a field and enter a patch of woods on a hilltop, pitched pup tents and prepared for the night. Another meal, making two today.

Another hike to the front. Jerry has retreated plenty of kilometers since he started on the 18th of July. We pass a field where cavalry must have charged as there are several dead horses there. Later a troop of French lancers trotted across a field, returning from the front. Our march ends at a little town called Chery-Chartreuve, where we dig in in a steep bank near the town. We sleep at night wondering what tomorrow will bring.

August 6. The day is clear and warm and observation balloons are up on both sides. All day we remain in our dugouts in the bank without disturbance.

At dusk we roll packs, fall in and hike through Chery-Chartreuve and then follow the highway to Fismes. We pass troops from the 4th and 32nd Division coming out. "What outfit Jack". "The 990th Division" or "Y.M.C.A. replacements" is the answer. We turn off to the left on a wrong road, then our 3rd Battalion passes us, we return, then on again toward Fismes. The jerky movements begin again, a few yards, halt, a few yards, halt, etc., and so on for hours. A soft drizzling downpour. On one halt I stepped into a foxhole beside the road to rest and my foot sinks in mud and water over my ankles. German shrapnel comes whining through the air occasionally to burst in the air close to the road. Our ears are tuned now for that shrieking noise that means a shell coming and we must dive to the ground if we care to live.

August 7. The hike continues in the jerky manner till about daybreak and we have travelled three kilometers. Orders are passed to lie in the ditches and sleep. Gratefully, I drop my pack and rifle, lay down beside them in the muddy ditch and drop off to sleep.

The sun awakens me about noon. Some are stirring and some still sleep. A ration cart arrives with a meal, then corn willie and salmon are issued for reserve rations. The Boche shell the fields and the roads intermittently all day but we are well protected by the ditch and only a direct hit would get us. Few men leave their shelter and then only when necessary.

A few unwise men from another outfit pitch a pup tent in a field about two hundred yards from the road. It looks like a foolish thing with German observation balloons up. The tent is not up long. A salvo of Boche shells whistle over our heads and makes a direct hit under the tent. The body of a man and the tent rises high in air above the smoke and dirt, twisting and turning and then comes flapping to the ground with a thud. One other man is slightly wounded. His buddies run in time to escape the other shells that burst. I read my New Testament; after a sight like that I need it. I pray to myself, the same may happen to me and it is best to be ready to go quick.

FISMES

Runners coming from Fismes say the town is full of gas. A call is passed down the road for stretcher bearers. The bearers run up but soon return for they were not needed. I am glad, for the sight of men in agony on a stretcher is not good for men ready to go to the front line. Yossolovitch is one of the stretcher bearers, one of the smallest in the company.

About 4 p.m., a mile away in the valley road a battalion of infantry in squad formation marches toward Fismes looking like a brown snake crawling along the ground. What a beautiful target in close order for field artillery. How could anybody be so dumb as to march an entire battalion this close to the front in broad daylight in close order? There is nothing we can do about it but pray for them. The brown snake crawls slowly on until hidden behind our hill so far unmolested but I cannot conceive of them getting through unharmed.

Dusk and we fall in again. Now we are going in and face the music and Jerry the fiddler making us dance. The 3rd Battalion has been in all day along the Vesle River and now it is our turn. I have that queer, empty, weak feeling in the pit of the stomach again.

Captain Miller, in command of the 1st Battalion, issues warnings about the gas in the valley and also that it is reported that the Boche have attached bombs to the end of telephone wires loose in the streets. We walk a mile ahead and see the town of Fismes in the valley below. A white cloud of gas and smoke hovers over the town but otherwise it looks peaceful enough. We turn to the right down a sunken road that crosses a field five hundred yards in width. A big German, swelled and bloated to enormous size, lay on his back with his hands raised high above his body. The road is good protection, the Boche had used it as a trench, and dug holes in its sides. Bandages on a dead man's head and shoulders make a ghastly sight in the twilight. He is not dead long enough to smell yet.

Past the sunken road is an old mill. It is almost dark, the sun has set but the sky is still pink. A salvo of three shells hits near the old mill and burst just before we arrive there. The reports echo and re-echo through the valley. We drop to the ground and remain quiet. Another salvo, each shell with a different shriek like a badly arranged trio. We are not close enough to the bursts for much effect except for stray pieces but we don't want any closer. The shelling lasts a few minutes then stops, we move ahead again closer to the old mill, the shelling starts again and we drop to the ground till it is over. When all is quiet we move into the blackness under the trees surrounding the old mill. We cross the mill race on a plank in single file. It is difficult to walk this plank in the darkness; a slip would mean a fall of twenty feet into the water bubbling and gurgling under us. The entire battalion, about eight hundred men, must cross this plank and it takes time to do this. Those already across wait in the road beyond, lying on the ground in case of more shelling. Then we cross a railroad track, then a narrow gauge track and up a street leading into the main part of town and halt again. Two fires burn lustily in the town sending a red glow into the sky. We proceed cautiously as it is not known yet if the Boche are clear out of town or not. We believe they still hold a part.

My part of the battalion is between two stone walls on each side of the street. We are not there long until the German artillery starts again in salvoes of threes, the same battery I believe that was firing on us at the old mill. The shells have the same discordant shriek, bursting beyond the wall to our left, sending a shower of steel clicking against the opposite side of our wall. We drop down to the street again and lie on the bricks. If a shell comes through that wall it's goodnight for us and they only have to raise the range a few yards and they will be dropping big stones on our backs. The strafing lasts a long time but there is nothing we can do about it but hope for the best. Another, heavier gun, starts and lands shells on the other side of the wall, adding to the commotion and increasing our danger. If any of those guns shift a little a shell may drop into a close packed organization and kill scores of men. But the Lord must be with us for the shells stick to their course just enough to save us. Why don't we move ahead and get out of this?

Captain Miller has left us to find the positions we are to take from the 32nd Division. The adjutant, Lieut. Galbraith, is worried for fear he is hit in this shelling. At last he calls me; I am to go with Rhodes and Pvt. Crist and find the captain. The detail, difficult and dangerous as it is, is a relief from hiding between two walls expecting the walls to be blown in anytime. The Adjutant issues instructions. Captain Miller went up that street ahead and expected to find the 32nd Division that had occupied the town that day. An easy assignment, a strange town, dark except for the burning buildings, the streets littered with fallen buildings, shell holes, poles, wires and other debris and we are not certain that the Americans do hold the town. He warns us again of wires that may have bombs attached to them.

We go ahead a block and start down a street leading to our right. A shell strikes a house ahead of us, we duck behind a building and watch, another shell and we hear a building falling, then another bursts in the center of the street sending its whining messengers of death by us. That is enough; Captain Miller did not go down that street. We take another street leading to the center of town. At first we are careful of the wires that snag us, and stop and free our feet. But that soon is too tiresome; at last we pull and jerk, bombs or no bombs.

"Halt, who is there," a voice challenges in a loud whisper. Sgt. Rhodes answers. "Advance to be recognized," the voice whispers again. We cannot see the man till we are near the voice when he steps from a ruined doorway, bayonet leveled at us. He is soon satisfied we are alright, glad we are the relief, and directs us to the next guard. In this manner we are passed from guard to guard. One guard informs us that a strange Captain passed and he directed him to their Battalion Headquarters.

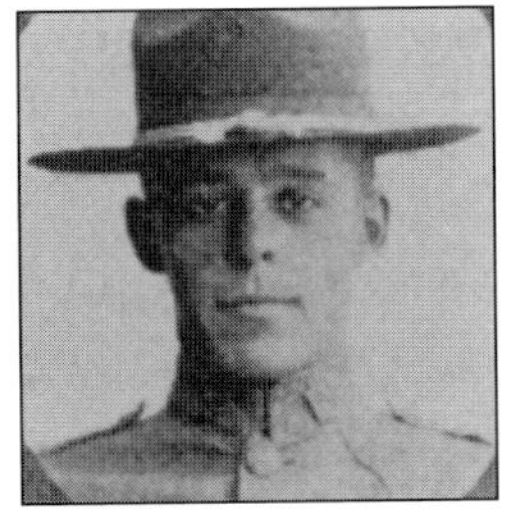

Sgt. Nellus Rhodes.

We leave the third ruined street. We should be stopped again. We halt to look around and take bearings but everything is quiet; too quiet. I glance at my feet and I am standing straddle of a dead American Soldier. Frightened, we duck into a doorway, fearing that this dead soldier is the guard that has been sniped or stabbed by a sneaking German. Sgt. Rhodes runs back to the last guard for information.

Crist and I remain watching from the doorway. Crist and I hear a noise in the rock piles across the street. Something IS moving, maybe Germans coming back to finish us as they finished the man on the sidewalk. We strain our ears, a few small stones rattle, our rifles are ready to fire. Something is crawling over those rocks towards us. Sgt. Rhodes returns from his visit to the last guard, hears the same noise and draws his forty-five. The rattle of stones is closer and then a cat crawls over the rocks. We laugh relieved. The dead man was not killed by a sneaking German but by shellfire this afternoon when this battalion came into town. Sgt. Rhodes has the location of their Battalion Headquarters, so we proceed down the street till halted by another man in a doorway where the headquarters is located. The guard leads us down a black hallway, lifts a blanket to the cellar where the captain commanding the battalion is. He informs us that Captain Miller has been there and gone back to his men, that we are to relieve his men and try and push the Boche out of Fismes entirely. This battalion was the one that we saw earlier today marching up the valley in the direction of Fismes. They had been untouched until they arrived in the town when Jerry cut loose at them. A few minutes here and we started back to our outfit.

Captain Miller was already back and we met him at the head of the troops marching into Fismes. It is now about 11:30 p.m. Past two burning buildings we march toward the center of town. The heat scorches us as we pass and rifle ammunition is exploding continuously in the flames. Beyond the burning buildings we turn left down a dark alley, then into a courtyard and onto a road where we halt and Battalion Headquarters remains there. The companies push farther into the town to remain for the rest of the night. "A" has been attached to the 3rd Battalion, which has been in action all day along the Vesle River to the left of the town of Fismes.

August 8. At one a.m. I am sent to bring up the ammunition wagon. Captain Miller shows me the map where they are located three kilos back on the road to Chery-Chartreuve. I must go back and find a place in the dark only by the memory of that map and bring them up a strange road to a place I never even heard of before. By now it is very dark and foggy. I start across a field but am soon lost among the trees but I keep on until I am on a road. There I am confused in directions as all I can see is dark, damp fog. I am to get those ammunition wagons up by daylight so I cannot take time to be lost. I sense rather than see the presence of another man, an engineer who shows me the right road and as it happens the very same road we came down earlier in the night. At the old mill I hesitate to walk across that plank but finally cross on hands and knees. A new fear in the sunken road, that dead German's lying in the road. I know he cannot hurt me, still I dread to pass him alone. It must be the fog. I climb the bank so I will miss the one lying in the dugout, sing a hymn to myself, then whistling the same hymn and thus fortified I pass on by him. But the fog has also blotted out his bloated body and I pass him unobserved in the dark and reach the road to Chery-Chartreuve safe, but not brave.

On the road I think of what a brave soldier I must be to be afraid of a dead German. My fears leave me on the road and I walk faster. About two kilos back three ammunition wagons are waiting to be guided to the front. It is now three a.m. and we will have to hurry for the drivers to get away before daylight. The drivers push their mules as fast as possible. We pass the sunken road, then down a hill to the old tannery I had seen on the map. Our artillery has been firing a barrage behind us and it doesn't seem to be going very far. I fear I may be leading these men and animals into the Boche lines. The drivers question me uneasily to see if I am right. At the tannery, dead Germans are sprawled all over the road and ditches, one with his face entirely blown off and the face lying in the road. A Dodge Sedan staff car is wrecked in the ditch. I worry more as our shells are bursting not far in front of us. Just this side of the bursts is the creek bank where we are to cache the ammunition. We hurry the remaining distance dubiously, pull off the road and unload as rapidly as possible; the drivers leave as rapidly as possible for it is now near daylight. I wonder if I am not caching this for the Germans.

But ahead the shells are bursting close so we must be almost on the front line. The shells whistle closer over my head as the artillery lowers the range and the shell bursts are closer. On the opposite bank of the creek men run towards me.

"What's the matter?" I yell. "Our artillery is firing into us and have chased us all the way back from the river." It is true, our own artillery hit first on our own front line positions and chased the men back and then lowered the range and chased them back further. I covered the ammunition with branches to keep the dump from being seen by planes and then follow the drivers on the run before our own artillery kill us. Pieces of their steel shower the field as I run. Hippensteel, a Scout from the 2nd Battalion, passes me swearing a blue streak at the dumb artillery. He says he has to run back two miles and plead with them to cease firing as signals and telephone messages have done no good. Must be a pro-German in command back there. I halt on a little bridge across the creek. In the main street of Fismes our infantry are running across the street. The gunners lower the range again; the infantry retreat sullenly out of range. I also must get out so

I walk along a railroad track to find battalion headquarters and report. Something caused the artillery to cease firing. We heard rumors later that a first sergeant killed his officer but never found out if it was true or not.

On the tracks I met a ration detail from "G" Company under Lieut. Friedenburg and offer to help in return for a little food. When I leave them at Battalion Headquarters, they give me a half load of bread with very little mold on it.

It is now about seven a.m. Battalion is in an old wine cellar beside the road leading into Fismes. In front lies a man torn to pieces, a gruesome sight, his head resting on his chin, eyes staring to the front, and a leg wrapped around his neck. He had been gassed the day before and laid there on a stretcher and a shell came along and finished him. I laid down in some weeds near him and tried to eat the bread, picking the good from the moldy. I cannot keep my eyes off that man. What if it is my brother, but no it is not. Then partly to keep from seeing him and partly to rest I close my eyes to sleep. A little kitten plays around me, purring and crawling over my pack. Such an innocent thing in this great war, but hardly more innocent than that dead boy over there. The kitty seems to comfort me and I stroke and play with it as it purrs contentedly beside me. Eyes closed again, it plays over my shoulders, its gentle paws so different than the harsh world. Someone kicks me on the foot, the chaplain of the 2nd Battalion, a Catholic priest. "Excuse me," he said, "I thought you were dead." I assured him I was not. "I am glad of it, we have enough as it is," he smiled back at me. Maybe the kitty thought I was dead also; cats are meat eaters and this kitty is well fed.

I rest and then look for my brother and report to Captain Miller the location of the ammunition dump. Captain Miller and Captain Phelps are still mad at the artillery for firing at our men as it stopped an attack the 2nd Battalion was to make on Fismette. I find my brother O.K. in a ruined building across from the wine cellar, just awakened and hungry. We pair off and eat a little breakfast then decide to build a dugout. In the weeds where the kitten played we dig a hole in the bank away from the Boche lines and protected except from a direct hit of course. But I believe I prefer an open hole to a building where stones and rafters can cave in on you.

I am not at work long until I am called to go on a patrol. Sgt. Moore and Cpl. Graham of the 2nd Battalion, Scouts and Clush and I of the 1st Battalion Scouts are to form the patrol. Captains Phelps and Miller

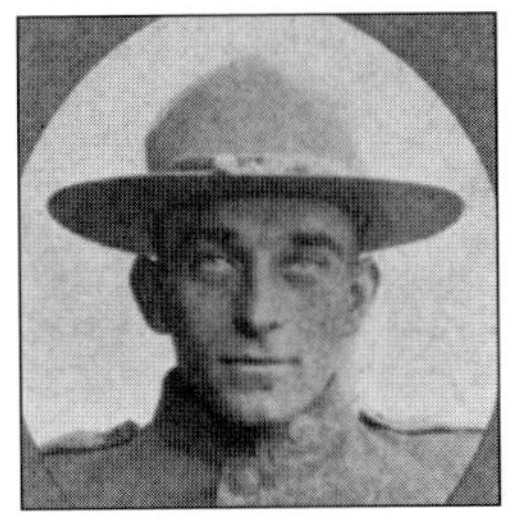

Pvt. William Clush.

explain the situation to us in the wine cellar. The attack this morning was stopped by our own artillery. The 3rd Battalion has crossed the Vesle River about a kilo to the left of Fismes and is holding. We must get Fismette, which is directly across the river from Fismes, or the 3rd will not be able to hold their gains. There is one bridge across in the center of the town and this is covered with machine guns. The river is filled with barbed wire and due to the recent storm is running high so it cannot be forded or swam. They want us to find a way across the river to the left of Fismette if possible. Burt Oudett has been down to the river during the darkness and claimed there is a small footbridge across. We are to find if there are trees that can be felled across the river in the same manner as the 3rd crossed. The 3rd needs our help badly.

Our patrol cuts across a field to the Main Street to the left of the town and halt behind the road embankment where the railroad crossed the road. Machine guns and riflemen are behind this bank and here form the front of our lines. Although in Fismes, our lines are much closer to the river. We explain to the machine gun sergeant what we are going to do and he promises to cover us. Then we raise our heads slowly over the embankment to survey the ground ahead. In front of us is a field a half mile wide and beyond that the river bank bordered by pine trees that we are to go to. The railroad goes directly to the river and then curves to the right into Fismes so it will give us a little protection if we stick close to its ditches and embankments. If we ever are to use our scout training it will be now as in broad daylight we have fine chances of being observed by the Boche across the river. Our worst bet is crossing the road where we must be upright but then if not observed we can crawl on our bellies in the railroad ditches. Sgt. Moore gives our last instructions, orders us to all lie down behind the bank and when he gives the signal we will all jump up, run across the road and dive for the bank and if not fired on we will keep on.

Moore gives the signal, we are off like a sprinter, a run and a dive and we are in the railroad ditch across the road. Once there we lie still and listen, no shots, so we must not have been observed. Then taking advantage of the ditch we crawl slowly forward on hands and knees and when the ditch is not high enough to conceal us we crawl on our stomachs. We do not have to be told as maybe there are snipers on the other side waiting for us to expose a small part of the body for them to drill. We rest often and observe both ahead and behind although we can see little above the ditch for we dare not look over the top. Two hundred yards down the track we crawl through a small break in the ditch and into a drainage ditch that follows the railroad to the curve. This ditch is just about large enough to hold a man's body and has the advantage of being concealed more than the ditch beside the track. More cautiously now we proceed in single file, half expecting a burst of machine gun bullets to come tearing up the ditch from the heights above the river. A half mile is a long way to crawl but it is the only way to do it. At last we reach the curve and so far have not been observed. Once we have passed the curve we are on a straightaway into Fismes with a good bank between us and only a few feet to the Vesle River. Here we hold a conference. All decide that the best thing to do is to jump over the railroad embankment and hope not to be observed and take the first cover we see on the other side. If we have not been observed we are all right but we dare not look over the top beforehand or we may be seen and they be ready for us. Again we dig in our toes to jump. Sgt. Moore signals, we are up and over and in two jumps are over the bank and slide to the ground. Of cover, there is none. We are lying in short grass fifteen yards from the Vesle.

A few pine trees are along the bank and could be felled if choppers could live long enough. A small foot bridge does cross the stream hardly a foot above the water line only a few yards from us but the water is deep and we can see strands of barbed wire. Across the river is the village of Fismette. Smoke is rising from a small fire and clothes are hanging on a line there. Our position is bad; at any minute we may be discovered and riddled with bullets. I hear a shout across the river and Sgt. Moore orders us all back over the bank. We run for life, jump the tracks and drop into the ditch on the safe side and still no bullets. But over our heads now German shells whistle through the air to burst on the rear of Fismes. We start the return trip on hands and knees. The return is more tiresome than when we came down. Halfway back the machine guns covering us begin to fire. We halt in the ditch, certain that we have been seen and a party of Germans are on the other side of the track coming for us. But then the guns are pointed down the road in the direction of the Tannerie so the Germans are in that direction. At last, tired of crawling we run the last two hundred yards to the roads, then over the road, panting hard, safe behind the embankment we halt to recover breath. The machine gun and riflemen behind the road are firing steadily at Germans who occasionally jump across the road from the bushes at the Tannerie, the same place I had passed this morning with the ammunition wagons. I was surely close then. This party of the enemy must have been working up from the river about the same time we were returning but on the other side of the track. The guns cease firing as no more Boche appear. I wonder if there could have been live Germans in that Tannerie when I passed this morning. Maybe the men in that wrecked Dodge car had been taken prisoners. The gunners watch closely for more Boche but no more came over. About a dozen were in the party. Our patrol then returns to Battalion Headquarters to report.

Hugh has been working on our dugout while I was gone. Five dead American soldiers had been laid on the road beside our hole covered with shelter halfs. Two men come to bury them on the bank above us. One, lying on a door is directly in front of us. The burying detail wish to roll him onto a stretcher. When they raise the door the body rolls out from the shelter half onto the stretcher face up. But there is no face for both face and chest have been blown away leaving nothing but blackened flesh and blood. The two men scream and run. We turn our heads and look into our hole. I cannot bear to look at that poor dead soldier again. At last slowly and gingerly one of the detail comes tiptoeing back and shakily covers the corpse with the shelter half; the other comes back and they carry him up to his shallow grave above us.

Hugh and I build a small fire for our dinner. We mix French hardtack and salmon and cook it and make coffee in our tin cups. But the memory of that dead soldier is too much for a good appetite. The other dead are carried away during the meal but I look away. After our dinner we dig the dugout deeper; now it should be safe for anything but a direct hit. Over us is a bank and across the street is a high stone wall that will stop fragments from that side. We talk of serious things that afternoon. About five we cook another mess of French hardtack and salmon, not much but the best we have. Hugh has found a can of German solidified alcohol, which we use for cooking.

A terrible barrage on Fismes starts in the early evening with several batteries of Boche artillery firing rapid fire. All around us the air is filled with whistling, rushing shrieks, explosions and dirt, stones and fragments. We dive into our hole just in time. There is nothing to do now but to take it and pray. Hugh insists that I stay on the inside of the hole. The ground sways and rocks with the explosions. I hug the earth and pray the agonized prayer of a soldier. "Oh Lord, keep them going a little higher." There is nothing to rely on but God, he is our only salvation. It seems that the very foundation of the earth is shaken by the violence of the explosions. The shell bursts are within a few feet of us and so rapid that we cannot count them. Stones and hot pieces of iron whiz into our hole and miss us by inches. All around the earth is erupting violently into the air, stones and dirt rising and falling in clouds of smoke and dirt. The fines on the wall opposite us disappear along with a section of the wall as a shell goes on through. The suspense is terrible, at any minute now we expect a shell to blow us into eternity or cave the dirt in and smother us to death. But the violence of it passes our hole as the Boche raise the range a hundred yards and then cease firing altogether. It only lasts fifteen minutes but what a long time. The quiet is like the quiet after a thunderstorm. Above us the dead buried today are uncovered and must be buried anew. I am glad we dug our hole where we did and I offer a prayer of thanks to God for keeping those shells as far away as he did.

Colonel Snyder of the 103rd Engineers passes as we raise our heads above the parapets of our dugout to examine things. He has a detail of engineers to put a bridge across the Vesle River, if possible. His men lie on the ground in front of our hole while the Colonel is talking to Captain Miller in the wine cellar. I am glad I do not have their job. These men had taken that barrage in the open and came through unhurt, though how I can explain except by the Grace of God. It was the most intense and vicious artillery fire I have been in yet and I do not care to repeat.

The engineers pass on into town. It grows dark. Over the bank a shriek and three men come rolling and tumbling down the bank. One, a shell shock, is fighting with two others trying to hold him. He strikes at them with fists and feet but at last they throw him to the ground and sit on him where he groans and writhes on the ground. They try and make him wear his gas mask as there may be gas around but he will not have it. At last they get him on his feet and push and jerk him back with them toward the rear. The man is crying and screaming as he is led away. It is quieter now. Hugh and I lay in our hole and talk. Brothers, we are very dear to each other now. I secretly wish he would be wounded, not seriously but enough to get him out of this mess. As for me I would welcome a wound, even a foot or a hand off, just so I am not going to be horribly mangled. It is not that I fear death or the beyond for I have always lived a good life but it is that awful sock you get before you die. I can understand now why a man is so happy when a bullet hits him in the arm or leg. A blighty is about the best a doughboy can look for in this war.

We have not crossed into Fismette yet for it is a tough proposition. The companies are along the railroad embankment near the river but the river separates us from Jerry. It is not wide, but the bridge is too well covered with machine guns and the river filled with barbed wire.

August 9. Our rations are low so early in the morning Hugh and another Scout and I go up to a cave beyond the sunken road where there is a supply. We are lucky: "D" Company's mess is there and they say it cannot be taken any closer. We eat well and carry off rations for ourselves. The dead German in the road does not scare me in the daylight and with some company. On the way back I see a man sitting along our path. It is a German soldier, apparently dead, but sitting leaning against his pack. We pass him up of course, being dead, but I passed this place later and he was gone so I believe that German was alive and playing possum.

A large batch of prisoners arrived that had been taken at the river. These men were caught as they had advanced down to the river bank to dig in. Our men on the tracks held their fire till they were on the bank and started to dig in and then opened fire killing and wounding several of them. Some escaped into the houses and these had surrendered. During the excitement some of our men had crossed the bridge into Fismette, obtained a foothold and sent the prisoners over to Fismes. On the way over the bridge their own machine guns had opened fire on them and several more were shot. About forty with two officers wait in front of Battalion Headquarters. Some of them are friendly and glad to be captured. A few of their shells burst in the town. These men are veterans and accustomed to shelling and they are amused when we duck if the shell is not close. I try to stand close to them and pass the shelling off as unconcernedly as they do but my knees have a tendency to jerk when the shell comes shrieking into our neighborhood. After they are marched away another captured German is brought in. A single American escorts him and the Yankee puts his pack on the Heinie's back, who carries it good-naturedly. The story is that a little German followed Red Eckroth into Battalion Headquarters and surrendered. Red did not know there was anyone with him till they asked him where he found his prisoner. Lieut. Ackerly and Cribbins of the Scouts were badly wounded today.

About two p.m. a runner brings word of a counter attack on our troops in Fismette. That town is now held by most of the 2nd Battalion and parts of the 1st. Since the capture, Battalion Headquarters is too far away. Captain Miller sends most of the personnel forward with Sgt. Major Kale. Lieut. Galbrath, Sgt. Mars, my brother and I go with Captain Miller. We cross the courtyard above us, then on to the Main street of Fismes toward the square but turn down a street before reaching the square as the Germans have been dropping big shells near the square for several minutes. Captain Miller and Lieut. Galbraith cross a street while we wait till they are across. A big shell comes down quickly with that terrible rushing noise and bursts in the center of the street entirely eliminating the officers from sight. Another one follows and we three duck behind a building till it

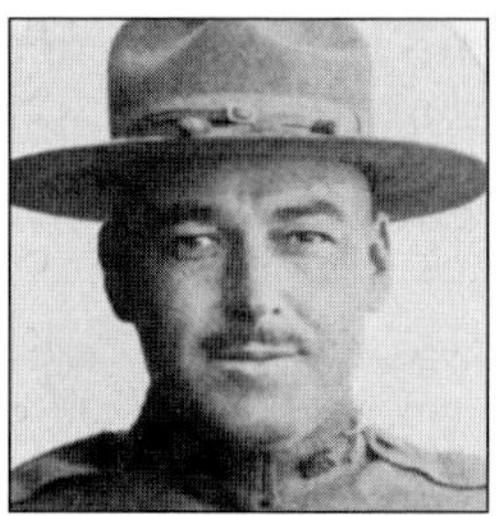

Lt. Charles Galbrath.

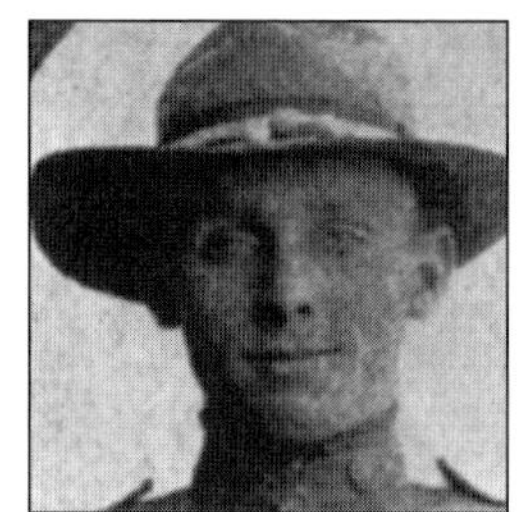

Sgt. William Mars.

explodes in the same place, then we run across into the smoke to pick up what is left of the officers. But instead we find them, not only alive but laughing. Relieved, we laugh with them. Later I found the reason for their good nature. They had found a barrel of German kimmel.

We followed them on a run from that dangerous square toward the river. We turn down a side street and an old lady runs across the street into a partly ruined house. Curious, we followed her and found she was a half crazy old French lady. I thought she must be entirely crazy to stay when she did not have to. Her house looked fairly neat and clean amid the debris of the town and I noticed that the houses in her vicinity had not been damaged as much as further up town. She cackled around and insisted on us drinking some black French coffee, which she made and served in small china cups that seemed out of place in the midst of a battle.

Captain Miller told Sgt. Mars, Hugh and I to go to the river and find out what is doing. We find Sgt. Major Kale and the rest of Battalion Headquarters along the river bank trying to find something to shoot at. Kale warns us to stay under cover as a Boche plane is up. Regimental Sgt. Major Powell had just dumped a supply of hand grenades near the bridge. He went with us back to Captain Miller.

The six of us then go down closer to the river and climb up a roofless house to observe. Seeing nothing, we go down to the bridge into Fismette. A Lieutenant from Company A shot in the leg yesterday and just going for first aid now comes limping across the bridge. He stops and informs Captain Miller that the counterattack was easily broken up.

Captain Miller says we will all rush the bridge together. I don't like his decision, for it is a straight run of a hundred yards and the Jerries should

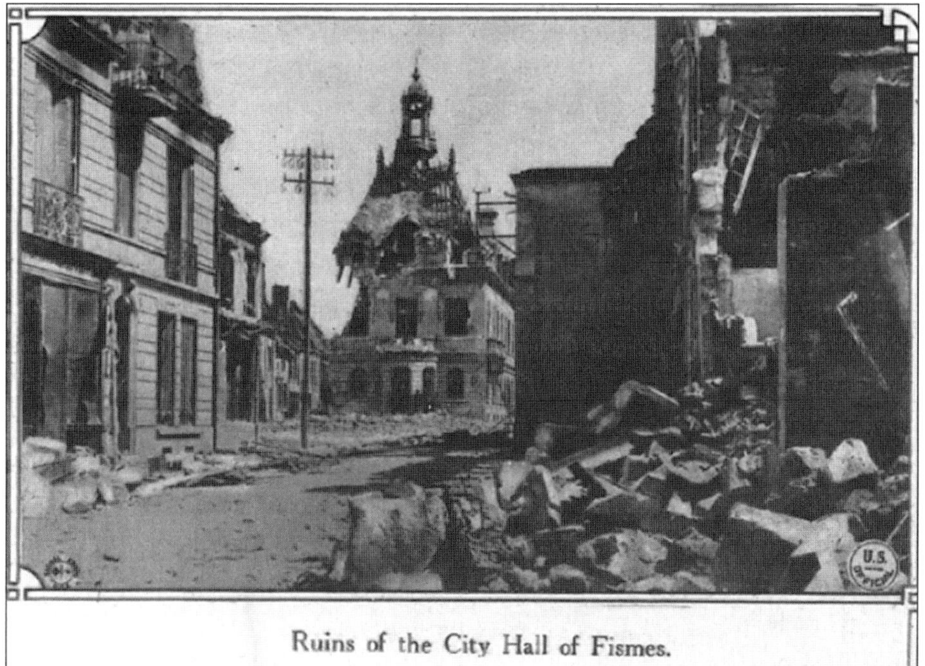

This photo appeared in the book *U.S. Official Army Pictures of the World War* in 1920. It may have served as the model for Harold Pierce's untitled painting showing the same location with doughboys advancing down the street and taking cover in the ruins. This street is likely that referred to on the previous page.

have machine guns up there. He commands to go and we start as fast as our legs can go, over the bridge past a big dud aerial bomb. I see my brother Hugh fall and I think he is shot but he has only jumped into a hole in the bridge and we all follow him to get our wind.

Two dead men are lying in the water. We climb out and run again to the end of the bridge and turn quickly to the left into the houses. Near the first house an American is lying so covered with rock dust he looks like a marble man. In the first building we find men of the 2nd Battalion. Captain Miller receives the news from the officers. Casualties have been high but we hold practically all of Fismette except a few houses still held by the enemy on the outskirts. Lieut. Landry and Lieut. Friedenburg are in one house we are in.

In one house Lieut. Saunders and Danny McClellan are upstairs sniping through a window. Several men of the 2nd Battalion in this house ask for cigarets. Now a few days ago I had a chance to get some cigarets and tobacco and put them in my pack and forgot about them as I do not smoke. These men have had no tobacco for two days and have been smoking leaves. I hand out packs of Camels and Chesterfields and know how the Good Samaritan felt. I am a hero, a saint, a philanthropist in their eyes. Such generosity cannot be imagined. But I save a few packs of Bull Durham for others. They inhale and relax. Lieut. Saunders and McClellan come down from their post for the treat. Saunders asks for a knife to cut notches in his gun saying he has seven. A man nearby wonders quietly how he is so sure of the seven as he stuck the rifle around the corner at arm's length and fired and could not even see the sights much less his "Victims."

Hugh and I walk back of the houses in the open field along the river bank. In this field the Germans were caught in the trap yesterday. They had dug shallow dugouts and put up machine guns and then our regiment had caught them in a murderous rifle fire. Their dead are lying sprawled half in the dugouts where bullets had caught them, some with their hands in air yelling "kamrad." A brilliant exploit, that sudden surprise enabled our regiment to get a foothold in the town. But there is nothing in the waxen faces of these boys in their early twenties of brilliance; nothing but the dirty cruelty of war. The men that shot them are not proud of their work and wish it could be avoided. In the heat of battle men do not realize that the enemy is only a scared, frightened boy like we are, killing for self preservation and because he has to and hating it as bad as we do. As he lies sprawled there, it is different. In their pockets are pictures of women and children who will mourn for their loved ones just as ours will mourn for us. I wish I could have met these fellows as friends instead of this.

The rest of Battalion Headquarters, under Sgt. Major Kale, Scouts and Runners are across now. Casualties are estimated at two hundred in Fismette. None of them have been carried across the bridge yet as it was too dangerous. Captain Miller says they can be carried back and says he will carry the first one and show it can be done. Officers try to dissuade him but he picks up a wounded man and carries him across the bridge to Fismes. The wounded are a pitiful sight; they have not been cared for except for field dressings. Two houses in Fismette are filled with the injured and dying. Now that Captain Miller has started, others carry them across. I believe that there are kind hearted Germans up that road for surely they can see them on the bridge.

I was going to assist in that work but a call comes for men to fill a gap in the lines. All the Scouts and Runners are taken. We run through the streets past another dressing station where two men are trying to lift Pvt. Mauro of "F" Company with an eye hanging down on his face. Then we go between two buildings and run up to a stone wall and drop down behind it. A dozen Scouts fill up the hole in the line there. An orchard is just ahead

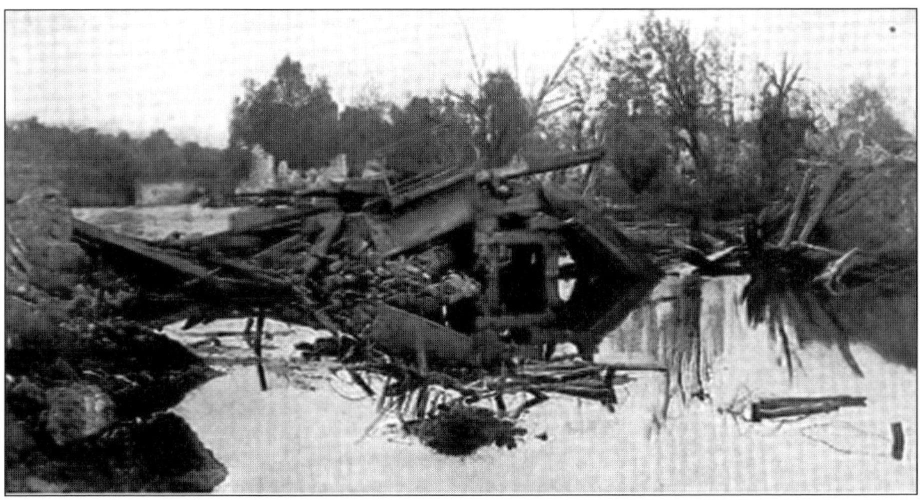

The destroyed bridge between Fismes and Fismette. Doughboys had to wend their way across it as they moved between the two towns, most often under fire. (*Center for Military History*)

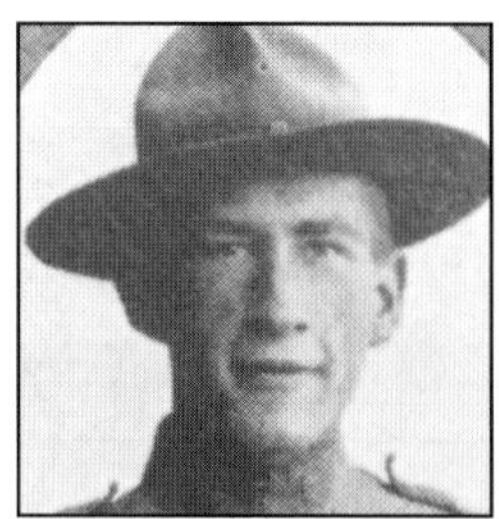

Pvt. John O'Day.

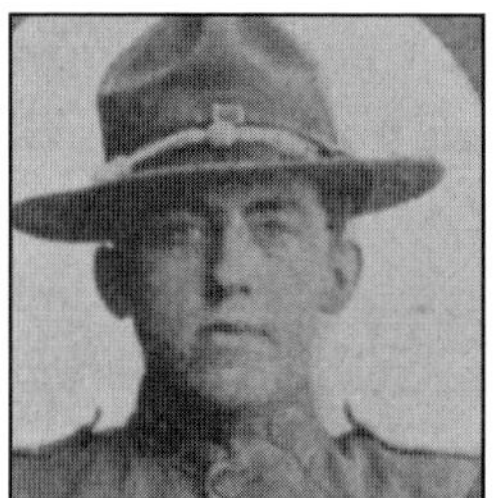

Pvt. Leslie Strauss.

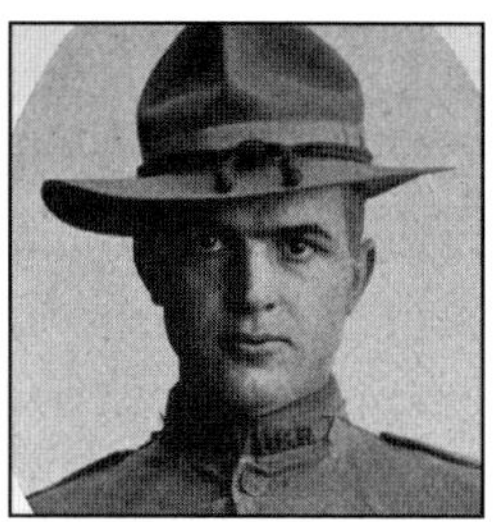

Lt. Philip Burdick.

so we cannot see very well but also offers cover for us. My brother, Hugh, lies to my right, Dellinger to my left, Smith, Strauss and O'Day left of Dellinger. To our right are men from the 2nd Battalion, about twenty, only their part of the wall is higher and they fire from the kneeling position.

Lieut. Burdick is walking up and down behind the line coolly directing the firing. He orders us to fire a shot occasionally but be careful of our shells for if the Boche shut off that bridge on us ammunition will be hard to get. The kick of the rifle feels good and I actually enjoy it a little as it is the first time I have fired a shot in the direction of the enemy although I cannot see anything to shoot at. A machine gun is ahead of us somewhere close and it lets go a few bursts. When it fired I would get down behind the wall. Hugh claims it is an American gun and does not get down although it is firing steady now and the crack of its bullets are plain now over our heads. I yell at him to get down but he laughs and fires another shot. I jump and grab him around the neck and shoulders and throw him to the ground heavily and light on top of him. Just then a leaf comes tumbling out of the peach branches cut by a bullet not over a foot over his head. He is willing to admit I am right.

The machine gun blazes away at the bridge trying to make up for lost time. The men on my right pop their heads above the wall and commence firing rapid fire although they only know the general direction of the gun, yet it may make him nervous and save someone on the bridge. The rifles snap and rebound off the wall. Then when the machine gun stops, they drop their heads behind the wall. Lieut. Burdick cautions them about their carelessness and again warns them to save ammunition. But the next time that gun blazes away up go their heads and again they answer it. At any minute I expect to see that machine gun rake the wall and take the lives of those reckless riflemen. The gun stops and they also stop. They are risking their lives but they may be saving the lives of those unprotected men on the bridge.

I see them pop their heads above the wall again and shift their rifles to the right, firing again as if the whole German army are marching down the streets.

Quickly I shift my Springfield to the right to get in a shot. As I shoot, a man from "F" Company next to me drops to the ground as if dead. I had the muzzle about six inches from his ear. He is out for a few seconds, then rolls onto his back, stares to the sky and asks me where he is hit. A sergeant next to him, whose ear drums were almost broken, curses at me but the one who was knocked out says, "Never mind buddy." I settle back of the wall ashamed but then my intentions were good.

Lieut. Burdick walks up to the line and informs us that news has just arrived that the British have broken through the Germans for the first English victory in months. The news was sent up by runners to encourage the men on the line. Then we see Germans running over the hill from Fismette and we hope that the Boche are retreating again.

Dellinger, Hugh and I commence a dugout back of the wall. Our section of the wall has been knocked down and it is only about knee high so we must lie on the ground all the time. A few minutes digging lying on our sides and it is easier to move around. While working a Boche shrapnel bursts close over our heads with a terrific report, which knocks me to the ground with its force. We crawl behind the wall confidently expecting a bombardment but none coming, renew the work on the hole with vigor. Later a Heinie airplane sails leisurely over Fismette, flying low but undisturbed, looking our positions over.

Dusk and there is still a lot of firing in Fismette lasting till after dark. Smith said he shot a German crawling through the peach orchard. I fired occasionally over the wall. On one shot the rifle bucked clear out of my hands. When I examined it I had shot the bayonet ring off. I felt lonesome without that bayonet but I still had a trench knife I could use.

After dark a number of flares go up seemingly from back of our lines. At first we think they are our own but the lights are of value only to the Germans. When they burn we lie low behind the wall till they burn out. These flares kept up hour after hour, annoying the outpost men till everyone believed it was German flares. Here in this town a house may be held by

Americans and the next one held by Germans, and have several times been in the same house together. But during the night a horrible, blood chilling shriek comes from our left. No shots, so some Yank must have reached the flareshooter with the bayonet. A moan or two and all is over and the flares cease.

As darkness is more complete the firing gradually ceases. The artillery fire a few shots behind us and we tremble in our holes knowing too well the habit this artillery has of dumping shells onto the infantry. But apparently they have the range a little better. We are not supported by our regular 28th Division artillery yet and the ones behind us have our wind up as much as the Boche.

Back of the wall we split into reliefs. One watches as long as he can stay awake, wakens the next man who in turn wakens the third man. In this way we spend the night. We sleep fitfully a few minutes at a time without blankets huddled together as the night is cool. Strauss back of the wall is hit by a bullet in the lungs, knocking him instantly unconscious. He lay there all night and the man next to him thought he was sleeping and did not bother him. Lieut. Burdick informs us that the 111th Infantry will relieve us in the morning if they are able to get over the bridge. He warns us that our situation is serious if they cannot come; so conserve our ammunition as much as possible.

August 10. I waken about three a.m. Behind me a line of men are lying on the ground, the relief from the 111th. They are to attack in the morning. We inform them quietly that we have seen Germans running over the hill the night before. But in my heart I pity them if those machine guns are still there and they likely are. I am glad we have a fairly good dugout to turn over to them and hope it saves some.

The 111th are in, we do not wait for orders as we surely are in a hurry to get out. Hugh, Dellinger and I stick together. We run through the streets of Fismette to get to the bridge and over it. Our artillery drops a barrage to protect the relief and prepare for the attack. Machine guns in the houses of Fismes keep up a continuous rattle. Flares are everywhere lighting up the place with a ghostly red light adding to the light from the burning buildings of Fismes. Across the bridge a line of men from the 111th are creeping into Fismette feeling their way. Going toward Fismes are a disorganized bunch of men from the 112th, knowing too well the dangers of that bridge, and hurrying as fast as they can to get out before hell breaks loose again. We three follow the line out past those poor devils going in, running, jumping, twisting and sliding over the ruined bridge but safely across in a short time. On the other side the Boche open up on Fismes with high explosives. We hurry through the streets while houses crumple and fall filling the streets with rock dust and smoke.

The roar is terrific from both sides. The horizon on our sides is lighted with the flashes of many guns while on the German side their horizon also plays. In the center our way is illuminated by the red flares and the burning buildings. Surely this is hell.

In the rush to get out I lose Dellinger and Hugh. Then up the street farther I am beside them again. At the square in Fismes a company from the 109th Machine Gun Battalion are lying on the streets, mules and all, as shells burst and houses fall around the square. We detour them and hurry down the lane to our headquarters of yesterday to run out by the old mill and the sunken road. But the Boche are shelling the back areas heavy, so we duck into our old dugout and lie down to wait till it quiets down. We are tired out, and noise or no noise, danger or not, we are soon sound asleep.

It is daylight when we awaken. Not a shot and birds are singing in the trees a different song than the singing of a few hours ago. We cross the railroad track, past the old mill, up the sunken road to the cave where the ration dump was and then start for Chery-Chartreuve where we expect to find the regiment.

RELIEVED

It is warm and we are tired and late for breakfast anyhow so we walk slowly. A field kitchen from another outfit gives us hot, black coffee, all that is left but the finest drink I have had in my life so far. The field kitchens of other branches all seem willing to share with a doughboy just coming from the lines and many of these men will go hungry to give food to infantrymen. The coffee perks us up till we are back to the valley near Chery-Chartreuve.

I approach the valley, dreading to meet "A" Company and finding out how many of my friends are dead and seriously wounded. I am almost afraid to ask when I see their familiar faces. But "A" has fared well again, only one killed, Barnes, and I do not know him well. Shorty Williams, the shortest man with the biggest pack, the life of the Company, a drafted man from Indiana, is badly shell shocked. A shell lit beside him and seemed to tear the insides out of him. But the names of the slightly wounded I hear with relief as they will be out of it for a while. "A" had spent the time in support of the 3rd Battalion to the left of Fismes. In our Scout Section, Strauss was the only one wounded and we hear that he was carried out by the 111th.

"A" Company's dinner consists of prunes mostly but they are good. Two sixteen-year-old German boys help serve, captured but not sorry, they remain for several days unable to get enough "f'weiss brot." Both stay with "A" and act as kitchen police. It is difficult to imagine these harmless kids as part of the terrible German army that has just given us a taste of their bite. I am glad they surrendered to someone who did not shoot them down without mercy. They should still be in school where most of "A" Company belongs.

Word comes hack that the 111th is having a hard time in Fismette. They attacked as we left but were scarcely up before they were knocked down. At our stone wall they made about a hundred yards, the only gain made but they could not hold it. The Boche counter-attacks with liquid fire but the 111th stops them. They will be lucky to hold Fismette.

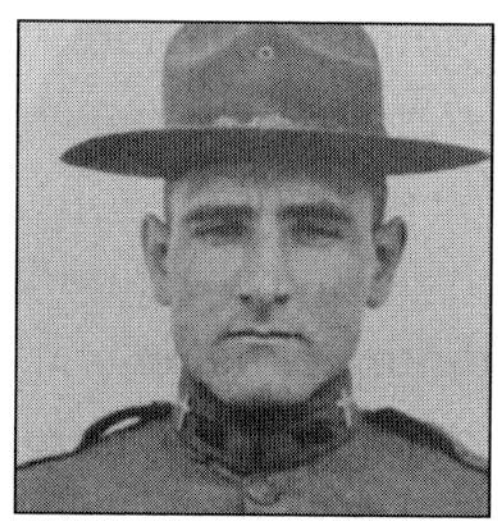

Capt. Willis Hall.

August 11. Sunday and Chaplain Hall has a church service in the valley. Formerly in camp, he had a hard time keeping his crowd. Today everyone crowds around to hear more about God. The rituals and ceremonies of churches are gone, we don't care for that, we want to find out about God and Christ, that being so many of us are going to meet soon. There is no mistaking the feelings of these men, they want to know God. No, they will not be found making long prayers in public or even trying to be pious. Yet today there is an awakened interest in Christianity. They are prepared to meet their God although they say little, yet in their hearts it is all settled.

We are mostly a Protestant regiment but Catholics and Jews are there. No difference in opinion when we really are close to God. Dogmas and creeds are done away with. We sing the old hymns such as "Jesus, Savior, Pilot Me" and "Rock of Ages" with fervor and they bring relief and comfort. Chaplain Hall preaches a short sermon but he says a lot. There is a God and we must serve him, we must do our duty, face death bravely and even be merciful as He is merciful. We may die, and many will, but if we have lived right, what is there to fear.

The service cannot last long, we may be discovered. The Regiment scatter to dugouts in the bank. At the meeting I had a sense of security as long as we were gathered to worship God, no shell would strike us. I know hundreds of men, including myself, were comforted. The cursing and swearing of camp life is not heard on the front. We are a serious lot. New Testaments are read in many a dugout this afternoon.

August 12. Dellinger, Hugh and I are still together but we are forced to move with Battalion Headquarters. We had fixed up a good dugout, covered with elephant iron, and now we hand it over to someone else and must make a new one. Where Battalion Headquarters is, the ground, soft a few yards away, is flinty and hard and digging is a job.

The day is clear and warm. Two of our balloons taking advantage of the clear sky are up a few miles from us. During the afternoon a Boche plane comes hedge-hopping over our lines and then makes a beeline for the first one. The anti-aircraft batteries in our valley come to life. Machine guns stream lead after him and the seventy-fives fill the air near him with shell bursts. The infantry even fire at him with rifles but he keeps right on.

The observers in the first balloon drop in their parachutes and float slowly to the ground. The plane circles the bag as the ground crew work frantically to bring it down, then fires a stream of incendiary bullets into it, a wisp of smoke, then the bag catches fire and falls a mass of smoke and flames. The ground crew is trying to bring down the second balloon two miles away. The Boche, finished with the first, starts with the second. The firing begins again but he is not hit. Again he circles as the observers drop, then another burst and the second bag is a mass of flames. His return trip begins through an atmosphere of bursting shells and streams of bullets from our rifles and machine guns. All at once near Fismes he staggers, turns over and then falls like a dead bird, end over end to the ground. The firing ceases, we have him, the balloons are avenged. But about three hundred feet from the ground, he rights his ship and flies away home, probably thumbing his nose at us.

He was not gone long till we hear the warning screech of coming German shells. Men scatter swiftly to their dugouts, but some are too late. We did wrong in firing at that plane, we gave our positions away. We stay in our holes and take it. It lasts about fifteen minutes with the worst hitting 3rd Battalion. One is killed instantly, others will die and sixty are wounded. Our quiet valley is turned into a place of dread again; we thought we were fairly safe here. The walking wounded leave as fast as possible. Ambulances drive up and take away their loads of seriously wounded with less seriously wounded hanging on wherever they can get a hand hold and those of us uninjured have to stay and take ours all over again.

August 13. Before daybreak the regiment is on the move. The tail end of the column is just about out of the valley when the Dutch bombardment begins. Behind us, growing fainter and fainter, we hear the screech and bursts of their shells but we are away, thank God. We hiked to Dravegny and pitched pup tents for a rest. We hope. The weather is good and it is a relief to be out of the forward zone again.

August 14. Washed clothes in a creek and analyzed the contents. They were full of contents.

August 15. Mailed letters and received letters from home.

August 16. Took a hike to Chamery and visited Quentin Roosevelt's grave. The Germans had placed markers on it and fenced it in with poles.

We eat three meals a day with cabbage and carrots each meal. If I ever marry and the wife made cabbage I will divorce her. I can stand the beef, goldfish, hard tack and corn willie but the boiled cabbage is too much.

We all have diarrhea and what time that is not spent at the latrines is spent going to and coming from the sickness makes me weak and tired. We drill a little to keep in condition. A dud shell lands directly in front of my dugout while I am inside and I am sent on a patrol to try and find a hidden gun.

An airplane fight between one German and two Americans. Air fights are so common we don't look up anymore. But this is a little different. They maneuver for a long time pouring shots into each other. Suddenly the Boche cuts in between them somehow and both Americans collide in midair. They seem to stand still, then locked in death's embrace, they drop. The fall is not pleasant to look at. They hit the ground a mile away and four men are dead. Pieces of the wreckage float down near us.

FISMES AND FISMETTE AGAIN

August 17. Orders to move again to the front and relieve the 109th Infantry. Following the 111th's turn in Fismette a battalion of the 109th were in and now we relieve them. The order dampens the good spirits of the men. It has only been four days since we moved from the dangerous valley near Chery-Chartreuve and we had expected more time to rest. Silently the men pack their few belongings. We have been on the front now nearly two months, just enough to know that the inevitable sometimes will happen.

I am to go with "A" Company to St. Gilles and there other Scouts will take them on to Fismette. The battalion lines up at dusk with "A" ahead and the other companies following several minutes apart. The officers are all ahead with Captain Miller and Sgt. Martin Henning, first sergeant in command.

Captain Miller and Sgt. Mars meet us at St. Gilles near Death Curve. It is now quite dark. The company halts and lies down in the ditches beside the road. Mars said it would be a good idea to get inside a small dugout in the road bank. He and I do so and we are no sooner inside than we hear a salvo of Boche shells screaming overhead. They burst about fifty yards beyond the road and "A" Company. Then for fifteen minutes the shelling is wicked but lucky for "A" most of the shells passed the road and burst in the field fifty yards beyond. Safe in my dugout, I worry for my friends outside. The shelling halts, but we stay inside fearful that it is only a lull to draw us into the open. But at last we emerge from the hole onto the road.

Sgt. Henning calls down the company lines to ask if any are hurt. Scott and Moore are both hit in the arm by fragments. Captain Miller informs me my work is finished and I can wait for Battalion Headquarters. I promise Henning I will see the two wounded men back to a dressing station. I bid him goodbye, wish them good luck, as "A" passes on toward Fismes, the last I will see of some of them forever. Scott, Moore and I start for a dressing station a mile back. They are not dangerously wounded but painful. Moore is just sixteen, nervous and ducks every time a shell comes near but Scott is older and cooler. We find the dressing station and their wounds are dressed and I remain there for the night.

August 18. I join Battalion at the cave above the sunken road a half mile out of Fismes on the hill. It is an ideal place as far as security is concerned but it is a long way for the Scouts and Runners. Nothing can touch you inside that cave and we have the advantage of getting something to eat, which the companies forward do not. "A" is in Fismette, "B" to the right of Fismes, "C" and "D" in Fismes. Upon my arrival Sgt. O'Connor put me to work making maps of the sector. We work between shell bursts as the Boche know this cave is used as a headquarters and they shell often. Thousands of flies and yellow jackets swarm and any movement is a signal to raise them buzzing in the air. When we eat, in order to keep the food fairly free we have to be swinging the food continuously. I thought I was shot today, I bit into a piece of bread and molasses and a yellow jacket bit my mouth.

My brother is also here. We build a dugout near the entrance to the cave, protected by a crevice in the rocks and reinforced with sandbags. The cave inside is damp, dreary and dismal but if the shelling is bad we will go inside. The day is warm and sultry.

August 19. Worked on maps again. Fismes and vicinity are shelled continuously, the Boche evidently aiming to completely destroy the town. Dellinger on Observation Post in Fismes, estimated with accuracy that in the eight hours he was on duty four thousand shells fell on Fismes, Fismette and vicinity. The town is covered all day with a pall of smoke and dust. Our own artillery fires often. And this is a quiet front, no big attacks at present, the line is stationary except in Fismette where the Jerries are trying to get "A" Company out. A platoon of "C" is with them now. Rather than losing ground they have regained all that lost by the two previous regiments. Fismette, a small town of a thousand normal population, is a bad place to be in right now. The houses are close to the river, which is not

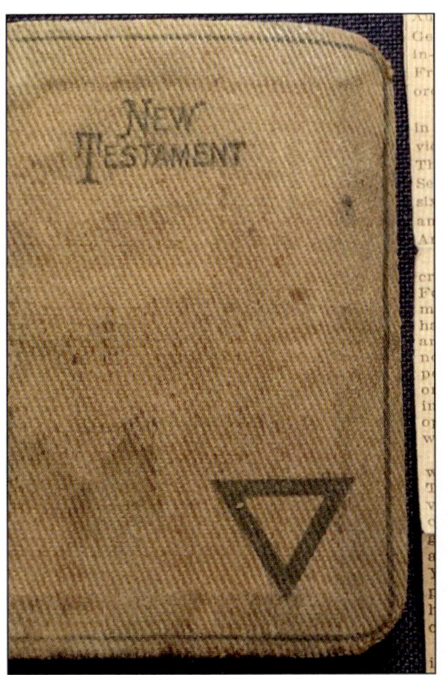

This is the Bible Harold Pierce carried in his shirt pocket throughout the war. He turned to it often for comfort.

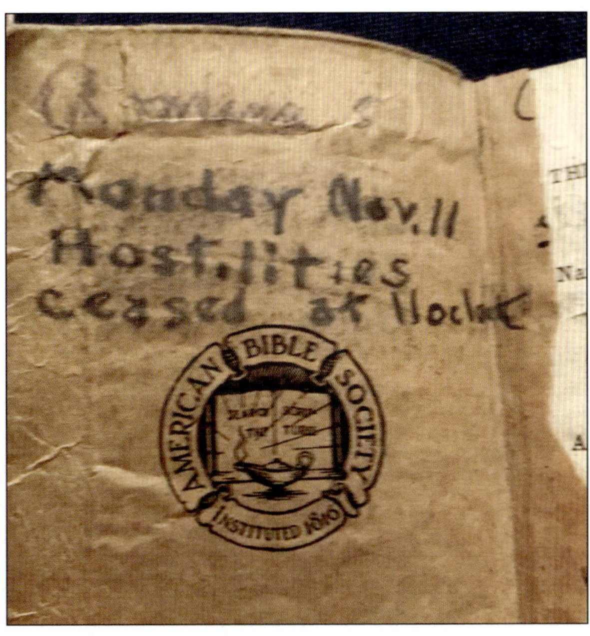

Inside the Bible he wrote down the best news: the Armistice.

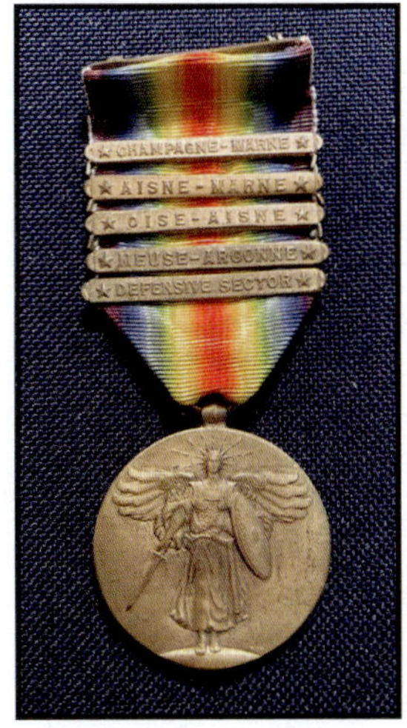

Pierce's campaign medal lists the four campaigns he participated in, much like the rest of the soldiers in the 28th Division. (*All photos this page courtesy of Brenda Pierce Simpson*)

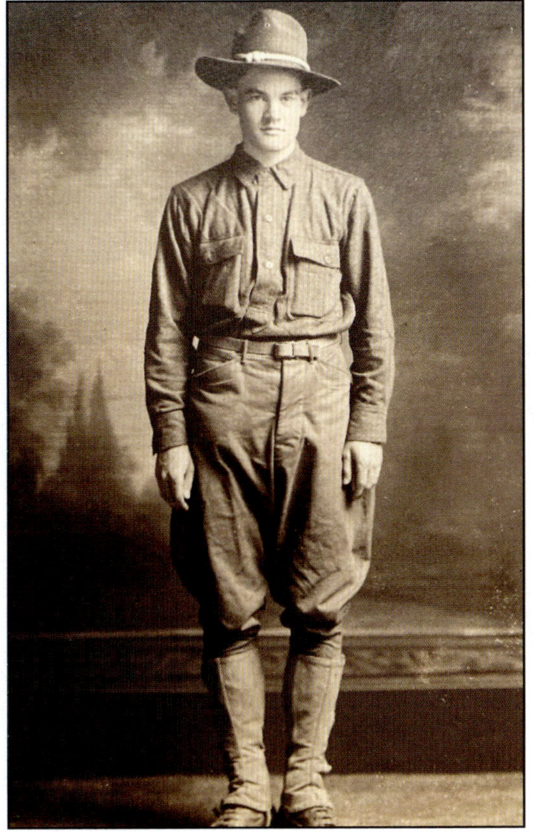

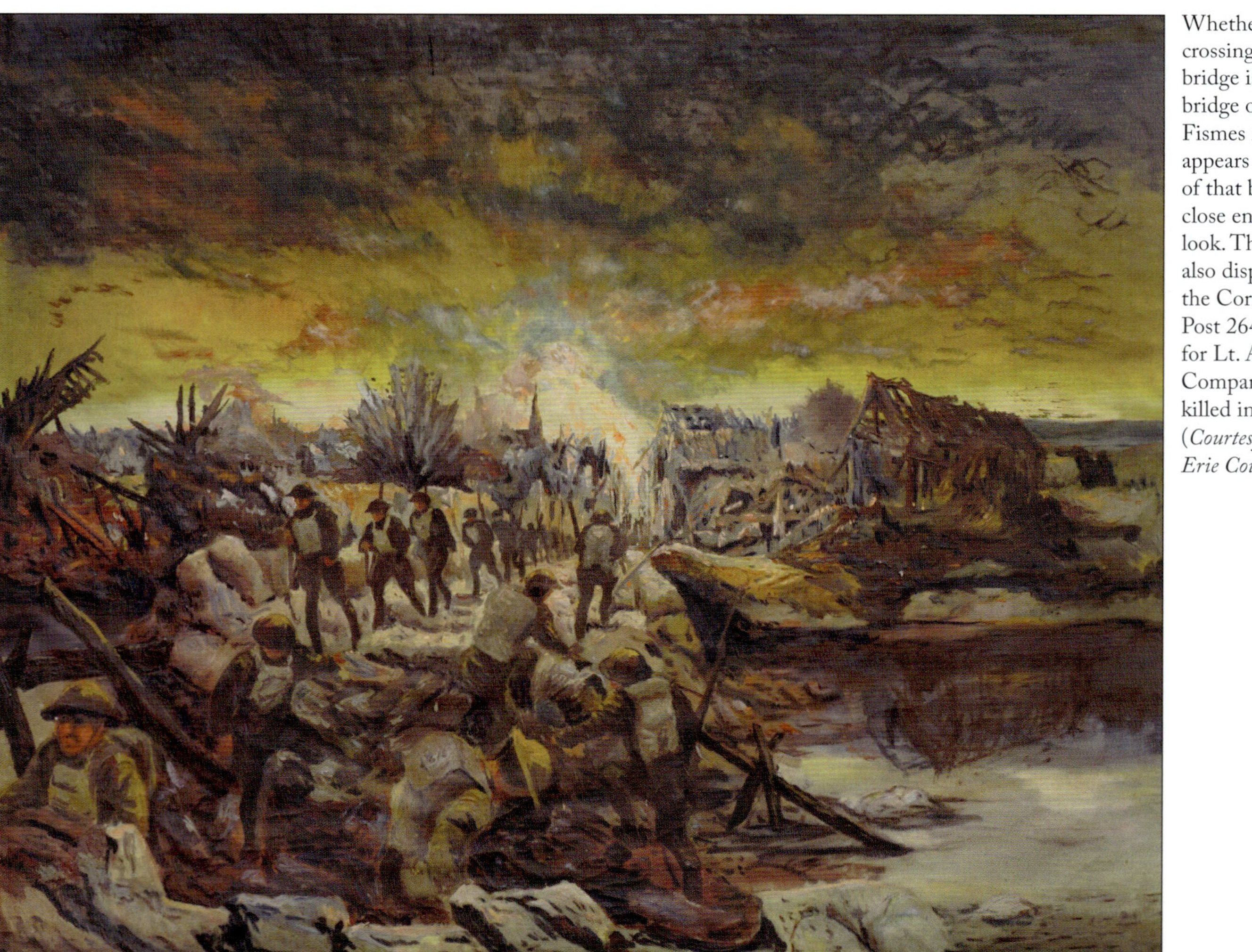

Whether this painting of troops crossing the ruins of a stone bridge is meant to show the bridge over the Vesle River at Fismes is conjecture now. It appears different from the photo of that bridge on Page 77, but close enough to warrant a closer look. This Pierce painting was also displayed for decades in the Corry, Pennsylvania, VFW Post 264 hall that was named for Lt. Archie Thompson of Company A. Thompson was killed in action August 18, 1918. (*Courtesy Hagen History Center, Erie County Historical Society*)

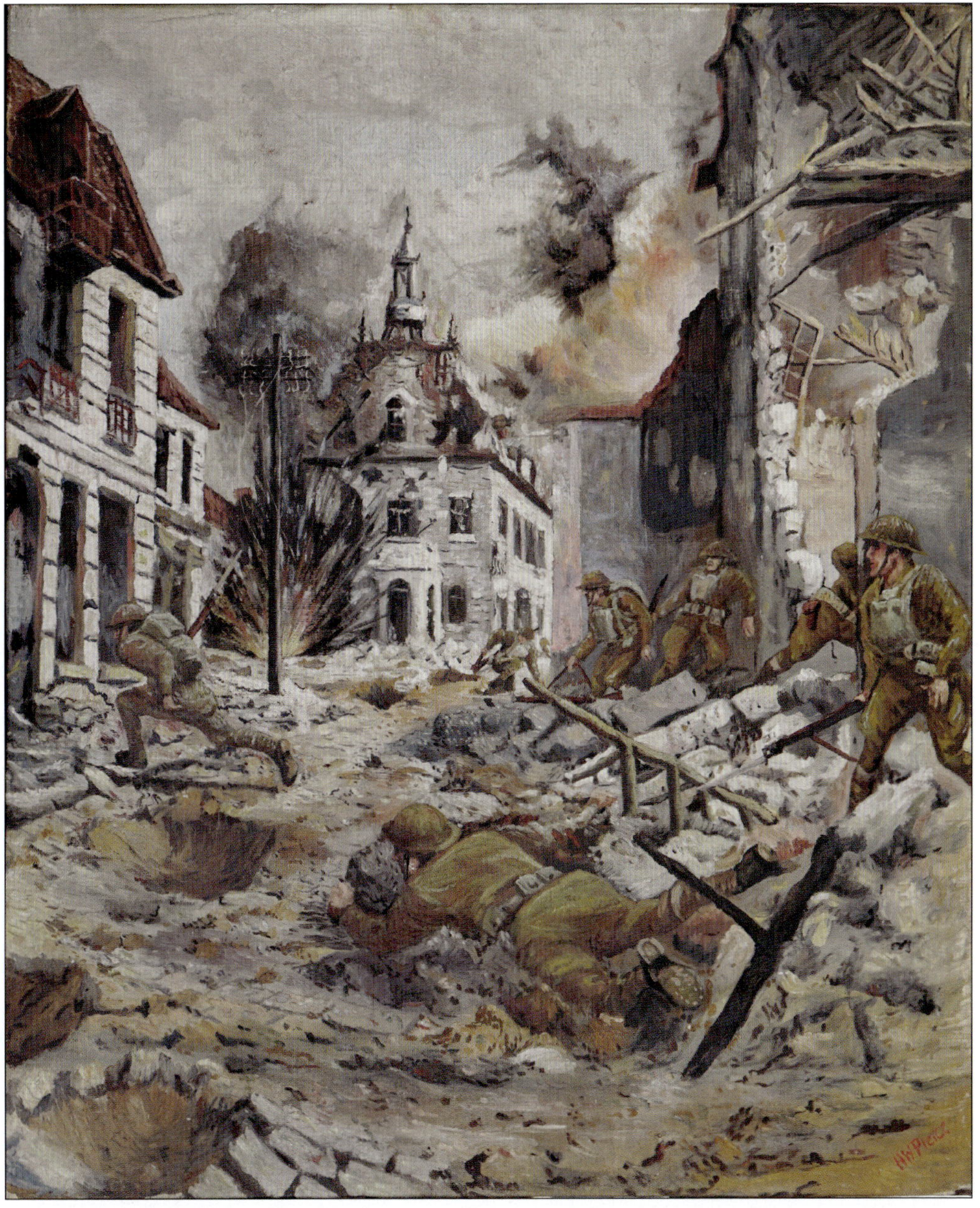

Fierce fighting took place in the town of Fismes in August 1918. This is Pierce's interpretation of the regiment's move through the heart of the town. The building in the center is the Fismes Town Hall. Other than the doughboys, this scene matches the U.S. Army photo shown on Page 76. Pierce didn't give a name to the painting. (*Courtesy Hagen History Center, Erie County Historical Society*)

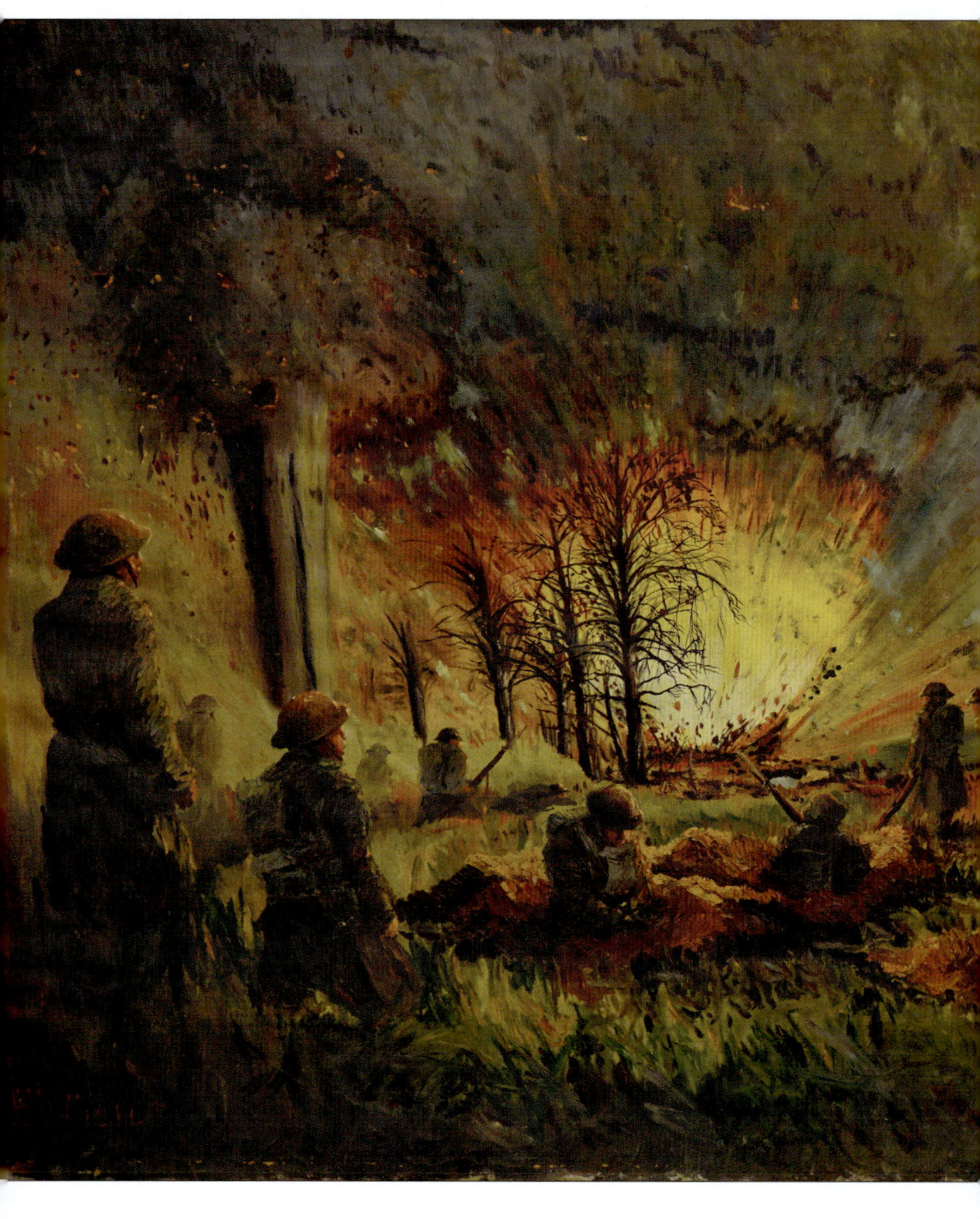

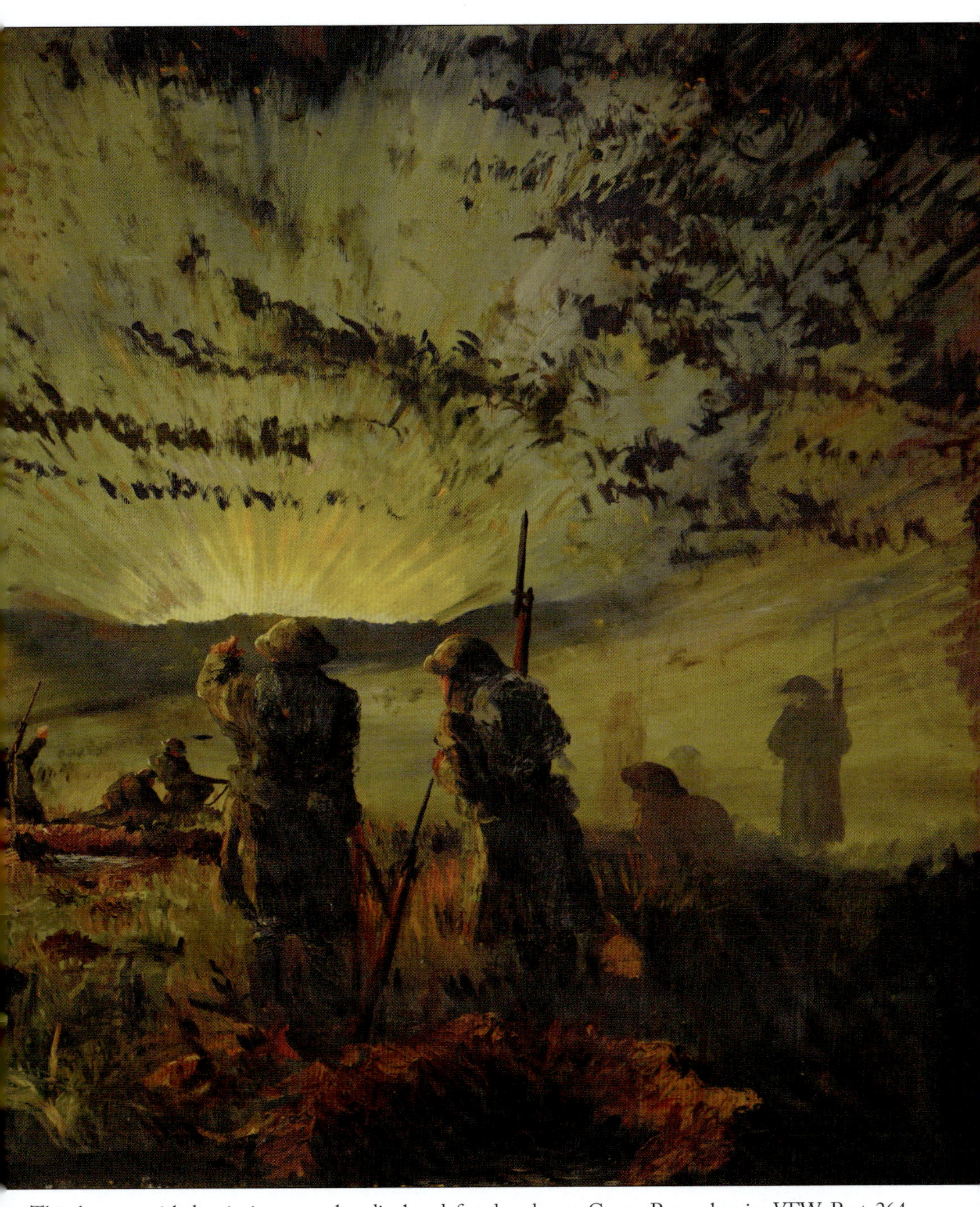

This large, untitled painting was also displayed for decades at Corry, Pennsylvania, VFW Post 264. (*Courtesy Hagen History Center, Erie County Historical Society*)

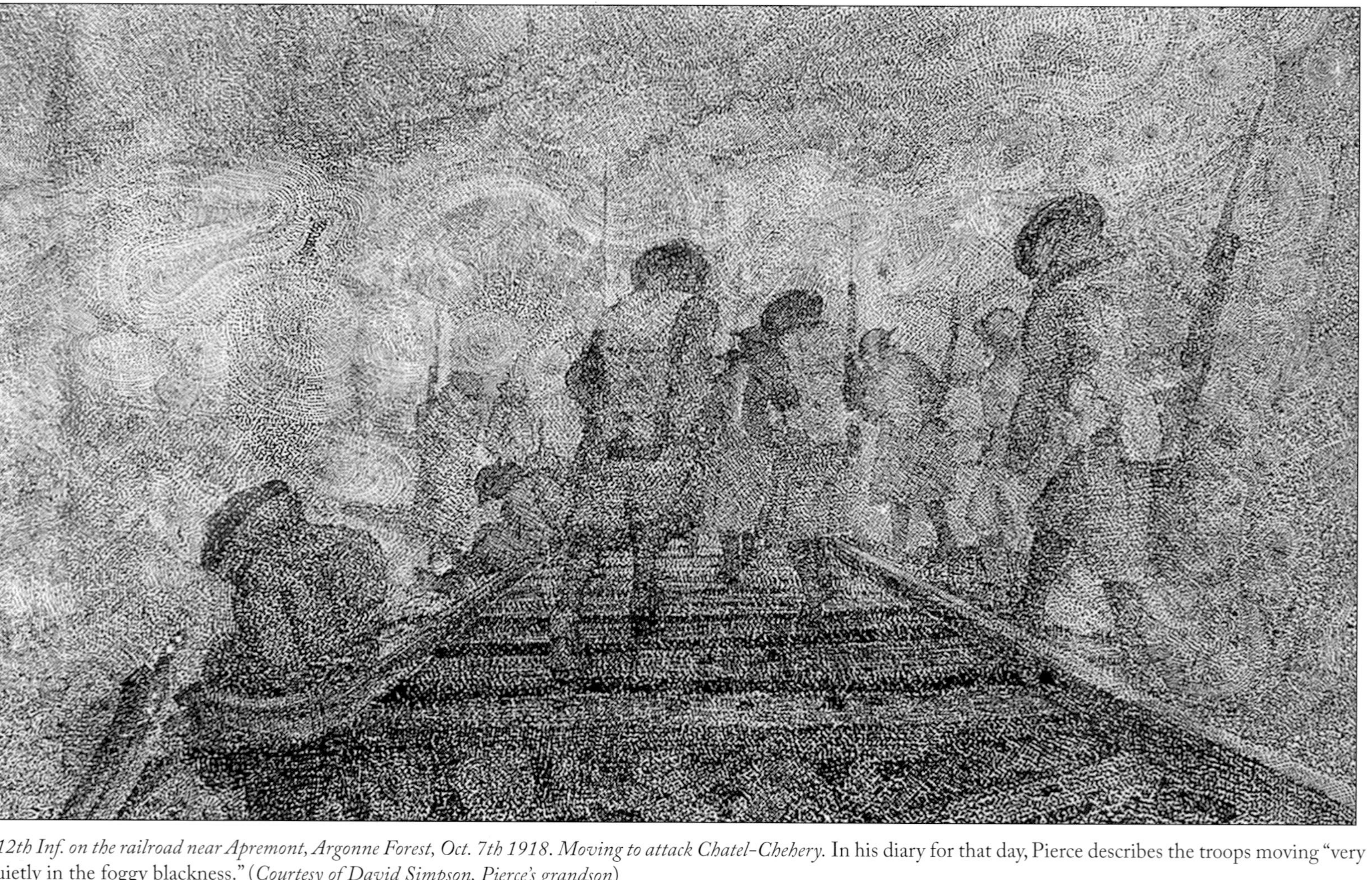

112th Inf. on the railroad near Apremont, Argonne Forest, Oct. 7th 1918. Moving to attack Chatel-Chehery. In his diary for that day, Pierce describes the troops moving "very quietly in the foggy blackness." (*Courtesy of David Simpson, Pierce's grandson*)

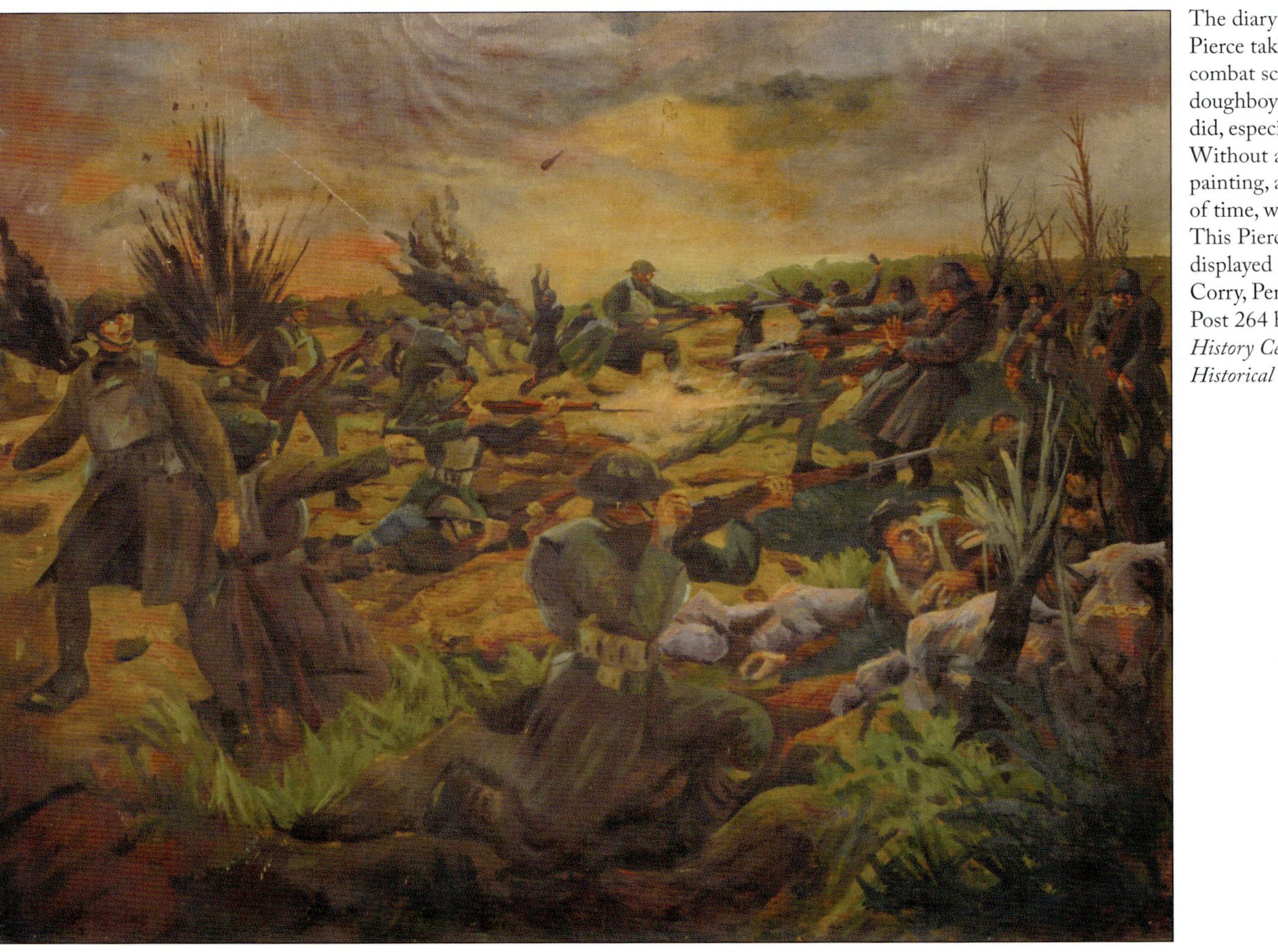

The diary doesn't record Pierce taking part in a close combat scene like this, but the doughboys of Company A did, especially in the Argonne. Without a title on the painting, and with the passage of time, we are left to guess. This Pierce painting was also displayed for decades at the Corry, Pennsylvania, VFW Post 264 hall. (*Courtesy Hagen History Center, Erie County Historical Society*)

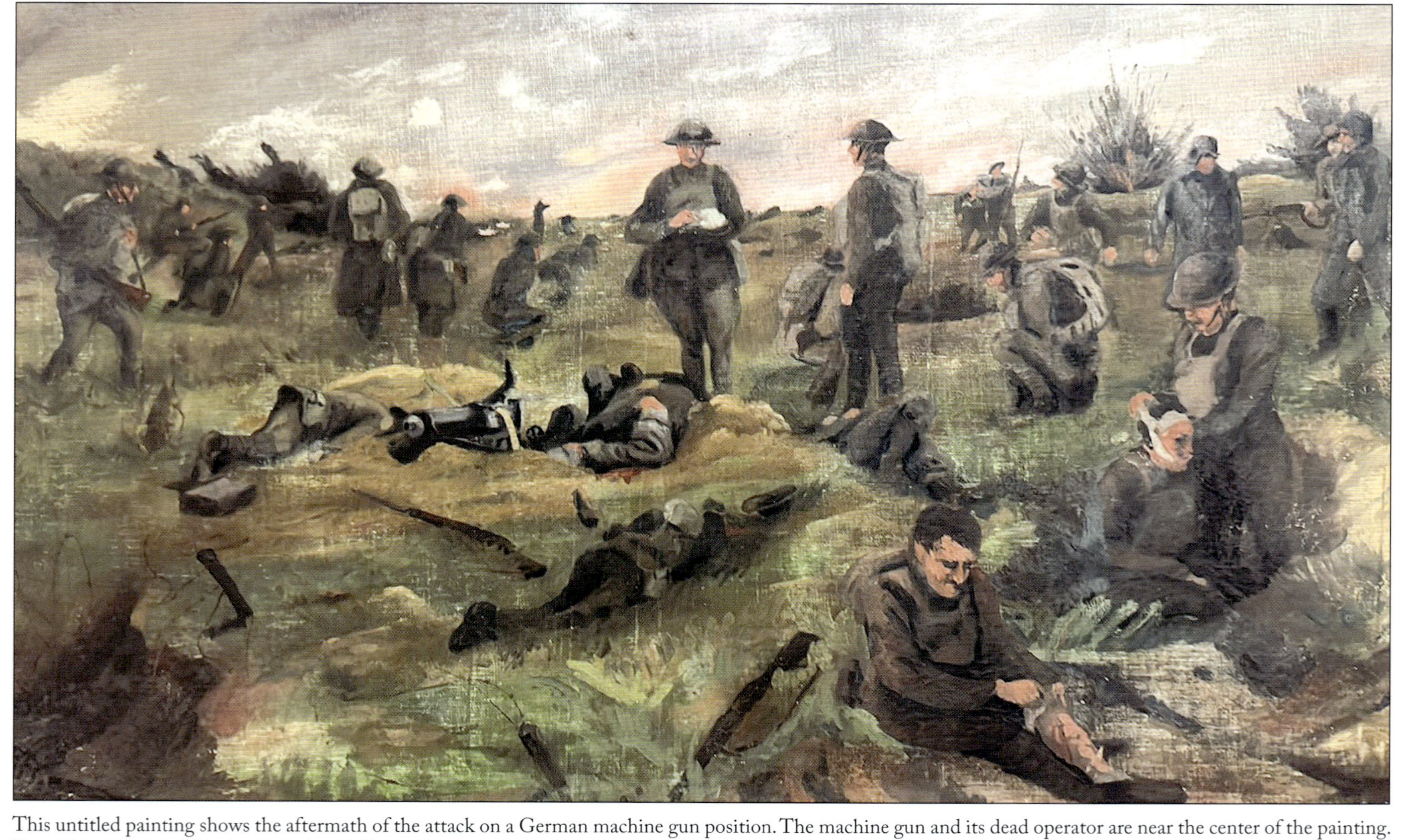

This untitled painting shows the aftermath of the attack on a German machine gun position. The machine gun and its dead operator are near the center of the painting. Doughboys, some of them wounded, and German prisoners now mix on the battlefield. (*Courtesy of David Simpson*)

wide but filled with barbed wire. There is the same ruined bridge and an old ruined stone dam to cross on and then a man must be fast. Meals are almost impossible except what a man can carry in his pack.

Jerry does not neglect us all day. We are driven into the cave often. Some men will not come out. A man from the Medical Detachment is killed near the entrance by a shell but I did not see him get it.

Tonight it is my turn to go for water. The spring is about three hundred yards from the cave. Men going for water take an armfull of canteens and hurry as Jerry knows where the spring is and shells it often. Hugh has been over a couple of times.

I take as many canteens as I can carry and run to the spring. My ears are open for that warning screech that means I must hit the ground if I care to live. Arrived at the spring I lay down inside the little hollow for protection in case one does come. The water gurgles slowly into the canteens. The moon is shedding its beautiful light over the hills and valleys of the Vesle. It makes a beautiful picture and I can scarcely realize I am at the front and may be killed any minute. I gaze upward at the sky and softly and prayerfully sing that old hymn.

> *"Lead Kindly Light, amid the encircling gloom,*
> *Lead Thou me on,*
> *The night is dark and I am far from home;*
> *Lead Thou me on,*
> *Keep Thou my feet, I do not ask to see, The distant scene, one step enough for me."*

The song is comforting. Maybe someday, I can look at the moon and a peaceful scene like this without expecting it to change suddenly into a night of terror, horror and despair. My canteens are filled. I grab them and hurry back to the cave where thirsty men need that water.

August 20. Ahlquist and I are given a job for the night. Sgt. Leinbach explains that we are to go out near Villette and Magneux, villages to the right of Fismes. A big German gun is supposed to be run up close to the line on a railroad track. We are to spot it by the flashes. Someone in

Paris figured that out. Orders have been relayed from higher authority so we must go, sense or no sense.

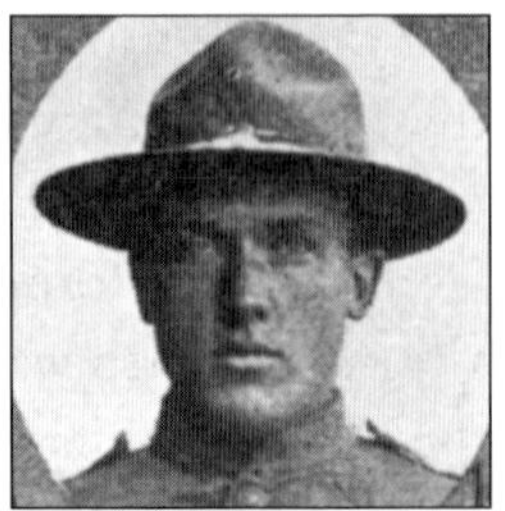

Pvt. Floyd Ahlquist.

After dark, we walk down through the sunken road, crossed the old mill race, then took the railroad track going close by the old Tannerie. Near the Tannerie a couple of bullets cracked over our heads but we pay no attention. We reach the road running through the Main Street of Fismes. It is a ghostly, unreal city of shadows and death tonight in the moonlight. The wreckage is more complete than before; the big town hall in the central square is almost demolished.

Close to the square I hear a strange sound faintly. I must be in a dream or is that piano music. Inside a ruined house, a piano is playing and a quartet is singing "My Little Grey Home in the West." It is beautiful, although unreal, in this place of the dead. The music is faint as we reach the square, then a quick run as it is shelled too often. I see the body of the 32nd Division soldier I had stumbled over the first night I was here, still lying in the place he fell, but now under the hot sun little more than a skeleton and a patch of grease on the pavement. Outside of Fismes in the country the road is filled with shell holes and debris. Puttee wrapped legs and futile dead arms stick out from fallen branches in the ditches and rotting dead Americans lie in the road where they had lain for weeks. We pass a crater in the road, thirty feet deep, where the Boche had undermined a culvert in their retreat. Beyond the crater we pass a half mile of woods. Beyond them we are not sure if our men are ahead or not though there may be a few outposts. We walk cautiously now; the moon is bright although the night is cloudy.

Suddenly from the side of the road, three men with bayonets leveled spring at us, almost pricking us with their points, demanding to know what we are doing here. Hands in the air we try to explain that we are Scouts from the 112th. They are of the 110th and want to know what we are doing in their sector. They had been on a patrol, saw us coming, concealed themselves in the ditch till we were close then jumped us. Finally satisfied that we were not spies they disappear in the direction of Fismes.

A little farther we find a good observation post where a railroad track crosses the highway. There we lie down behind the embankment, heads just over the cut ready with the prismatic compass to sight it on any flashes that appear on the opposite hills. Everything is quiet. Then an American battery opens up, lighting the horizon, and shells screech over into Heinie's land, just a few rumbling shots and then quiet. An hour of weary watching goes by in which we have seen nothing. Then an American machine gun on the hill back of us sweeps the Boche line. It is only the regular, routine fire but it wakens a German machine gunner and he returns the fire splashing bullets all over the countryside, then suddenly he turns them directly up our cut, sending a shower of bullets all around us. We roll quickly to the bottom of the ditch and flatten as flat as possible, while a few inches above us his bullets snap and crackle. Possibly he has discovered us, but there is no danger of us getting up, not even a few inches. He swings the gun across the countryside again, then another burst above us and he ends. We remain in the ditch a long time, he may be just waiting for us to get up.

At last we back slowly up the ditch, crawl cautiously over the bank and remain concealed a few minutes, then out onto the road back to Fismes. On the road nothing happened and we concluded the machine gunner had not seen us leave. Their seventy-sevens shelled the woods ahead of us intermittently and we can see the smoke drifting slowly away in the moonlight. But before we reach the woods the firing has ceased. We hurry through them lest he start again, down the crater and out to Fismes. As we near the town they are dumping G.I. Cans, otherwise the two hundred and tens, about a nine-inch shell. We walk slowly into the deserted streets, the big boys hitting on the square every two or three minutes. Ahead the square is white with dust and smoke. A man from "D" Company in a doorway calls to us and we stop for a few minutes. He says if we time it right we can get through the square. So we walk closer and duck inside a doorway till the next shot registers. As soon as the rocks are down we are off on a run across the square. Our calculations are wrong; in the center of the square another big one comes for us. Straight down on us, with a horrible rushing noise, increasing in volume as it is closer, I turn wildly, looking for cover then drop beside a block of stone tossed there, praying frantically. Ahlquist drops behind me, as the shell with a last mad rush bursts in the house beside us, sending huge stones, timbers, pieces of shell and all into the air around us. Before the pieces had started down we are up and running down the street in terror with a descending shower of slugs hitting the streets. Two hundred yards down the street another one comes into the square and we turn and look over our shoulders to watch it burst. This one bursts in the center of the square, exactly where we had been a few seconds ago. I hear a zooming noise and a large chunk of steel swishes past my head a few inches away, hits the pavement, bouncing and clicking on the stones till it stops a hundred yards in front of us. We burn the air from that awful spot and do not stop till we have reached the edge of town near the railroad track we came down earlier in the evening.

"Get down here, do you want to be killed," a voice unmistakably New Yorkish, yells at us from the bank beside the road. We see men crouched in holes below us. Panting heavily we sit down on top. "What for?" we ask between gasps. "The Germans will see you," they say. "There is none around here," we answer still on top. "Yes, they are in the Tannerie," but we laugh at that. "In the Tannerie, why we just came by there a few hours ago." They still insisted there were Germans there and we sat on top of the bank and argued with them till a bullet did crack over our heads and we thought better of it and dropped behind the bank with them. Although the sergeant in charge considered us too dumb to understand he explained that they were a part of the 77th Division and tonight they were to make an attack on the Tannerie. I told him they should surely capture it as there were no enemy in it. They were waiting for a barrage to start.

Although we do not believe there is anyone in the Tannerie we decide to go past our old headquarters in the wine cellar. Once there the barrage the (New Yorkers) were waiting for started. But someone had made another mistake. The fire is about one thousand yards short and nowhere near the Tannerie but directly across our path. Ahlquist and I crawl inside the dugout my brother and I had made, the second time it has come in handy. Then a German barrage started from the opposite direction both advancing and it looks as if they would meet where we are. Rather than be there when both are together we decide to duck through the American fire. But just as we are close to the line of bursting shells, a rocket from our cave whizzes into the air warning the gunners to cease firing. The shelling stops and we run as fast as possible before they start again, across the track, by the old mill, up the sunken road and to the cave to report.

August 21. Captain Miller was not well pleased that we came in so soon. I thought we did quite well but he seemed to think we should have stayed till morning. He does hate to send us back and I won't volunteer and if we are sent out again we will go out in some hole and stay till morning. But he does allow us to eat some food Hugh had saved for us. The Captain comes out of his hole to order us out again, but as he does a roar comes up from the valley as a heavy German barrage hit the valley and the sunken road. The Captain dove for his hole and I considered the matter ended and for once in my life I was glad the Germans shelled. I went wearily to my hole in the crevice and lay down between the rocks and sandbags to sleep with pieces of steel whizzing harmlessly over my head. I am just dozing off amid the noise when a shower of dust and rocks precede a man's body sliding over the bank to drop on my ankle. I hear the valve of his gas mask flutter and I reach for mine. It is Percy Beebe, a runner from "A" Company. He has just run up from the sunken road where the shell fire had caught he and his pardner. His team mate decided to chance it in the sunken road. We keep him in our hole till the shelling is over. His pardner does not come; no wonder, in the morning he is found dead in the sunken road.

I sleep late that morning and remain close to the cave or near a hole and most of the day inside the cave. The events of the night before scared me more than I would like to admit.

August 22. I am to visit all the companies in the Battalion and secure their map positions. I start early in the morning alone. As I look into that valley I think of the Psalm, "Yea, though I walk through the Valley of the Shadow of Death, I will fear no evil. Thy rod and Thy staff they comfort me." Surely I am going into the Valley of the Shadow of Death. I dread most the run across that bridge into Fismette. I approach the bridge warily, ducking from house to house, then wait under cover and scout the bridge. There are more rotting bodies now than before. I say a long prayer, then run for dear life across that dangerous spot. Not a shot. Cocky Morrell is in a ruined house near the bridge with a machine gun and he directs me to Company Headquarters.

Captain Graff asks me what's wrong with Battalion, what do they expect of men. Someone had given the wrong impression of "A" Company, said they were scared of their lives but who wouldn't be in a place like that. He gives me the map positions, which showed that "A" … had regained all the ground lost by the other regiments.

Sgt. Thompson and Pvt. Freeman were killed by one pounders. Groves and Shaw were killed crossing the street in an attack. There were others but these I knew best and many wounded.

Fismette is a city of the dead. At every turn and corner they lie, some now only bony skeletons. Germans and Americans side by side, on top of the ground and half buried by the debris. A few have been buried but hundreds have not. The stench is sickening, flies and yellow jackets everywhere and men must live here. Buildings are leveled much more than when I was here before. The entire atmosphere is dismal and terrifying, surely the Valley of Death. I see many friends who quietly greet me, not in the loud boisterousness of camp life but every bit as sincere. I wish them luck and hope they will be out soon. I hear with relief that some are slightly wounded; always it seems now that when we hear of them we are relieved. I am in a hurry to leave this misery and death trap but do not want my comrades to know it so I linger longer than necessary. Captain Graff does not take long with the map positions, then I can go. I dread that bridge. I bid "so long" to my friends, then close to the bank of the river with the rock piles between me and the Germans only a few yards away, till I am ready. I scout the bridge from behind a ruined building again, picking out the best cover. Suddenly I spring out and run, expecting to be shot, reach the other side safe and take cover in buildings on the Fismes side of the river. The bridge is only about seventy-five yards long but the time spent on it seems ages. From then on I run up the street, ducking from cover to cover, doorway to doorway, resting frequently, afraid still of a killing burst of machine gun bullets, till at last the square where the danger of rifles and machine gun bullets is over.

I have already taken "C" and "D" positions in Fismes; next is "B" beyond Fismes toward Villette and Magneux. After a lot of running and ducking from cover to cover I find Lieut. Pond in a hole in the woods close to the big crater. Back at "C" Company Chaplain Hall is waiting to go up to the old civilian cemetery and locate the grave of a French officer. We find him buried close to a row of black crosses of Germans killed when they swarmed down from the Aisne earlier in the spring. This duty finished I return to the cave, going by the old mill and the sunken road. During my absence a German shell hit our ammunition dump, starting a fire and exploding the shells, the explosions keeping up for hours.

"Yea, though I walk through the Valley of the Shadow of Death, I will fear no evil." This thought has been buoying me up all day. Not a shot or a shell near me all day although I did spend some time fearing plenty of evil. With this thought in mind I thank God that no evil did befall me this day.

August 23. The 3rd Battalion is to relieve us tonight and we are to go to Death Valley in support. I remain close to Headquarters all day. About 10:00 p.m. the 3rd comes tramping over the hills and the relief is effected without any trouble. The night is quiet, unusually so, a beautiful moonlight again. We hike over the hills above St. Gilles to Death Valley, which does not resemble its name lying peacefully in the moonlight. We drop our packs and sleep on the ground.

DEATH VALLEY

August 24. My brother and I dig a good dugout in a bank on a line with the dugouts of the rest of the Scouts and just above Captain Miller's dugout. Death Valley was well named, the support line and every bit as bad as the front line. It is well to remain close to the dugouts as we will be shelled at any time during the day or night whether we need it or not. A battery of the 107th Field Artillery is above us on the hill with other batteries in the woods and valley. One battery of 155 howitzers of the 108th Field Artillery is farther down the hill. These are the batteries supporting the troops in Fismes and from our own 28th Division, much superior to the ones that first supported us in Fismes when they hit our front line as often as they did the Germans. Our meals arrive before daylight and after dark and there is enough left for another meal at noon. At least we will eat more regular. A good clear cold spring of water is not far from our dugout. Artillerymen during lulls in the firing drop down for a chat. They wish to hear the stories of the front line from the doughboys. The redlegs are our best friends now. They know we have it much harder than they and they are kind and sympathetic, dividing their food with us and even giving us all at times. When passing through their guns going to the front they always say, "Good luck doughboy," or "God bless you doughboy, we will help you all we can," and other encouraging words. Returning from the front when the artillery spies the doughboy he is always sure of sympathy and consideration. Although they have it plenty tough they seem to think we have it worse. Our own Pennsylvania artillery have all our confidence for we know they will help all there is possible.

August 25. A fine day. Hugh and I write letters home. Dellinger and I secure permission to go to Dravegny where our field kitchens are, mail the letters and visit "A" Company for a dinner. It is good to eat a meal off the stove.

We are experienced veterans now. Wherever we go our eyes are constantly looking for cover. A second sense is always at work, searching the fields and roads ahead for holes, depressions, ditches or cover of any sort to fall into if need arises. We dread flat level places and will travel farther to be near a bank or ditch. When we pass cover we hate to leave until we have sighted the next cover. Our ears are tuned for that warning screech of approaching shells or the crackling of bullets over our heads, which means that we must throw ourselves to the ground if we care to live. Our instincts are for self preservation; these instincts will be with us for years in civil life and we may shiver and duck unconsciously if we hear a noise like a shell.

We are more accustomed to the front now. A shell must be close or it is passed unnoticed. A bullet must snap to scare us. We are not as liable to adjust gas masks at the first pretext, first we must see the shell burst or smell the gas. The gas alarms do not travel for miles as they did a few weeks ago. Things that worried us at first, now we pass unnoticed, and other things that at first never worried us we know now by their bite to avoid. We guard helmet, gas mask and shovel more than the rifle. But still the front is not a nice place to be.

While we were away today the Boche gassed our spring. He dropped mustard gas near it and ruined the water. I taste a little and can taste mustard. It looks so cool, clear and healthful as it gurgles out of the hillside but misery hides within it. The men in the companies are digging trenches on the hills at night for a strong support line. Parties go out every night to remain and work till daylight and sleep during the day if the Germans will let them.

August 26. Sign the payroll and watch bursting shells. One makes a direct hit on an artillery ammunition dump on the hill opposite, setting fire to the dump. It burns all day with shells bursting every few minutes. The spot is shunned for days.

Overhead at night German bombing planes pass in the darkness. We know they are Boche by their peculiar hum of the motor, which rises and falls. Our own planes have a steady hum. We get in our dugouts and cower in the ground, the hum is overhead, we wait dreading a bombardment, but they pass and we relax. Some place, Chateau-Thierry or Paris, is likely to be bombed tonight.

FISMES ONCE MORE

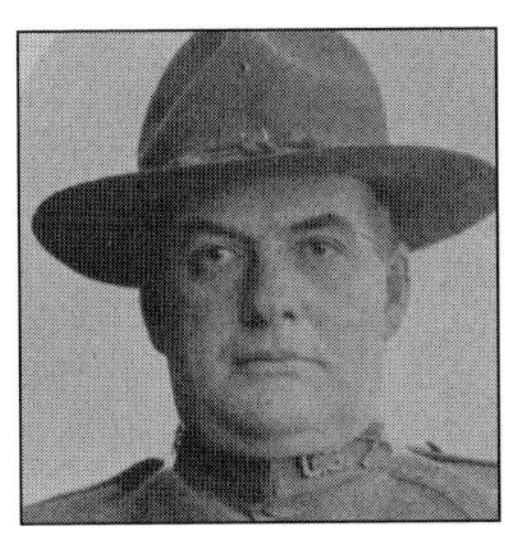
Capt. Lucius Phelps.

August 27. Terrible news from the front. "G" and "H" Companies of the 2nd Battalion had relieved the 3rd Battalion on Fismette early this morning. The 3rd Battalion had just left Fismes after being relieved when a terrible attack opened on Fismette and since then "G" and "H" have not been heard from. Word has just come that Captain Phelps, commanding the 2nd, has been wounded and Captain Miller is to take his place. We hear the news with dread, two whole companies annihilated. It may mean another big German drive in this vicinity.

About 2:00 p.m. I am picked with a dozen other Scouts to go into Fismes and with 1st and the 2nd Battalion Scouts find out what has happened across the river. We go to the cave and there find Captain Miller. A few men, about thirty, had escaped from Fismette, the last to come about ten this morning.

Captain Miller calls Kightlinger, Clush and I. We are to go into Fismes and Fismette if necessary and find out for sure what has happened. We must leave our identification and not take rifles, just forty-fives. I hand over my letters and other identification to "Big Mike," the Captain's dogrobber. "Big Mike" looks sorrowfully at me and says, "Goodbye Pierce." Captain Miller shakes hands with us, his eyes say, "Good luck son," but he cannot trust his voice to speak. Thus encouraged and enheartened we set out on what they seem to think is our last mission.

The Germans are shelling the sunken road now. We lay on the bank above the road timing the shots. A shell comes over about every thirty seconds and usually lands just beyond the road. We have a hundred yards to run until we are sheltered by the road and from then on we can travel in comparative safety except for a direct hit in the road. At last, decided to risk it, we move down to the edge of the embankment and lie flat on our stomachs till the next shell bursts. My heart is beating fast; if our calculations are wrong we are going to be out in the open for that next shell. I have time for a short prayer but my prayer is so mixed up with a dirty little song about the private life of a woman named Lulu that I am afraid it does no good. All day this song has been running through my mind so much that I cannot get my mind on my prayer. The next shell is whining in our direction, flat on the ground we dig in our feet to start as soon as its pieces have whizzed by us. "Crumph," it goes, the pieces whistle over us, we are up and away, a hundred yard dash in which I never tried harder for speed, ready to dive, equipment banging and breath coming hard. "My Lulu was arrested."

We reach the protection of the sunken road yet we do not stop. We slow down at the old mill, then cross the railroad tracks. A 77 shell comes toward us, we flatten out till it bursts, then on again. Lulu is humming through my head and I try and switch to "Jesus, Savior, Pilot Me." Another shell; we slide on the ground as it bursts. I come up with Lulu and run on again. I roll into another depression to let the next shell burst, then on again, up and down, across that shell-swept field, a few yards, diving, on again, up and down, up and down between shell bursts, trying to get rid of that dirty little song as I do not want to die with it on my mind, frantic, scared, panting and sweating, between trees and through bushes, over and into shell holes, by dead men and horses, till at last we have passed through that shell fire unhurt but exhausted. Ahead is the old wine cellar we had used for Battalion Headquarters before and we run inside. A man went in ahead of us, hit in the wrist in the shelling we came through and is now lying on his back faint and sick. I lie down on a sack to recover my breath. It is terribly hot and the sweat rolls off me, I feel myself fainting also, the dugout swims around in blackness and my head drops over to my knees too weak to hold it up. Bad food, diarrhea and dysentery, gassed water, and gassed air, overwork and strained nerves are not the best of training for a run of a mile that we had just made. But I do not go clear out. I soon recover and outside of a little weakness, all right.

A French officer is there that can talk English fluently. He calls us outside and shows us a big air battle over Fismes. There several planes a mile high are twisting and turning at each other and faintly we hear the rattle of machine guns.

Lieut. Ostendorf in Command of "E" Company says that all of "G" and "H" have been killed or captured but that twenty-five or thirty are back safe. He does not know much of what happened only that shortly after they relieved the 3rd Battalion a terrible artillery fire was leveled on Fismes and Fismette and "E" Company could not go to the support of the men in Fismette. The bridge especially had been heavily shelled. He directs us to an "E" outpost closer to the river. A German machine gun is placed to fire up the street leading from Fismette. We jump across the street before they can fire and find the squad in an old building. Most of the men are in the cellar. We climb to the attic, one of the few houses that still has one, where two men are observing. They have seen Germans all over Fismette and there can be no Americans still resisting. The last firing was about ten this morning. A few men come back about ten and one was killed by a shell in the street and his buddy had his feet blown off.

I look through my field glasses between the rafters. Fismette surely is occupied by the Germans now, I can see them in several places and they seem unmolested and unafraid. It is about five hundred yards from where I am and I can see it must have been a terrible fight. There are actually piles of the German grey and in one place there seem to be three men piled on top of each other. The dead were plenty when I was in that town last but now they appear doubled. "G" and "H" fought to the last and the Boche paid a terrible price for that victory.

We could not gain any further information by going farther ahead as we are certain there is no chance of any Americans still holding out there. We pick up the French Lieutenant at "E" Company headquarters and he accompanies us to the old mill. We return to the cave again and report the sad news to Captain Miller. What worries us now is that they will want us to recapture that town. I take back my letters and identification from Big Mike; the job had not proved as dangerous as we thought. After reporting I went inside the cave to rest if possible. The roof is not high, only two or three feet at the most, and we must crawl on hands and knees and lie down. The light from the entrance extends only a few feet and then candles are used. But candles are scarce and there is so little light inside that one is bumping his head on the ceiling frequently. The candles are conserved with great care, the wax all gathered again and wrapped around a string to be used again.

As I lie on my back the roof is only a foot over my head and I feel as if imprisoned in a casket. I almost decide to go outside but bad as it is here it is much more dangerous outside and inside nothing discouraged and homesick, my brother is back in Death Valley, maybe I will never see him again. I have an almost irresistible impulse to run out of that cave, over the hills to Death Valley to be with him again. I reach for the jackknife my kid brother gave me the day I left home and it is gone; almost, it seems, the last connection with home. I feel on the ground in the blackness but it is useless. A great wave of homesickness overcomes me and I roll over on my side fearful lest I cry.

In my New Testament maybe I can find comfort. Opening it I find a letter a lady from home had given us the day we left home, a letter that we were not to read unless we were absolutely feeling hopeless. If ever I felt that way it is now. The letter reads: "Brave Soldier Boy: We are saying do we know under just what conditions our neighbors are laboring? Are we quite sure that were we placed under those conditions we might not see things in a different light? What one of us is wise enough to say whether or not another had done what was best under his circumstances? So to save life and make peace let all find our God, with His help we must each work out our own salvation. Unless we overcome our sins, punishment will overtake us. So let us choose today whom we will serve, our God, with his loving protection, we shall keep our flag clean and pure. Your friend." I think of the lady Mrs. Brown at home with two lovely daughters and it brings a little cheer and a feeling of home.

I have no blanket, having only brought my combat pack, but a fellow from the 109th Machine Gun Battalion shares his with me. He is friendly, realized that I am homesick and need a friend to talk to. The lieutenant of the detachment of machine gunners has a basket of food brought to him, which he divides with all the men in the room and I receive a share including some grapes. They all sing, "One, Two, Three, Four, sometimes a little bit more, Ein, Zwei, Drei, Fier, I miss the one that's near." The song cheers me almost as much as the letter; maybe things will be better soon and I will survive to see my home yet. The lad who had shared his blanket with me is sent out into the rain to take his turn on a machine gun and though I have only met him tonight and do not know his name I dread to have him go as much as if I had known him all my life. I hope for a wound, not a serious one of course but enough to get me out of this mess. This war will go on endlessly and a man cannot survive long unless he is disabled. Silently I pray to God for help and to be ready to leave this earth bravely.

Outside dimly, muffled explosions echo, where the Germans are trying to hit the entrance to our cave with Nine Point Twos. So far we have not taken them seriously. Finally a louder roar and over our entrance the rocks and dirt slide down and with the dust entirely blot out the entrance. A shell has hit above the entrance and we may be imprisoned in the cavern. Every candle but the one in my room is blown out and the men are frantically trying to see and find out what chances we have of getting out. We can dig out in a few hours at the worst if no large rocks have entirely blocked us in. The dust settles a little and a speck of daylight appears at the opening, then a man near the front yells not to worry for we can still crawl out. I lay over on my side and try to sleep.

About 10:04 p.m. I hear someone calling, "Pierce." I lie still, perhaps they will pass me up. If they find me I will pretend I was asleep. With only one candle in a cave it is almost impossible to find anyone and now a runner has to almost hogtie a man in order to hold him. The men of the 109th do not know my name so I am safe with them. Others have goldbricked before so why not I, it will only be some fool errand and I did enough for one day. But the runner calls so often that at last, more out of sympathy for him, I answer, "Here." Captain Miller wants me again, the runner says. I crawl through the blackness of the cave, wiggle through the small hole the shell left for the entrance and report.

Outside a soft, misty rain is falling. Kightlinger, Vogel, McClellan, Clush, two others I do not know, and I are to go with Lieut. Saunders into Fismes again and patrol toward the river. We walk the well known track again, the sunken road, the old mill and the railroad tracks to Fismes. Near the track a shell comes at us, I dive for the ground and fall into a shell hole on my helmet and do a head stand.

Our first stop is the "E" Company Headquarters where we leave Lieut. Saunders, and Sgt. Pat Slayers of the 2nd Battalion Scouts escorts us to the "E" outpost again. I am always glad to be with Pat, he is like a father, almost thirty years old. We remain at the outpost for hours, nothing has happened, we know the Germans hold Fismette so why go any further.

August 28. We remain at the outpost till about one a.m., enough time to make it appear as if we had actually gone to the river, then start back. At "E" P.C. we pick up Lieut. Saunders and three officers of the 103rd French Mortar and start for Battalion Headquarters. I am third from the last in the lineup, Clush behind me and Kightlinger bringing up the rear. For some time the Boche have been shelling the area back of Fismes and the cave with the big 210s, one coming over about every five minutes. Out on the road we hear a big one coming but apparently going over our heads. But suddenly it seems to turn, louder and more horrible comes the rushing noise, straight for us, it's onto us. I flatten out though I feel it is hopeless, it is going to be a direct hit. There is a terrific explosion a few feet back of me, the concussion passes over me in a great rush of wind and dirt and black smoke envelopes me but I am unhurt. Kightlinger was there where it hit, Clush too is probably dead, if alive it is a miracle. I rush back through the smoke and Clush comes scrambling toward me unhurt. I yell, "Kight," but no answer. The road that I just came over has a hole big enough to bury several horses. The rocks and dirt thrown up by the explosion are just falling when I see Kight's body against the bank, but he stirs, jumps up and runs toward me. Quickly I assure him that he has no serious wounds at least and thank God that he is alive. The thing that lit beside him picked him up and threw him against the bank, stunning him but that was all. We burn the air to the old mill where we find the rest of the patrol, resting and waiting for us. Further examinations show that none of us are even wounded, another miracle. We wait at the old mill till a few more shells burst and then rested, start up the sunken road.

Lieut. Saunders lies for us beautifully to Captain Miller. He says he went to the "E" outpost and that the rest of us went to the river. We Scouts are brave men and that Captain Miller should be proud of us. White lies save a lot of trouble and maybe a life or so. We are sure at least that Jerry holds Fismette and we may as well let him have it. I am sure I don't want any of it.

Late in the morning I wakened to find the cave deserted. Outside a man told me that Battalion Headquarters moved to the wine cellar in Fismes and everyone was to report there. Still I loitered, determined to take my time in reporting. At last, I hurried into town and reported to Captain Miller in the old P.C. Most of the Scouts were at the "E" outpost and I was sent there. We had an observation post in the attic with a few men on duty and the rest stayed in the cellar. The cellar was quite safe as the house had been hit so often the stones had piled so high a shell could hardly come through. It was said that in this cellar a German and an American lived for several days together until the American outfit was relieved and then he had taken the German along with him. (This could be Cpl. Edward Cribbins of "G" Company. He had a similar tale.)

We were not in the cellar long till the remnants of "G" and "H" companies, who had escaped from Fismette, came in, about thirty men in all out of two hundred and thirty. They were a tired and dirty lot. One said he was sure he killed twenty Germans and stopped because he was ashamed of himself. Another had his brother killed beside him. They had escaped over the dam after fighting until there was no hope and when everything was ended they had run. All the rest were killed or captured. Most of the captured were wounded who could not get away. There were probably seventy dead of the original two hundred and thirty.

One man estimated a thousand Germans attacked. They used everything including liquid fire and the town was so filled with smoke and dust they could not tell friend from foe. The shell fire on the bridge was so heavy that all the runners were killed in crossing. No one could support them, their signals could not be seen, caught in a trap with no help. Ahead the Boche, behind the river filled with barbed wire.

The Germans attacked first in mass formation and they beat them back. But they lost so many men in the first attack that it left a weak spot in the line that could not be plugged. The second attack came and again they thought they had stopped them from the front when suddenly they saw Germans in their rear.

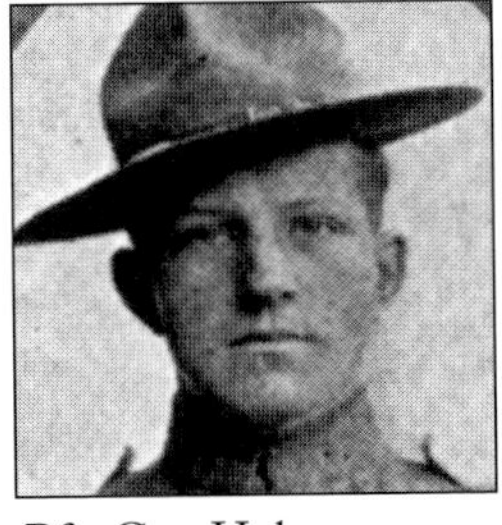

Pfc. Guy Hoke.

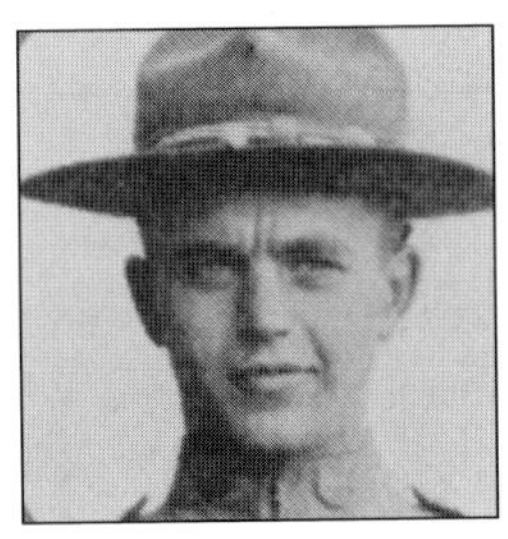

Pvt. William Freed.

Then it was all over, they fought with bayonets, clubs, fists and feet and sometimes five or six Germans on one Yank. It took the Jerries six hours to get the last twenty men out. Lieut. Landry was killed, the last seen of him he was emptying his automatic into them. It was a defeat but no disgrace; if all the German victories come as hard as this they will soon tire of victories. I believe it was the hardest fight American troops have engaged in in France.

These men could not stay awake long, they went to sleep in exhaustion in all sorts of grotesque positions. I also slept later beside Hoke and Bill Freed.

August 29. Awakened by a runner, and Freed and I are to report to Battalion P.C. Just as we arrived at the entrance a shell whistles close and we dive inside as it bursts close to the wine cellar. It started then, a regular hail of shells. The Boche observers have likely learned this place is a headquarters. They are close, one lights directly in front and bursts like a close bolt of lightning, filling the cellar with smoke. There is already one hole in the roof where a 105 shell came through but it was a dud, Major Smathers being in the place at the time. It is a nervous situation as we lay on our stomachs on the floor. The fire gradually dies down without a direct hit and we are all alive. Then I am not wanted at all.

A man in the headquarters wants to shave me to keep his mind busy. The shelling may start again any minute but I chance it for a shave. Clean faced I feel much better and return to the outpost. The Boche have a machine gun at the bridge now to fire straight up the street. In crossing the street one cannot loiter, but we make it into the outpost again. Bill Freed and I are unemployed for the morning so we decide on a little sniping post of our own. The Boche in Fismette have not been molested since they drove our men out. We select a house on the main street that still has an attic, climb three flights of wobbly stairs up, where we can have a good rifle rest. Fismette is about six hundred yards from us, our sights we adjust for that distance. We do not have long to wait. Two Boche soldiers leave Fismette and start to walk leisurely up the road. Bill takes the one on the right, I take the one on the left. I have been taught that it is an honorable thing and my duty to shoot these unsuspecting men in the back. We take our time, the sights are lined properly on the feet to hit into the body. The squeeze begins, I am trying to kill my first man, the thought makes me waver but I bring the sights back. The rifles crack and recoil, we look for lifeless bodies but the two men walk on as contentedly as before. We are piqued, those shots were so far away the Heinies were not even worried. Two bolts work, two more shells in place, two fingers squeeze the triggers again, two rifles crack again and two Germans run for cover. This time we were closer. Although I pretend to Bill that I am greatly chagrined over our failure, secretly I am glad the enemy escaped. Sniping is a dirty business but then all war is that way.

We do not have long to wait. A shell lights in the yard next to us and throws a shower of steel through our rafters. We may have been discovered. We hurry down the rickety stairs, plenty of time coming up but the down trip made in two jerks of a lamb's tail as more shells burst outside the home. Across the street we run into a cellar where men from the 109th Machine Gun Battalion are and there we remain till the shelling is over, then ducking back across the street and safe in the outpost and glad to leave off sniping.

I have scarcely eaten since I left the cave yesterday and there are no rations at the outpost. Bill and I volunteer to go to the cave for some. I am used to this route now, the road, the railroad track, the old mill and mill race, the sunken road and the cave. I have traveled it at all hours of the day and night and know when to run and when to walk. At the cave we find hardtack, corn willie and one can of baked beans. We put it all in a bag and carry it back to the outpost. Our reward is the can of baked beans, the others can have the willie.

Bill Freed, Bing Johnson and I are detailed to patrol to the river as soon as it is dark. But just before we start, Jerry unleashes an attack with one pounders and gas in our vicinity. Sgt. Faust of "E" Company was in the street and a piece of shell hit him in the nose. We all drop back into the cellar, the gas drifts in, we put on our masks and place blankets over the entrance to keep the gas out. Sgt. Faust is in a bad way, blood is running in a steady stream from the wound in his nose, the gas is in the cellar and he must adjust that mask over his sore nose or be gassed. We wear the masks a long time and my throat becomes dry and cracked. Outside the gas has cleared but inside the cellar it still hangs low.

Sgt. Pat Mayers is in front and when he returns the patrols are going out. I lay with the sentry in the doorway, remove my mask and wait for friend Pat. At last the guard and I hear something coming in front, the noise comes closer but we cannot see anything. The guard challenges, "Halt, who is there," but no answer. We hear small stones crunching again, the guard challenges again with rifle ready to fire. I caution him to wait a little longer. Another noise, another challenge and a little stage whisper returns, "It's me." "It's Pat," I tell the guard.

Three patrols are going out. Pat has the center, Vogel the right and Bill, Bing and I the left. It is several hundred yards to the river bank. We are to simply go ahead and learn anything we can. We sneak ahead quietly, staying in the dark places along the walls, waiting often to survey the ground. Slowly we draw near an old ruined factory and explore it but there is nothing there. We find nothing further down so we return about midnight. As we near our lines a nervous gunner fires three shots from a Chau-Chaut over our heads and then realizes we are friends. We report directly to Battalion. Pat Mayers, Vogel, Granger and I, men in charge of patrols, gather to talk to Captain Miller and give him the information we had secured.

Captain Miller asks if barbed wire could be placed down the streets and we all answered yes. That was a job for the Engineers and let us out. But the Captain said the leaders would go with the Engineers and help the detail and protect them from surprise while they were putting up the wire. So Pat, Vogel and I start for the Engineers' dugout. Just beyond the square a big shell, another nine-incher, comes rushing at us. I dive behind a pile of rubbish while it bursts. I am sure it has killed Pat behind me. I run back calling "Pat" but he comes through the smoke unhurt.

August 30. A platoon of the 103rd Engineers was there but the Lieutenant in charge is not anxious to wire those streets. We of the Infantry do not coax him or hurry him, we are not anxious either. The Boche shoot up those streets too often. We wait an hour, the dugout is comfortable, the Lieutenant is responsible now, I wish he would refuse to go. Then they only have enough wire for one street and they will take the main street. That was the one Pat had and lets me out. Another wait, then the Lieutenant reluctantly gives the order for the platoon to start on their detail. Vogel and I accompany them to the square where we warn them of the machine gunner near the bridge, then prepare to rush across the street to our own cellar and be rid of the Engineers. But Sgt. Leinbach is there with the look of a job in his eyes. "Where you fellows been?" "With the Engineers," I answer, "we're going to help them put barbed wire down the streets." I can sleep if he falls for that. "No you're not. You're going on patrol." Vogel and I argue with him that we are needed with the Engineers but it is useless.

Bill Freed, Bing Johnson and I start out again, but before we go we inform everyone on that line we are going as we don't want any more Chau-Chauts coming at us. It is reported that the Germans are bringing up men in trucks and building another bridge across the Vesle and we are to try and find out if it is so. We walk down to the factory where we had been tonight. From there on we proceed cautiously. One foot rises slowly, feeling for footing before the weight is put on. We lay in the shadows and dark places to observe in all directions, then on to the next shadows and so on till we are close to the river. The machine gun at the bridge rakes the street next to us often and we hope that they have not caught Pat and the Engineers. Now we crawl on hands and knees, close to the railroad track that follows the river. In the street a wagon with a large stone has been left. Arrived at this place we halt to rest and observe under the wagon. The machine gun fires up the next street again, the flashes plain now, just over the bridge, then he shifts and splashes into the rocks close to us but we are too well protected.

There are no signs of a working party at the bridge although several times I can faintly hear a few trucks moving on the other side of the river. Suddenly Bing Johnson coughed, the very worst possible thing to do. Startled, we whisper to him to watch himself, but rather than stopping he lets loose a regular fit of coughing, not little muffled wheezes but real bellows that sound like thunder to us in that setting where the snapping of a stick may bring down rifle and machine gun fire galore. Bill and I try our best to make him stop but it is of no avail. Then my own throat tickles, from the gas likely. I stifle a cough myself, then I am seized with a fit of coughing. Between the two of us we are making altogether too much noise. A fit such as we are having would be annoying in any society, but on patrol close to the enemy machine gun, it is terrorizing. I hide my face in my arms to muffle it, try and stick my hand in my mouth but the coughs come till I feel that I am blue in the face. Finally I take an old rag that I have used for handkerchief, dish towel, and what not and stick that in my mouth and though it does not stop the coughing it muffles it a little. By now Bing is over his spell. Then I take a drink from my canteen, a hard thing to do as canteens make a ringing sound but not as loud as my cough. The water eases the tickling but scared and weak for I thought I would choke to death. Three thoroughly frightened young men be still as mice then and observe our vicinity. Apparently nothing has happened and our only danger is that a passing patrol may have heard the coughing, but if they have we are not molested.

The first grey hints of dawn appear, nearly four a.m. and we must be returning. Cautiously we ease from the shelter of the wagon and sneak over to the opposite wall, then for a few hundred yards we take advantage of every cover, sneaking again from shadow to shadow and rock to rock, keeping ruined houses between us and that machine gun at the bridge and then inside our own outposts again. We report no working parties along the river, hearing the trucks and the location of the machine gun at the bridge. It is daylight when we are back at the cellar to sleep.

At noon Bill and I awaken. Bing Johnson said we were relieved and we were to report back at Death Valley again. There was no one at Battalion P.O. but Jensen and he said they were all gone so we took it for granted it was so. Hoke, Freed and I started for the Valley to rejoin the 1st Battalion. On the hill above St. Gilles we found a tree of ripe, red cherries, making a delicious change from the diet of hardtack, corn willie, salmon, etc., that we had had occasionally for the last few days.

I rounded a turn in the bank in the Valley and there was my brother in his dugout. Gratitude and joy registered on his face when he saw me. He thought I was dead as he had not heard of me since I had left for Fismes. He had packed all my things to send to mother. He is so well pleased I cannot do anything. I am mentally and physically exhausted, little sleep and little to eat, dread and horror present all the time and I am grateful for the kindly attentions he gives to me. I also am glad to see him as Death Valley is well named and he was in plenty of danger. I look forward to a night's sleep tonight and a little chance to recover. Once the strain of the front line service begins to wear off a little the nerves are more ragged and unstrung than when actually at the front.

I am in for a terrible disappointment. At nine p.m. a German barrage commences on Death Valley, driving the working parties away from the trenches they are constructing and into their dugouts. Hugh and I are in the dugout, preparing to sleep. Another man passing by jumps in with us also. Death Valley is living up to its name. All over its length and breadth high explosives send up geysers of smoke, steel and dirt. The fire averages six shells per minute. Gas shells mix with the H.E.; we can tell them by their wobbling sound and the "plop" when they explode followed by the humming of the nose as it flies after the explosion. Shells burst on all sides sometimes within a few feet, once a direct hit on the second dugout from us but no one was in there.

I am soon a nervous wreck. I lose control as the bombardment wears on into hours. The strain of the last week with this added is too much. I cannot lie still. I want to scream and run and throw myself. My gas mask irritates me and I am on the verge of tearing it off, gas or no gas. My throat is dry and cracked from the mask but the saliva runs from my mouth and swishes around on my face. When I hear the whistle of an approaching shell I dig my toes into the ground and push on the walls of the dugout, trembling when it bursts, then in agony waiting for the next shell. My body is trembling all over like St. Vitus dance, tense when they come, rolling and turning between shells, moaning and groaning. Can't the Germans see I have had enough, they can have France, America, the whole world if they want it. I am licked. The awful thought strikes me, that over on the other side are men who are firing these guns with the express purpose of killing me, that if they knew their range was not correct they would change to drop these killing charges directly on me and exult when they blew me to pieces, that if I was wounded they would not stop but would try and finish me entirely. I realize I have no right to expect mercy for our side do the same to them and they that kill with the sword shall be killed by the sword. I pray to God for help but the prayer seems to do no good, the bottom has dropped out of everything and even God may have abandoned us.

Back in my brain just a slight sense of reason holds me from running upright into the fire and tearing my mask off. I know that my best hope is to stay as far down in that hole is risible. My brother and the other man watch over me to keep me from doing anything rash, yelling words of encouragement and saying that it would soon be over. But the minutes drag into hours and the hours drag into eternities. At last a lessening of the shots, they are not coming as fast now, then suddenly a quickening fire which fills me in terror of a new bombardment and at last apparently it is over. It is nearly midnight, quiet again and we have been shelled three hours, a feeling of peace like the quiet after a storm, someone removes a mask and cautiously sniffs the air, another and another mask comes off and men breathe the free air again as the gas has blown away. My trembling ceases, devoutly I thank God that he has carried me through the most terrifying time of my young nineteen years of life and utterly exhausted mentally and physically I drop off to sleep.

August 31. I waken refreshed, a little weak and ashamed of my weakness the night before and wishing for orders to leave Death Valley. We took a punishing last night and they were till morning removing the casualties, which were mostly gassed. The artillery and machine gun battalions suffered more than the infantry. Most of the men were in dugouts or they would have been much worse. Within a few feet of our dugout are several new shell holes, and some must have just missed our hole in the bank.

DELOUSED

September 1. All the 1st Battalion Scouts that had been on the extra tour of duty with the 2nd Battalion in Fismes are allowed to go back to the kitchens. What a holiday, the only drawback is I must leave my brother in Death Valley. Hoke and I together hurry out lest another barrage will keep us in. "A" Company serves us a good meal, hot from the kitchen, the first in weeks. Bachman is there shell shocked, shaking and unable to control himself and claims he will return to the front as soon as the shivering stops. I can understand his feelings since the last barrage when I also was shaking all over.

Dinner finished, we go to a delousing station at the Abbaye de Igny. A shower bath, a shave, clean clothes, haircut, new socks and underwear, chocolate bars, I am in heaven. I have worn my old clothes six weeks without a change and no bath except a little cleansing in a creek once. And now cleaned, refreshened and heartened, I am actually patriotic again. What a difference, the itchiness and dirty greasy feeling gone, the new underwear clean and soft on my skin, the cooties so greatly diminished they are not bothersome. The 110th Band plays a concert and how good the stirring marches they play. I am a soldier of my country and proud that

I have fought. Today is so different from hiking, fighting and starving. I am a human being again, maybe there is hope even for doughboys. We hear rumors of a big rest camp back at the Marne where the 28th Division will go to recuperate and drill. Then to support that theory we hear that the Battalion will be out of Death Valley tonight and will be back with us. So after another meal, we Scouts find a clump of pines to sleep in while waiting for the rest. We watch till dark, then after dark the heat lightning on the front, a little fearful that it is only another foundless rumor and that the Battalion is not coming and that we may have to go back to Death Valley. At last tired and sleepy we lie down on the soft pine needles and sleep.

September 2. The Battalion passed while we slept and is now near Coulonges. We rejoin them in the woods above the town. We are out of shell range except for the long range guns. It is good to be this far away. The guns boom in the distance and the horizon is lighted with flashes at night but aside from that everything is quiet. We have three meals a day, cabbage and carrots, potatoes, slum and corn willie again. And more diarrhea and dysentery.

September 3. Hoke and I hike to Chamery and visit again the grave of Quentin Roosevelt. The Americans have placed a new enclosure around it, replacing the one the Germans placed. They had treated him with more respect than they will me I am sure.

September 4. I visit the delousing station again and go to the movies. I cannot have a bath or new clothes as mine are too clean. There was a dentist's office there and I had them working filling a tooth for me. While in the dentist's chair a runner came through yelling for all men of the 112th to report back to their organizations. That can only mean one thing, another move. I hope it is back to the big rest camp.

As I feared though, the regiment starts to hike in the direction of the front. We go in the direction of the front but to the right of Fismes, passing villages that apparently had not been touched. One lay in a valley so peacefully in the pink sunset with all buildings intact and just a few shell holes. But on the hill a kilometer away the light artillery is speaking again. We are in the forward zone again for now we move in short successions of starts and stops. On one halt Sgt. Denning faints. Ed Bowers remains with him when we move again, but he soon recovers and is soon trying to keep up again.

THE VESLE

September 5. We do not hike many miles, yet we spend the night on the road in a succession of stops and starts till early morning, when we stop by a big bank near Courville and sleep.

In the afternoon I am selected to go with Chaplain Hall and a detail to bury the dead along the Vesle River, I do not relish the prospect. We walk about a kilometer, the enemy shells the road ahead and the chaplain called off the burying detail. A sensible chaplain I think as I return to my dugout in the bank.

September 6. I am again detailed with Chaplain Hall. We walk to the top of the hill ahead, the enemy shells the road again, I look at the chaplain hoping he will call it off but today he says nothing about returning. On the hills beyond the Vesle we can see men of the 109th, 110th and 111th busy chasing the Boche to the Aisne. Fismette is recaptured and they are miles beyond that troublesome town again. Jerry is retreating to the Aisne, fighting delaying rear guard actions. Batteries of seventy-fives are already across the Vesle in some places firing direct fire much closer to the infantry than artillery usually goes.

We locate the dead by the smell. Along the railroad track we find a pile of decaying flesh and parts of a blue uniform where a shell had hit a French foxhole. The detail digs a grave as I search two packs for identification. The chaplain makes a cross and writes "One unidentified Frenchman." The grave is completed and the men start to roll the pile of flesh in. "Say, this fellow's got three hands," one man exclaims. Two men instead of one. The men roll the parts of two bodies in, the chaplain crosses out the "one" and writes "two" on the cross. I hold a perfumed handkerchief that I had found in one of their packs to my nose. I had always thought of the French as being effeminate for carrying perfumed handkerchiefs, now I know the reason.

We search the road and vicinity for more bodies. Yesterday this was "No Mans Land," where the unburied dead had lain for weeks. Our search is interrupted by a low flying plane, an American at great speed whizzes over us with a German on his tail peppering him with a stream of tracer bullets, the telltale smoke passing over our heads. I duck but the danger is over. The Boche had evidently swooped down on a low flying American plane and the Yank could only take to his heels. He puts on all the speed he can and escapes after the German had driven him well into our lines.

Then shells interrupt our work, bursting viciously along the road. We run for an old stone quarry and take cover in dugouts, where the shells burst harmlessly. We remain in the quarry until the shelling ends, listening to the chaplain talk to us, eager for his message, "Where two or three are gathered together in my name there am I in the midst of them." The shelling ended, regretfully we go back to our dread work. We bury five Americans that afternoon, none of which we can identify. They were probably from the 110th Infantry but now hardly more than skeletons. I use the perfumed handkerchiefs often.

Slightly wounded French and Americans pass in a continual stream all afternoon. Today's casualties are high in our division but not many dead or seriously wounded. Medical men comment on so few deaths in so many hit, caused mostly by machine gun bullets that do not tear the big holes the high explosive shells do. About nine hundred men in all today in the 28th.

Late afternoon, the chaplain calls off the detail and we start for our own positions in the rear. As we arrive on top of the hill, we turn for another look at the regiments across the river still advancing and now miles north of the Vesle. A German ammunition dump, burning all day across the river, explodes with a terrific roar, sending clouds of smoke and timbers hundreds of feet into the air, a terrifying but beautiful sight against the pink sky.

We are just going to sleep, my brother and I, when we hear an explosion on the hill. Startled we jump up thinking it is artillery fire. A Boche plane dives at us, a whistling noise is in the air as his bombs drop to explode on the hill nearby. With a rush he is over our heads, another terrible whistling, louder and louder, the bomb hits the ground, springs into air and bursts above our heads, a fierce, rocking concussion, a hellish burst of light and flames, an invisible power with stunning force drives us into the ground and it is over. Terrified we cling to the ground, our only support now, expecting more death to drop from the sky. Yet, bad as it was not a soul in "A" Company, where the last bomb hit, was scratched.

The sound of the motor recedes while we wait trembling for his return, a little more free as he passes us entirely and we sit up to take stock of each other. Another miracle that no one was hurt.

The Boche, however, is not gone, he is only circling, the noise of his motor returning to finish the job grows louder. Hugh and I squeeze into a small dugout in the bank expecting this to be the last. It is the last minute for some but not for us, the plane swoops low overhead headed for the woods where the Field Artillery are camped, there is that awful whistling again, blast after blast after blast as fast as a machine gun rocks their woods, smoke, flames and trees rise into the air in an awful conglomeration, the quiet again as the plane speeds away and the souls of boys he has slaughtered speed on to their eternal reward. Screams of horses mutilated and dying for a few seconds, then a voice on the air sings out, "All's well" and relieved I go to sleep little realizing the havoc that had been done so close to us.

RELIEVED

September 7. The French relieve the 28th Division. Rumors again, a long rest in a quiet rest camp. we may even go to the States as instructors, wild, silly rumors, but anxious to believe them and hope they are true.

We have breakfast and hike away from the front, past a row of about twenty men covered with blankets, victims of the air raid last night and for whom the relief came too late. Twenty dead, one hundred wounded and seventy horses killed, the roll of one airplane when it cuts loose. We hike to our former camp near Coulonges and rest in safety now. The front has been pushed back miles more; only the planes can get us.

September 8. We hike to the rear early in the morning in the rain. When the regiment passed me I could realize the ravages of war. "A" Company is in the best condition, about one hundred and seventy men of the original two hundred and fifty, "B" about one twenty, "C" about eighty and "D" about one twenty. "G" and "H" of the 2nd Battalion have fifteen apiece left of the original two hundred and fifty that started about the beginning of July. Of course not all are killed, wounded, gassed or captured. Some are still straggling, some transferred, many sick, many A.W.O.L. and a few actual deserters. Each company now averages about one hundred men.

The companies look like platoons as they pass. That worries me. Two months of fighting and three fifths of the men gone, what will it be at the end of the year? What chance do I have if we keep it up? And this slaughtering each other in the name of God and our country may continue for years. It will be hiking and fighting, starving, exhaustion, terror and horror and the only hope is that some kindly bullet or piece of shell will nick us just enough to get us into a hospital. I cannot hope for death, as some have, though at times when I looked at the dead lying peacefully I have wondered if they were not the luckiest after all.

We have undergone a change in discipline also. I notice that the loud shouting, cursing, mean officer and noncoms are quiet. The stiffly military men are also in the background. Military courtesy means little at the front. Discipline cannot be maintained by threats of court-martial under fire. We respect the man that gives the order, his ability and courage and the regard he has for his men, not the bars on his shoulders. The officers recognize the difference also. We have found that our superiors bleed the same as we, pray in fright, they fear and they run as fast as we. It is more dangerous to be an officer judging by the casualties. And they have found that the inferior private that caused them the most difficulty in camp by his lack of discipline is now the bravest and most dependable soldier and the good soldier who saluted properly and said "Yes Sir" in the best military manner may now be very hard to get out of a dugout and very scarce when an attack is to take place. Discipline, which I had heard was the backbone of the army, in the sense that we had always thought of it before, is entirely gone. Who would not rather be in jail than at the front; surely the jail. Leavenworth scares us not at all, it would be heaven compared to the front. Why we remain is a mystery, certainly not because we fear the officers who are as scared and as anxious to get away as we. Yet most of us stay and face the music. Anyhow the sham and blustering of military discipline and courtesy is gone. What officer can decently punish a man who has been in a shell hole with him under fire. He and the private are buddies, no caste now, the bullets see no difference and the shell does not inquire. My outfit marches by and I fall in and continue the march. Patriotism is at a low ebb, the air raid finished that. What soldier could love a country that sends him into a hell that we have been in? What if the Boche do win, they probably would be as considerate as anyone.

We are passing a ruined French village where the refugees are just returning to their homes. A few women wave at us. Bitterly I think of the men that have died and suffered that they may have their homes back. Then standing on a bank I see two little French boys, smiling and waving, sweet and cute in their horizon blue. We also gave them their home back and they are thankful. The men in my regiment that died also gave those little boys their homes back. I cannot feel bitter about that. It may have been worth it to return the smiles to their faces.

Behind us have been many of these children, lovely women, the aged ones and we have also protected them. Yes, no matter how hard, it is still the young man's duty to form a line and fight back the barbarians to protect these people so that some day our own may have safety and protection. Christ suffered and died and set an example to die by. Instantly the smiles on these boys' faces have changed my thoughts to wholesome manly thoughts and I resolve that I will not descend to those weak things again as long as it is my duty to fight.

Our hike takes us back through the Forest de Fere, the scene of our first attack. The beautiful scenery does not remind us of the horrors of that day little over a month ago. It would be a fine place to camp. But we pass through, then on to the Marne near Jaulgonne and camp in the woods on the heights above the town. It rained a steady, soaking drizzle. Hugh, Dellinger and I pitched pup tents, first scraping off the wet top soil, then lay down to sleep.

September 9. A beautiful day. My brother and I hike to Jaulgonne. It is still partly wrecked and deserted with only a few of the inhabitants back. The church still showed the snouts of German field pieces through the windows, where they had abandoned their guns in their hurry to get away.

On the way back to camp we find a large sack of sugar. We make fudge over the fire, a crude mixture, sugar, a little chocolate and canned milk, but as good as I ever tried at home. We concealed our treasure for candy is a luxury worth stealing.

Our camp is in the woods, wet still from yesterday's rain, a little muddy and miserable but safe from airplanes cruising around. We can see for miles the beautiful Marne valley. Fast passenger trains remind us that there is still a civilization, a strange contrast to this same place a few weeks ago.

September 10. First call sounds early and we are to move again. A hard, cold driving rain is falling as we roll our wet shelter halfs in the packs and march down the heights to our kitchens in the valley where we are to receive our morning meal before the hike. By daylight we are on the march, heads bent to the storm, raincoats soaked entirely through, then the clothes underneath soak up the cold rain, the shoes swishing from the water inside. But somewhere is the big rest camp where all will be rosy again. I have a small, half blanket, which I throw over my head and shoulders to keep some of the water out. We slog along in a running stream of mud and water which at times is over the shoe tops. There is little bantering, everyone is too miserable.

We march till twelve o'clock and wonder if we are going to eat. It soon develops that we are not. The afternoon wears on, the rain lets up, occasionally a shower but not as bad as this morning. Then when the clothes had about dried another heavier downpour accompanied by a high driving, cold wind. Once more the clothes are soaked. The rain lasts a half hour and then turns much colder. Muscles stiffen from the cold and fatigue of the hike but no sign of a let up.

At four p.m. I am famished. Orders that no man dare fall out for any reason. We are passing through a forest where a few French refugees, driven from their homes north of the Marne, had taken refuge and built shanties. I manage to undo the strap on my puttees so that one will come down, which will force me to fall out and roll it again. When the company has passed I roll it quickly and run over to a shanty and ask for bread. They were able to give me only a small piece but refused to take money for it. I was ashamed to take it as the poor people had very little. Saying "Merci, merci", I ran and catch up to my place in ranks. Late in the afternoon the rain stops entirely. We hike through the large forest and finally halt near a hunting lodge a few miles from Epernay. Under the trees we pitch tents. Fires are started, large roaring bonfires around which men crowd to dry out. With the clothes dried, cheerful spirits return. Rations are issued to cook ourselves. Over the coals steaks are broiled on sticks and potatoes baked in the ashes. Later the bonfires are started again, men crowd around, songs are sung. The forest is full of thousands of men and the woods ring with their songs. Things could be worse, at least we are out of shell range. The spirits of young men are hard to keep down and then there is the rest camp coming, maybe this is it. But we are also tired from ten hours hiking in a cold rain. Plenty of wood is piled on to last the night through. We roll in blankets feet to the fire and sleep.

September 11. The woods are full of blackberries so I gather enough for a meal, dessert after the broiled steak and baked potatoes. This is a French National Forest, the temporary home of many refugee families, living in small slab shacks little better than the dugouts at the front.

September 12. We remain in the forest till evening and then a long night appears. We wait in the ditches beside the road till dusk when long lines of French camions roll up and halt. Thirty men to a truck, we pile in.

The first few hours are not bad as we are still fresh and the scenery is wonderful in the night. Surely now we are headed for the rest camp but why do we travel by night. Standing becomes tiresome but there is not room to lie down. We are finally a mixture of men, packs, rifles and equipment, half standing, impossible to sleep with the truck bumping and swaying in the darkness without lights. We have no idea where we are going and at last in that state of insensibility, half conscious but never restfully asleep that is so common to soldiers. The ride goes on for hours and hours of this torture.

September 13. Near daylight the truck train stops and we disembark stiffly and wearily and drop into the ditches to snatch a little sleep. Bodies are cramped from the unnatural positions and the jolting. At daylight we move into a small village called Scrupt. I am assigned to a billet in a barn but by the time I get there everything is taken but the horse stall. The horse stall would be fine but the French farmer's horse is going to be there.

We are given limited rations to cook again. Those that have money buy from the farmers but we have not been paid since June so that source is slim. I manage to ward off hunger on the small bits of rations issued. This must be the rest camp and I am content to stay and never get up anymore.

The night comes on and I am very tired. No sleep on that truck the night before. The horse stall is big enough if he would only stay over on his side.

There are no other places and he looks like a kindly, considerate old horse and he has enough straw for both of us. Then too tired to even worry, I lay down under his feet, close to the manger and go to sleep.

September 14. He was a good horse. I am even clean and if he stepped on me I was too tired to notice it. The French farmer had a good laugh when he saw me there. Once awake I leave the stall to friend horse.

Rations were more plentiful today. I enjoy cooking steak on sticks when we have the time. The St. Mihiel drive is on. French people are on every corner talking excitedly. The Americans have crashed through and wiped out a large salient the Germans held for four years. The French are incredulous. In three days the Yanks have kicked Heinie out of a section of France that the French could not budge. Many prisoners and material taken and the American loss slight. We may be heading there.

September 16. Drill. Then pay day. With two months' pay I bought plenty to eat. The wine flowed and the crap games again. Boys who had reformed under shell fire and sworn they would never shoot crap or drink liquor are at it again now that the scare is over. They will reform when they go up again. Some go to Vigny-le-Francois where there are plenty of women and wine. Others hearing the wonderful tales of the women of Vigny decide to go tomorrow.

September 17. More drill and cooking over our own fires, the weather is good and I feel better. The kitchens caught up and cooked us a meal tonight.

But we roll packs again prepared for another move. Another wait in the evening beside the road. Still the rumors of a large rest camp. Some say it's to the front. Others argue it can't be the front as we have no replacements. The arrival of the trucks stop the arguments and we pile in for another long tiresome night ride.

It is the same old story of a truck ride, no place to sit in comfort, bumping all night on a hard floor, swaying and jerking, jostling and grumbling, equipment prodding with the jerks. fatigue and bad tempers all night when the minutes are hours and the hours like a day. At last again, a jumble of men and equipment nodding in a half doze, miserable, cramped and disgusted.

September 18. Early in the morning we stopped in a forest near Revegny and went to sleep in the ditches and the woods beside the road. Evening and we line up to hike. We do not sneak off in the night to rest camps, it is the front again, probably a quiet front where we can rest and recuperate. The night starts well, a beautiful moonlight evening. I am even glad to hike on a night like this. We pass through a village and a sign points to Verdun. There we must be going to take over the front. Verdun has been quiet since 1916, not so bad.

A few clouds appear and soon hides the beautiful moon. A few raindrops fall, then more and then a steady rain. We don slickers and plod along, the rain increasing in intensity as the night wears on. The lines of men cease to talk, heads bent in that position of a tired man while the feet keep up the steady rhythm as the hours drag on with rests infrequent.

Chapter 6

The Meuse-Argonne Offensive

Editor's note

With the Aisne-Marne offensive over and the great bulk of the AEF now formally under General John Pershing's full command, plans went forward for two offensives. The first was at St. Mihiel to eliminate a German salient. The 28th Division did not take part in that successful campaign. Rather, it was pulled back from the line, given some rest and then moved into position for what would become the U.S. Army's biggest – and bloodiest – offensive of the war, the Meuse-Argonne campaign.

The 28th Division was one of the three divisions of I Corps at the left wing of the American front, much of it the Argonne Forest. Pershing's plan was to push through on a broad front and ultimately reach the Hindenburg Line and key transportation points, including the city of Sedan. French Field Marshall Ferdinand Foch also saw this campaign and others along the Western Front at the same time as the way for the Allies to break the German army once and for all. He even thought the September and October fighting might end the war in 1918.

More than 1 million U.S. soldiers, airmen and Marines, along with 135,000 French troops took part in the offensive. Over the next 47 days, American losses amounted to 26,277 deaths plus 95,786 wounded, the highest of any battle in American history. The brunt of those casualties fell on infantry units like Pierce's A Company of the First Battalion, 112th Infantry Regiment. When the offensive began on September 26, the 112th had 77 officers and nearly 3,000 men fit for duty, according to James A. Murrin, author of *With the 112th in France: A Doughboy's Story of the War*. When the regiment moved to the rear on October 9, it had dwindled to 10 officers and just over 500 men. For A Company, command changed hands four times as company commanders fell. For four days command fell to First Sergeant Martin Henning until Second Lt. Thomas Smail took over.

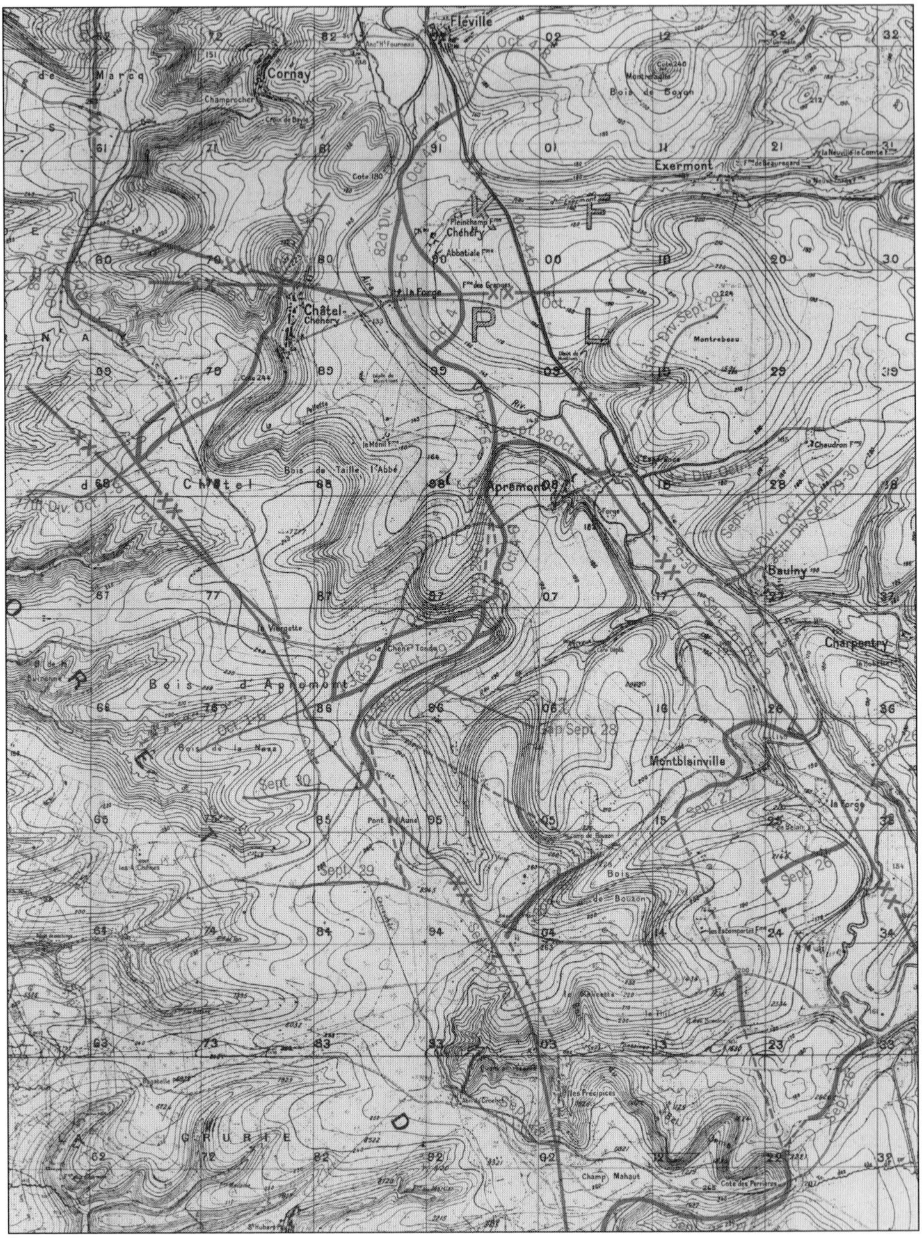

The 28th Division started the Meuse-Argonne offensive on September 26, 1918, at the line shown at lower right. In 13 days of fighting until its relief, the division fought its way northwest, shown on the upper left on this contour map. (*28th Division Summary of Operations in the World War*)

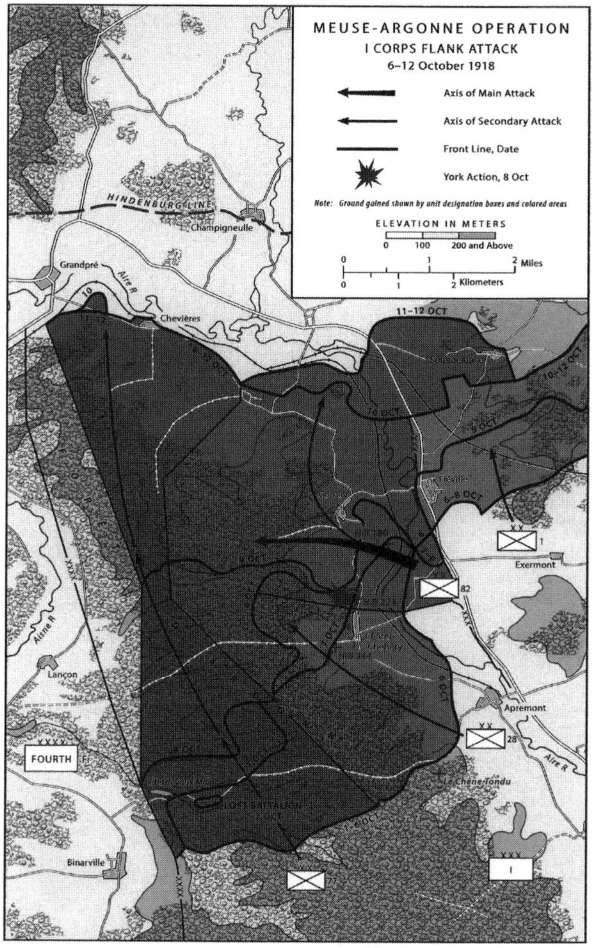

This map shows the second part of the Meuse-Argonne offensive, beginning October 6. For the 28th Division, this was the final push. Near the lower left is the position of the 77th Division's Lost Battalion. The Keystone Division's push helped relieve the pressure on the Lost Battalion and ultimately led to the capture of several key objectives. (*Center for Military History*)

The first phase began on September 26. Nine American divisions went forward along a jagged, 30-kilometer front. They were advancing into territory the Germans had held for most of the past four years. The Germans had used that time to prepare thoroughly. Machine gun nests, pillboxes, artillery batteries, hilltop observation posts, fields of barbed wire, and more awaited the doughboys. Four years of war had stretched German manpower to the limit, but those fearsome defenses all concentrated on the ground the Americans would have to cross, made this a deadly venture.

The 28th Division was among the experienced (and blooded) divisions that had learned how to fight. For its soldiers, including Harold Pierce, those battlefield experiences often proved lifesaving. Still, even with those skills the Meuse-Argonne took a heavy toll. The American command leadership had not learned all the lessons and relentlessly pushed the soldiers against the German defenses. As the infantry made attack after attack, American logistic support barely kept the front line soldiers supplied. Long lines of trucks could barely move along jammed roads.

The American First Army staff planned for a 16-kilometer advance on the first day. All along the line, including the 56th Brigade's sector, which included the 112th Regiment, met intense machine gun fire that cut into the advancing soldiers. Still, the brigade advanced five kilometers. That was a good showing compared to many other units that day. The 28th Division continued to attack day after day until October 3, sometimes going so far its flanks were left unprotected. Attacks resumed October 6. The 112th fought bitterly for Chatel-Chehery, Hill 223, Le Chene Tondu and Cote 244, capturing and holding them until October 9 when the 82nd Division relieved the exhausted 28th Division.

Pierce's account of the battle is gripping as he describes being pinned down by German machine gunners. When American machine gunners and tanks come to the rescue of the riflemen, the reader can let out a sigh of relief. And then come hunger, thirst, exhaustion and horror. The battle goes on and on. Through it all, the doughboys go forward. Bloody as this offensive is, it is a victory.

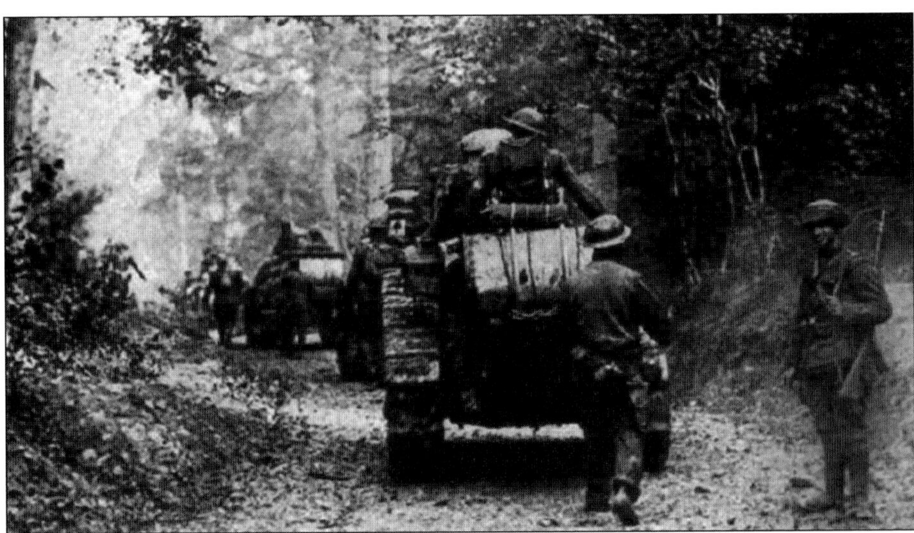

Keystone Division tanks move forward near the town of Boureuilles. (*Center for Military History*)

Chapter 7

The Argonne

September 19. At midnight the march still continues, and a few men, the first to give up, drop down exhausted. From then on the hike becomes another endurance contest, the pace quickens rather than decreases, there is no talk, no grumbling even. The mind is deadened, it seems that for ages we have been placing one foot in front of the other in the tracks of the man ahead and this will continue forever. Men walk more asleep than awake. Again the pace quickens and men who cannot increase falter, stumble to the side of the road and are asleep as soon as they drop. The road is wavy, ahead is a snake-like chain of men who have lost their formation but still keep walking in the rain. They are dropping faster, many in their tracks, often we stumble over a man unable to stay up longer. The strain of two nights of truck riding and riding on dysentery-seared bowels was too much.

It is nearly daybreak and I have stood it all night. Sgt. Leinbach, Ed Bowers and I are the only ones still in the Scout Section. Bowers and I decide to fall but Leinbach says he will stick it out. We stay a little longer, then through the woods we see a building, the temptation is too much, we drop out of ranks, crawl into an old wooden French barracks and are sound asleep on the floor exhausted by one of the hardest hikes I ever was on. It is noon when we awaken. The hike had stopped about one hundred yards further so we stood it to the end after all. A French canteen serves hot chocolate, we are issued food and iron rations. The rain still falls softly. Stragglers of the night before catch up in ones, twos and small groups. Frenchmen inform us that this is the Argonne Forest, quiet for a long time so we are here for a rest. Our division has had plenty, now they will recuperate us on an easy sector and recover our nerves, rid us of diarrhea and dysentery and other ailments. That is the way they do with exhausted divisions everyone says.

The evening and our battalion is to go to the front. Replacements from the 48th Infantry join us, about forty men to a company, making each company about one hundred and fifty men, a hundred short of full strength. Lieut. Randall Houghton, who has just received his commission, says it is not far to the trenches we will occupy. The hike starts cheerful enough. Hoke, Oudette, Freed and I in the same rank. Hoke is carrying a can of tomatoes and he and I are going to drink the juice when we are thirsty tonight. The Argonne Forest is a beautiful place with the moon shining through the tall trees.

But the hike keeps on for hours. Lieut. Houghton says it is not far. We pass a place where men are placing a battery of long range naval guns. "A quiet front" someone snorts in disgust.

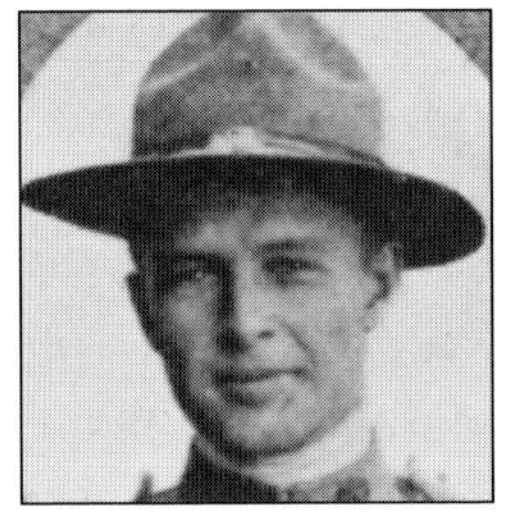

Lt. Randall Houghton.

September 20. It looks like repeating last night's hike. Lieut. Houghton has stopped saying it is not much farther. We rest beside the road and when we move again, Hoke has left the can of tomatoes. He does not discover the loss until we are too far to go back for it. I could shoot him, all that good juice gone and I am thirsty.

Sometime before daylight we halt and our Battalion Headquarters move through the great trees to halt in a ravine as the companies move forward to occupy trenches on the hill above. The moon shines through the tree tops, making bright patches of moonlight on the forest floor, the trees dark, silent black streaks against the moonlight sky. It is quiet and still, hardly a chance of war. Quietly we lie down to slumber in the peaceful woods.

When I waken I settle in a shack at the end of a communication trench. It is more like a picnic ground than a battle front; now we are holding a quiet sector. I am glad, war like this is not so terrible. People live long and are comfortable on fronts like these, there are no shell holes, no terrible scars, no ruins, no rotting dead bodies, just a beautiful leafy forest of evergreen and hardwood, as quiet and serene as the woods back home.

September 21. Regimental Headquarters comes in and battalion vacates the nice shacks for the trees. Gayvert and I make our bed under a wooden bridge. But at night it rained and the water dripped through the planks, the stream rises and we are forced into the open, cursing Regimental Headquarters for taking our comfortable shacks.

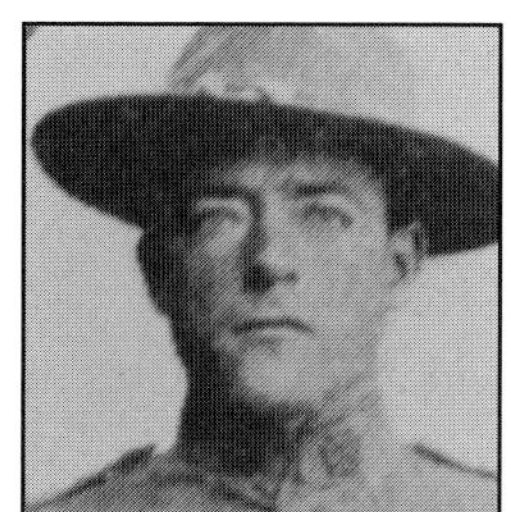
Pvt. Clifford Gayvert.

September 22. I am sent to locate the supporting artillery. I find plenty mostly big guns. That is funny: if this is a quiet front why are they bringing so much artillery. Already there is more than the night we came in. They are piling up huge piles of shells for the heavy guns. Battery upon battery of French and American guns are going in. I do not like the looks. It can mean only one thing, another big drive. A French soldier says we cannot lick the Germans in two years and we will do well to do it then.

September 23. A man from "A" Company was killed accidentally in the trenches today. A corporal, his gun loaded for inspection, threw the bolt home without looking in the chamber, pulled the trigger and killed one of the new replacements next to him. His body is now lying in a dugout near us. The rats have been chewing his face and we run in occasionally and chase them away. It is our first experience with trench rats for till now our service has been in open warfare.

I sleep in the shack at night listening to the patter of little feet and the squeaking of the rats. I feel a little foot on the edge of my blankets and a rat crawls cautiously up my frame. My hands are on my chest, I wait till Mister Rat is on my chest and then suddenly hurl him crashing against the wall. Squealing the rat runs followed by his companions and the rest of the night they leave me alone.

September 24. I am twenty years old today. For celebration, Lieut. Lapaze, now in charge of the Scout Section, sends me back to Regimental Headquarters for Instruction Books. That is encouraging. The drive may not start if we are going to start training. But the big guns back there are becoming too numerous. The seventy-fives and Trench Mortars are moved up on a line with the infantry, using light narrow gauge railroads that run everywhere in the woods. Artillerymen are working in the tree tops, sawing them partly through and holding them in place with wires. A great many guns are concealed under the branches of this forest, either we attack or they expect a big German attack.

September 25. In the afternoon Dellinger and I are detailed to Regimental Headquarters back a few miles to make maps. We report to Lieut. Abel and find scouts from other battalions there. We have a large pile of maps and we trace on them what our regiment is to take. It is a long job. Lieut. Abel explains that everything is now in readiness and that we are to start the biggest battle of the war. At present we are only waiting for the "Zero" hour, which may

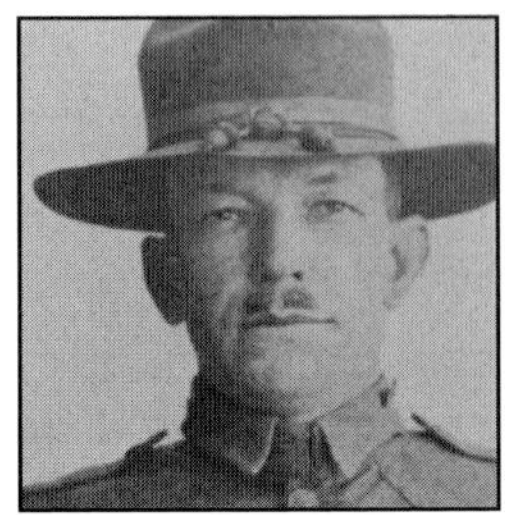

2nd Lt. Louis Abel.

be tonight or it may be several days yet. I cannot feel any elation. Will my brother and I survive and how many of my friends must go?

A few heavy guns boom their preliminary shots. Scattering booms continue during the evening and the early night. Above eleven p.m. Lieut. Abel appears and informs us that the "Zero" hour is set at five a.m. tomorrow morning and the army will jump off then. He hands Dellinger and I the barrage sheet for our battalion with instructions to see that it is in the hands of Lieut. Colonel Bubb, our new Regimental Commander. This barrage sheet is the schedule for the artillery to fire as we attack. I hate to leave Lieut. Abel, he was a fatherly sort, strict but straight. I have a feeling it would be good to be near him in the next trouble as he is so sure and dependable.

Going back to our forward positions the roads are jammed with traffic. The 110th Infantry is dodging in and out of the trucks, caissons, ambulances and what not that fill the road to the front. Only two of us and we can make better time. The heavy barrage is not well started but there is plenty of gunfire from the heavies to let you know there is a war going on. Surely a big event is coming off. We arrive at the forward O.C. and give the maps and barrage sheet to Colonel Bubb. He is very quiet and cool and jokes with us about the coming drive. He seems like a very good officer, not stuck up, friendly and kind. Nervously we stand around. A private asks the time and the colonel obligingly pulls out his

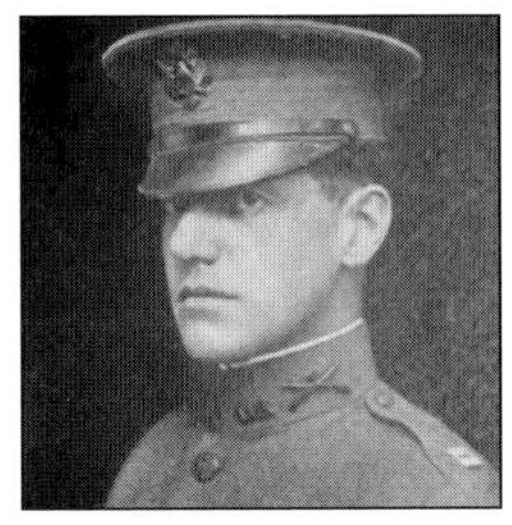

Lt. Col. John Bubb.

watch and gives the lad the correct time. A long range naval gun just back of us lets go and the concussion nearly knocks me to the ground. I walk down the communication trench to have a wall between me and that gun so the concussion will not be so bad. My brother comes along and sits with me. We are lonesome and afraid and pray again to God for help in this battle. Many boys are praying all over this same battle front although many will not admit it.

September 26. About midnight the 1st Battalion under Major McCoy is ready to move to our places on the front. The Frenchmen are leaving as we start, no doubt tickled to death that we, not they, are going into it. The artillerymen have pulled down the tops of the trees and already there is a constant roar from the cannon firing through the trees.

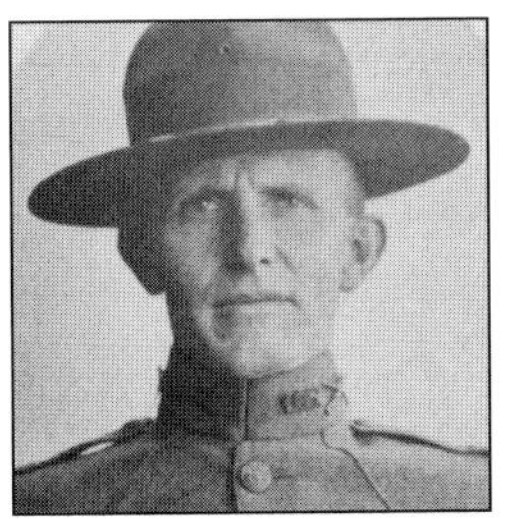
Major Fred McCoy.

The battalion moves slowly through the woods. Concussions rock the forest, we walk a few steps and halt. We must hold our hands over our ears and keep the mouth open or the eardrums may burst. We stop by things that look like logs and suddenly they belch flame and a blast of air and noise hits us. The din is terrific as we go farther ahead among the six and eight inchers. The sky for miles is lighted by a steady, flickering light, caused by the constant fire of thousands of guns. One can hardly imagine that there are enough guns firing to keep this glow in the sky. This glow and the flashes of cannon light the forest as plain as if a great fire was burning. The smoke and haze is heavy like a fog. Millions of dollars are going into this barrage tonight. It seems impossible that anyone on the German side could survive this fire. The Boche retaliate little, although with the din of our own guns we could not tell them anyhow. One shell did land in the Trench Mortar platoon, blowing guns and men into the trees and wiping out the entire platoon. I am soon exhausted from the smoke and the shocks and my head aches terribly from the concussions. But at last after what seems hours we are through the heavies and the roar recedes a little although still loud enough to make us yell at the top of our voices to be heard.

After passing through the heavies we file through the lighter seventy-fives. They have not opened up yet, their fire is reserved for the attack when they will lay down a barrage in front of us. Beyond the guns we reach a road and halt. Down the road a clanking noise grows steadily louder and then through the darkness and smoke a line of tanks, looking like a herd of elephants with their tenders, pass slowly by us. After they pass we move off again. It is close to the zero hour but Major McCoy is not sure if we are in the right trench to jump off. He believes the French front line is farther ahead. He calls for Scouts and Smith and I are sent to find the front line. The seventy-fives have opened their barrage and we are late. Then the machine guns behind us open with a continuous cracking noise a few feet above our heads, deluging the Boche line with a hail of lead. To me their fire sounds to be hitting close in front, but orders are orders, we must find the old French front line. I believe the next line is the Germans.

Smith and I are dubious when we find no lanes cut through the barbed wire and it is a common fact that in the second line lanes are cut to let men in and out. Yet we scramble through the best we can and then cross a field a quarter of a mile wide. The field has every appearance of not being used for a long time, tall wet grass, no paths and I am sure it is really "No Man's Land". The fog is rising slowly, the air is full of passing shells and crackling bullets and over the hill in front the shells are bursting. Beyond the field we enter a gloomy, damp woods filled with barbed wire. The two of us try to pass through it but after going about a hundred yards without a break in the wire we decide to return. I feel certain that this is the German wire.

Major McCoy still does not believe we are in the right position. It is nearly the zero hour, only a few minutes to go, the fog is rising faster, the seventy-fives are firing the barrage and he still insists this is the second line. The Major then sends me to the left to find the 2nd Battalion. After several minutes I find soldiers walking through the woods and they direct me to Captain Miller. "I don't know where in hell we are but all we're going to do is go ahead and find something to shoot at," he answers me when I asked him where we are and what he is going to do. The 3rd Battalion is to the left of the 2nd and neither have contacted the Germans yet. As quick as I can, I return to the major and report but he still thinks we are wrong. I do not care to jump off either, but I hate to think of the other two battalions going ahead and being enfiladed because we did not attack. I am sure this is the right place but I am not the major. I would be glad to stay here and never attack. I will not be sore by staying here. I find a small dugout with a bunk and tired as I am I decide to lie down and relax till some move is made. I will not go to sleep, just rest.

I come to with a start. I had slept, noise or no noise, and it is broad daylight and I am alone. I had no sooner stretched out than I was asleep. Outside a man runs down a path and when I overtake him it is Eddie Brenneman. He had been asleep and just wakened in time to see the last man go. We soon catch the tail end of our organization. It is quiet now, the barrage is over, no retaliation and our men are simply walking ahead through the woods. A mile or so ahead the battalion deploys in an open field to the right of the forest and then remains on the ground. Some officer has a bright idea. Scouts are to be sent in front and lead the companies, staying about two hundred yards ahead of the first combat groups. I am picked and with another scout take positions in front of "A" Company. I feel like a sore thumb sticking out away ahead of everyone. Over our heads Boche shells race and burst near a wagon train a mile behind us. A man from the 109th Infantry escorts a German prisoner through the line and when asked where he got him says, "Go on up and get one of your own, there are plenty of them up there." Instead of pushing forward, we assemble again and march in close order to the front. Major Smathers meets the head of the column and hikes with us forward. It is still quiet, hardly like the opening day of a big battle although we have advanced about three miles already. I cannot give my battalion much credit as we waited too long to start. Late afternoon finds us with the 2nd and 3rd battalions. The 3rd had taken a trench and captured a lot of discouraged prisoners. One said, "What's the use, we build fields of barbed wire we think no one can cross, and these Americans they take one jump and they clear it. There is no use of us trying to fight men like that." A man in the regiment passed a wounded German boy, shot already in the stomach, and when the boy begged for "wasser" he murdered him in cold blood. The 2nd found something to shoot at and something that shot back. Wounded men pass by us as we wait near the top of a hill, one man in terrible agony having been sprayed with a machine gun across the shoulders on both sides but missed all vital spots. He is full of holes and will live and if he can stagger along no one will carry him. To our right the 55th Brigade took Varrennes in fifty-five minutes considerably in advance of the French predictions of five days.

Night and we lie down beside a battery of German seventy-sevens abandoned today. A battery of our own seventy-fives unlimber near us and fire a few shots over our heads. I meet Lieut. Randall Houghton and talk to him a little. We attended high school together. Davie Lett and I cuddle together for warmth and talk of our home and wonder if we will ever be back. Both are very serious, we know that today is only the start and that in the next few days we are going to have tough sledding. Lieut. Abel was killed shortly after the jump off this morning, a bullet hitting him through the heart. Yet casualties have been light, the Germans are squelched, but they have a way of popping up again.

I hear my name called and Bing Johnson and I are detailed with "D" Company to lead them through the forest tomorrow with the prismatic compass. We find them in the darkness along a woods road and report to Lieut. Rippey Shearer who orders us to stick with him in company headquarters.

The night is chilly and dark. We have DO blankets and only our raincoats to cover us as we entered the fight with only combat packs. In the ditches we cuddle together, Bing and I, and cover with the raincoats and keep as close as possible to get a little body warmth. We sleep fitfully and several times during the night get up and run up and down the road to get warm. Off in the black woods to our left a machine gun duel starts, flares go up and a few spent bullets come whispering through the air. We had expected artillery fire but it seems that the Germans do not have much. A night of apprehension, cold, foggy and dismal, and tomorrow we will be in another attack and the Heinies will be better organized.

September 27. The morning is cold and foggy but the fog is a blessing as it affords us cover. As daylight appears we deploy at the foot of the hill. The 2nd Battalion is on top ready to attack with "D" in support. Connecting files lead back from the front line to the support and when these connecting files move off we will follow them. We have an advantage in the fog as it is so dense now that men fifty yards away cannot be seen.

Just before the attack a runner approaches Lieut. Shearer and Lieut. Zacharias of "C" Company who are standing together, ordering them to report to the rear to attend a school. Two broad smiles appear on both faces and without another word they lock arms, wave goodbye, and hurry happily down the road, the rest of us watching anxiously. To be relieved just before an attack, such good fortune, but not for me. The connecting files ahead of us move forward, the "D" commences the climb up the hill through the wet soggy woods. There will be no danger till we are over the crest. We near the top and just then the Boche machine guns must have seen the advancing first wave as a burst of machine gun bullets passed over the level top of the hill. We wait a short time dreading those last few feet of climb. But slowly I start up again, close to the top now and another burst rattles over our heads and the ricochet bullets scream off into space, young tree above drops, cut in two and a long white scar appears before my eyes in a tree just to my left and a few feet above me. If I had been there I would have received them. We lie down and wait till the fire stops. A lieutenant springs over the top and we follow. Now we are on the broad level top and the Germans are somewhere ahead in the fog. We walk forward always on the lookout for holes and depressions to drop into. At every stop we lie down. The air is filled with rushing, snapping, cracking sounds, sometimes close and sometimes far away as the Boche fire blindly into the fog hoping by luck to get someone. Ricochet bullets scream horribly when deflected by a twig or blade of grass. Dimly through the fog we can see the files and combat groups moving slowly. When they move we move, when they halt we halt. The rattle of the machine guns ceases suddenly as the gunners realize the men ahead are getting close and they have taken their guns and retreated to a better spot to set up again.

We come to a woods road, the men ahead stop and take refuge behind trees, and I remain on one knee. I can barely see the figure of a man behind a tree fifty yards in front of me. Suddenly a crackle of bullets and in front a man screams, then flops into the bushes, his throat gurgling, moaning, kicking and thrashing around. His kicks gradually cease, a long sigh and it is all over. It was the bugler from "F" Company and he got it through the neck. I lie down on my face and shiver and cover my head with a blanket I found this morning to keep out the sound. Bing Johnson also crawls under with me and though we realize the blanket is no protection yet it will keep out the sights. The firing dies down again, the 2nd has chased them off the top of the hill. The support lines move into the ditch by the side of the woods road where we have a parapet for protection. The 2nd moves down the hill and by the sounds are having a tough time but the connecting files we have been watching remain where they are. The fog rises and machine guns probably from the next hill rake our hill top and we remain below the parapet for protection. The 2nd are down in the valley but when they start up the next slope the machine guns stopped them. The 1st Battalion is trying to get around the foot of the hill to our right. By nine a.m. all are stopped although the rifle and machine gun fire continued for hours. We have gained about a mile.

We wait in the ditch all morning. Up till noon the fire was close enough that we hugged the ditch tight. I eat a part of a can of corn willie and give the rest away. Yesterday I ate one can and a box of hardtack and now all my rations are gone. The meat makes me thirsty but the water in my canteen is gone.

A German airplane sneaks over as close to the tree tops but in the fog we cannot see him, then turns around back of us and passes over again. Two bombs explode above our ditch but the fragments miss me. Men scream and thrash around in the bushes in agony. Four are hit but none killed, the worst injured being a red-headed runner from "D" who has several holes in his body. The other three are less seriously hurt and can walk but the runner has to be carried on a stretcher.

About noontime, Lieut. Flynn, now in command of "D", sends me forward to find out what has happened. The firing in the valley has quieted down to a few bursts of machine gun and rifle fire occasionally so it is evident that those in front are not advancing. The fog has raised except for a little mist in the valley. Large trees and rocks fill the valley and as I descend the hill I can see men lying quiet behind them. I jump from cover to cover, tree to tree and rock to rock, until I am half way down the hill, and then discover Captain Miller behind a group of trees. At the same time he spies me and jumps from behind a tree and waves frantically for me to go back. His actions are enough and I turn and hurry a few yards up the hill and drop into a shallow trench the Germans left. I remain there several minutes to watch so I can report a little to the Lieutenant. But the men behind the trees and rocks remain motionless, Captain Miller does not move, so at last I conclude that there are machine guns ahead too strong to be rushed and the Battalion is definitely stopped. Some of the motionless men will never move again and those that are alive are quiet for they do not dare to move and unless the guns are flanked they will remain till dark.

Finally, I returned up the hill, from cover to cover and reported to Lieut. Flynn. He decided we would remain where we were.

In the afternoon a stream of wounded men started coming back, those lightly wounded running and jumping, those more painfully walking slowly and carefully and a few seriously hurt being carried on stretchers. One man shot through the center of the body between the heart and breastbone was laid down to rest near me. At first glance I thought he was a man from home but after a closer look I saw he was a stranger to me. The two men carrying him started an argument, one saying he would be dead in five minutes and the other insisting on taking him on. The argument became quite heated while the poor fellow on the stretcher, when conscious, looked on and tried to talk. I bent down to hear what he was saying but could not make out a word. His eyes would focus on me for an instant and he would try to speak and then he would be unconscious again. But I could see during his conscious moments that he realized what the argument was and though he could not talk his eyes plead to be carried on to the hospital. I took his side of the argument for him and the stubborn man who had insisted on carrying him won and he was taken on although I watched them expecting to see a dead body rolled to the ground before he was out of sight. But he was carried on and did live. The next man was shot through the face and unconscious.

Two men came from out of the bushes, one running frantically down the road shot through the arm and the next man walking slowly and deliberately. The first man bent over and holding his arm stopped beside us and yelled to number two to hurry. "If that man hurried a little it would kill him," he remarked to us. "What's the matter, something hit you?" The wounded man turned angrily at his questioner, "Now that's a hell of a foolish question to ask me, can't you see something hit me, why ask such foolish questions?" Meanwhile the second man had been walking slowly toward us, apparently uninjured. "Where did you get hit?" we ask. "Oh, in the peter." Everyone but the wounded man burst into a roar of laughter and he just smiled a sickly grin. The laugh relieves some of the tension of the day and from then on we are easier.

As the afternoon wore on we could see to the right in the level valley units of the 109th and 110th with tanks pushing on from Varrennes. They captured Montblainville about two miles away. As for us we were hung up for the day. One thing fortunately for us is the lack of artillery fire from the Germans, a good sign that they were surprised. Only one battery of three seventy-sevens have been working from their side in these two days and one of their batteries that had likely worked against us yesterday is now safe on our side of the hill.

Harry Brown of "A" Company was killed today. Scouts Ahlquist, Hall and Smith were on a patrol that extended far into the German lines, where they captured a one pounder and two Germans. Returning they were fired on, one German killed, both Smith and Ahlquist wounded and Dille Hall and the other prisoner escaped. Casualties in the Regiment have been heavy today especially in that valley ahead, "F" Company especially being hard hit.

At dusk we fall in again, we cannot go ahead so we are going around them. The 111th will leave a Battalion to hold this hill. Those in the valley in front must wait till after dark to leave their cover where they have been hiding all day. Many will be left to be buried when and if they are ever found. As darkness settles we move down the hill we had climbed this morning and wait for the rest of the regiment.

At last, late in the evening we start a slow cautious advance, moving short distances, halting frequently while the advance guard scouts ahead, making a few false starts and returning in the open country to the right of the Argonne Forest proper. Each time we halt we drop to the ground to snatch a few minutes sleep and then the officers and noncoms waken us with kicks and jerks. This lasts all night, no relief, little sleep, and nothing to eat or drink. Yet the night is quiet, no rifle or machine gun fire and the artillery does not bother. The ground we are operating on is that near the advance of the 55th Brigade today and is not well reconnoitered yet.

September 28. Early morning, a chill cold fog, uncomfortable yet a blessing as it will hide our movements. The column halts in a valley between two rolling hills, the companies break away from the column and move to their appointed places and then deploy in combat groups. The entire hill ahead is covered with men ready and waiting to attack. So far in the Argonne I have only carried a forty-five automatic but as this looks like business I pick up an Eddystone rifle and bayonet with ammunition lying on the ground.

The advance starts as the first grey rays of light break through the fog and darkness. "A" and "B" is in the first wave, "C" and "D" in the second. We go over the top of the first gentle rise as our artillery behind us drop a few shells several hundred yards ahead, not a heavy fire, about one battery firing. On the hill top the fog clears a little and I can see to our right the entire regiment moving in combat groups and further to the right the 109th and 110th are keeping pace with us. To the left the Argonne Forest, dark, damp and forbidding, to our front about two miles away a large steep hill with an observation tower on top, our objective for today, and between us and that hill a semi-circular spur of the Forest lying directly across our path. I am with Lieut. Ogram at Company Headquarters.

We pass a road and then through an orchard where two dead German soldiers lay. Sgt. Leinbach relieved one of the bodies of a German Luger. Beyond the orchard an open field going down a gentle slope and the first patch of woods directly across our path about two hundred yards from "A" and "B". The woods to the left are closer now. The shelling is still very light.

Suddenly a terrific burst of machine gun fire from the front and the left flank. We have walked into a trap and three or four guns have us. The entire battalion, whether shot or not, slides to the ground for cover. But there is none but the tall grass. "A" and "B" try to answer them with rifles but the guns are concealed too well and the unequal fight is soon over. They are too close to run away and too far to rush. It would be suicide to rush and it is suicide to shoot back. The field is covered with tall grass, good hiding place but no protection, and as level as a floor. Men cling to the ground desperately trying to take advantage of the little irregularities in the ground and trust to God. Wounded men are thrashing around, men are dying and no one dares lend a hand. Some try to run and are shot down. The wounded scream for stretcher bearers and first aid but none can come. The suspense is terrible as the machine guns rake the field and though we are hid by the tall grass, yet grass is no protection. Any movement brings a burst of bullets, men soon learn not to move a finger. It is early morning and unless help comes we are doomed to lie here all day.

In one way I am fortunate. At the first burst I slide back of a bush, concealment but no armor. A few minutes after the firing began I start digging. Lieut. Ogram is beside me with a big chew of tobacco, lying half supported on his elbow, apparently not excited. I lie on my side and start the hole. Bullets crackle a few feet overhead. The Boche gunners sweep the field from left to right, then back from right to left. I can hear the crackling coming closer and I push myself as low in the ground as possible, the crackling misses my head by a few inches and passes on. I dig furiously, a few shovels full in front of me, the crackling returns toward me, dust flies in a line coming at me, the bullets are over my head again, snapping viciously, they are over and I am digging again. Every shovel full goes in front, the gun shifts again and is coming back, it will get me this time, the dust spurts are close. Will my little pile of dirt be enough? They are above me, then on again. I shovel frantically, a few more and I will have six inches of dirt. the bullets are swinging back at me, my helmet is not right, if I lay my head to the side and flat on the ground my head is not so safe, if I point it to the ground my shoulders are not covered. Inches count now. They are over. A few more inches of dirt and I am safe. I hope there are no rocks in the ground. Lieut. Ogram chews and spits. The wounded cry "first aid." The gun swings back at me, am lower in the ground, if they missed before they should miss now. Pray the agonized prayer of a scared doughboy, "Oh Lord, make them raise the range." The hole is deeper. I will throw a little dirt in front of Ogram. It seems like hours till my hole is a foot deeper but it is only a few minutes. At last I am safe from the guns, more than a yard of dirt in front and if I lie still they cannot hit me. But Lieut. Ogram needs dirt also, so from my safe place I toss him some and then give him the shovel. Now it seems the guns cease their raking the fields and only fire occasionally when they see movements.

For four hours of terrible suspense we lay in that field at the mercy of those guns. Then to my left a bunch of men rush up to our line and throw themselves on the ground. It is our machine gun company coming to help. I watch them anxiously, expecting a blast that will crumple them to the ground but apparently they are on dead ground where the Boche gunners cannot see them as well as us. On a line with "D" Company and in full view of the enemy it appears to me, they set up their guns. How long will they last? Behind us in the orchard another brave machine gun crew rushes forward and plants a gun behind a tree. The one pounder platoon also set up guns in the orchard.

The Boche gunners are kicking up the dust on the hill above us again near the machine gun and the one pounders. But to the left our machine guns are rattling, a steady strong, hard persuasive note. The dust spurts on the orchard stop, that gun opens up, the one pounder "chugs" and in the woods in front an eruption as the first shell bursts near its edge. Sweet music. The crackling above us is the same horrid note but oh so different. I am half relieved; if our gunners can only hold out we are saved. Anxiously we watch but they are going at it harder than ever. Jerry is weakening, he fires seldom now.

Another sweet sound, the soothing screaming shriek of seventy-fives from a battery just set up behind us. But their range is not good, too close to "A" and "B" and they must get up and retreat or be hit by their own shells. The Boche take advantage of the confusion to pepper them some more. But the artillery adjust the range better and soon that forest is in eruption. Machine guns, one pounders and artillery are evening the score now with the doughboys still in the middle.

Another note in the orchestra, the clank of tanks, the sweetest, softest music of all. I lie down in my hole with a sigh of relief and relax. It's all over but the shouting and I thank God fervently. Over my shoulders I see them rumbling slowly and irresistibly on and then a new danger, the Boche artillery shells them. But undaunted they plod on, slowly through our lines and lumber on into the woods. The Boche gunners have packed up and run long before they are near. Our firing dies as the tanks disappear in the woods.

And this although it takes a few minutes to tell, occupied at least six hours of the worst suspense a man can be in, when he knows that at any minute the contents of a machine gun may be turned on him and there is no defense.

The wounded that can walk get up and run to the rear, the more seriously are carried on stretchers and the dead are left on the ground. "D" had only one killed and he was just a few feet ahead of me, "A" five, "B" seven, "C" two, but they with the wounded took nearly half the battalion. Those of us left waited on the ground for further orders. Lieut. Ogram still chews quietly, occasionally giving an order as coolly as if on the drill ground.

In the afternoon orders to advance again. We must take that hill, Le Chene Tondu. "C" and "D" move to the front, "A" and "B" the second line now. Silently we start to move. I wonder how many minutes I have to live and what death will be like. We do not worry about these woods now, it's the next ones and that hill. Bodies of young men that only a few hours ago were alive and afraid mark the line of "A" and "B". For them it is past, they know now what the great mystery is. We cannot stop for the dead although some are my best friends.

The woods are silent now but beyond is where the trouble will be as we know from experience that Jerry has just retreated far enough to set up his guns again and that frowning, ominous hill with the observation tower will be hard to take. The tanks have cut wide lanes in the saplings. Beyond the woods we move into another open field where we may get the same dose as on the other side of this field is another patch of woods rising gently to the hill. Our luck seems to hold or the tanks must have run the Germans a long way for we cross this field and enter the second patch of woods. Yet somehow the suspense is just as bad for it is just as nerve wracking to walk along in silence expecting to be drilled any second as it is when actually under fire. I almost wish that blast would start and get it over with. There is nothing like the uneasy feeling of being out in the open and walking directly at someone who may be aligning a rifle or machine gun at you at this very moment.

We reach the woods at the base of the hill and start the ascent. Over our heads the battery of field guns sends its first salvo to burst on the hill. One gun is firing short, so short that when it fires the front line must take cover. More suspense. The infantry scramble through a knotty mass of underbrush and at last are ready to climb the steep pitch. No enemy fire. A small steep field and then the hill, cliff-like and surely hell will open now. But outside of our own short shell we are not molested. Lieut. Flynn, in command of "D", waves on with his cane, he does not seem like the man I saw running in the Forest de Fere, as brave and cool as Second Lieut. Orgum. The ascent of the cliff part begins. Soldiers grab roots and pull themselves up, digging their toes in, backs bent to the climb and still no fire. Slowly and wearily we climb and behind us in three miles of ground we have reclaimed since morning.

Cpl. Hilts at the head of his combat group is leading now and just going over the top. Suddenly from the bushes not fifty yards ahead a machine gun cuts loose a burst of about thirty shots and then ceases suddenly. It was "A" Company men he was firing at although "D" was closest. Just then the short gun fired behind us, the shell whistled at us on the hilltop and burst not fifty yards ahead and right beside the machine gunner. There is a rush of men forward, an old man is sitting behind his gun, men shoot him through the body but it is too late, that short shell blew the top of his head off and for once we, not the old German, were lucky when our own artillery fired short.

I am with the first line on top of the hill and we halt for a moment. Rifles are popping to the right where "C" is flanking the hill. Suddenly a perfect Babel of jabbering and yelling begins and German soldiers hands high in air and "Kamerad" on their lips burst from the woods and run toward us. "C" had flanked them and they run to us to surrender. They were a frightened bunch of poor old men and their motions indicate their feelings as they plead for their lives. We have suffered much at the hands of these men today, many of our friends lie unburied in that field, no wonder that some are in favor of shooting them down. A few search them for souvenirs and steal their watches. Lieut. Ogram says, "Boys, treat these old men like you would want to be treated if you were captured." Shamed, some men hand back watches. One old man explained in poor English that they did not shoot at us and we should spare them. Somehow it does not seem right to be fighting these grandads and we assure them we will not kill them. Smiles of relief appear, details are appointed to take them to the rear and we turn our attention to the front.

Several of "D" are in a sunken road. A skulking German in the deep under growth beyond the road throws a potato smasher grenade that bursts in the road with a white cloud of smoke. Lieut. Flynt is down writhing in agony and another man is slightly wounded. Lieut. Ogram rushes forward and I follow with Sgt. Merton and Company Headquarters. The lieutenant is badly wounded in the stomach. Firing breaks out again, men rush forward to get the sneaking Dutch man but he is gone. Rifles pop over the sunken road for the woods ahead may be filled with the enemy. The lieutenant is placed on a stretcher and carried away but he is dead before morning.

The command is "forward" again. The top of the hill is covered with thick woods and underbrush. We move slowly over the sunken road, ducking from tree to tree and rock to rock. Another machine gun opens fire on us from the front filling the air with that horrid crackling again. All around us we hear clicks as they hit the rocks and trees and the screams of the ricochets. Men drop down behind what cover they can find, fire a few shots, then jump up to the next cover. In that fashion we advance about two hundred yards. The Boche gun fires short bursts and though we are unable to see him we fire in his general direction hoping for hits. The men are firing coolly, the regiment was never more calm and collected under fire. Those ahead firing along the ground and those behind firing into the tree tops. The "Pom, pom, pom" of the Chau-Chauts mixes with the rifle fire. Men are fighting in the true American spirit without commands or instructions; in fact there have been very few orders today, just enough to start us out.

I have gone out with Lieut. Ogram, now in command of "D". The fire is too hot and we drop behind some rocks at the base of a beech tree. To our left is a wooden building. He directs a squad to attack but before they can be ready I run over and look through it. I would rather take the chance as one man does not make the target and I was quite sure there were no Germans in it anyhow. It is late evening and we have gone far enough for one day. The machine gun fire is still too heavy and the advance halts. The men ahead must keep quiet and only those with excellent cover dare fire.

The Machine Gun Company have been doing nobly today under the leadership of Pvt. Fairall. Another queer quirk of American discipline. The company has lost all their officers but Fairall appears to be in command. He had been a sergeant but was reduced for shooting craps. Now with two machine guns and about fifteen men he comes up the hill, walks quietly ahead, then breaks into a trot till they are at the farthest man, mounts the guns and their chattering adds to the noise of the Boche gun and the rifles. Almost instantly the Boche gun quits but Fairall has a bullet through his arm.

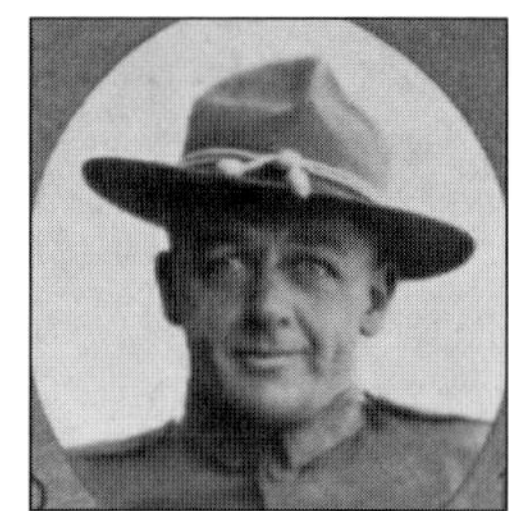

Sgt. George S. Fairall.

With the machine guns covering our retreat, Captain Graff, now in command at the battalion, orders all companies to retire to the sunken road for the night. Without hurry or excitement the men rise from their positions and start to walk back while Fairall's guns maintain a steady fire. A few parting bullets whizz by. A man near me grabs his arm, winces a little, smiles wanly, but says nothing.

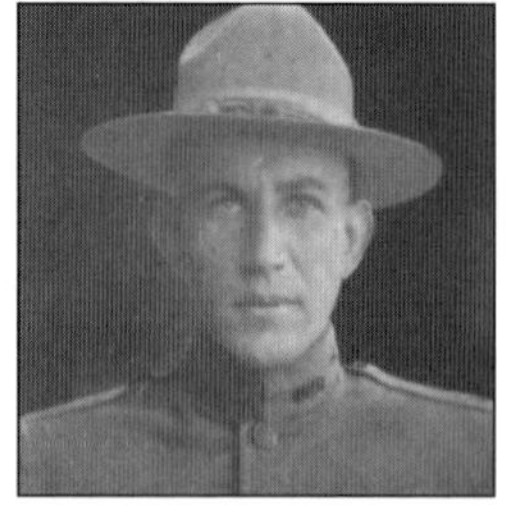

Capt. John Graff Jr.

Several are holding arms or limping but none seem dangerously wounded and none further killed beyond the sunken road, which is a miracle. As we retreat I cannot feel admiration for my regiment today.

I vault into the sunken road near the old dead machine gunner sitting with his fingers still clutching the trigger guard. A man searches him and takes his pocketbook and hands it to me for I am with the "Intelligence". But there is little except a few "marks" and a picture of this same old man in the center of a group of children. Probably a school teacher in the Fatherland. His kindly old face peers out from the center of the group. The old fellow back of the machine gun is the same but his beard is unkempt, his face is more lined but there is still a sad, kindly look on his face. It is hard to believe that this old teacher had killed my friends with that same gun and that he also tried to kill me. But it was his duty and he died believing he was doing right. Enemy though he was, I hope his soul is in peace.

Ahead in the dusk Fairall's machine guns chatter and more seldom the Boche gunner lets loose a strip. The guns are in an exposed position but in our sunken road there is good protection. It is growing dark fast. Reliefs of two men each are appointed, one to watch while the other sleeps. With the darkness comes rain. It is soon so black a hand cannot be seen in front of the face. The wind blows in the treetops and the rain drips from the trees. A man stumbles through the darkness. "Whersa 'A' Camp" an Italian voice asks. I recognize Tony Albina and call him to me. Tony is sore at the other stretcher bearer. He was trying to get a wounded man out of the field and the other bearer ran and Tony is carrying the wounded man alone. I advise him to stay with me for the night as in the darkness he will not find them and I need a man to work the relief with me.

The rain comes down harder and little rivulets run down the sunken road. There is no place to lie down except the muddy bottom of the trench. I watch, although I can see nothing until I am too tired to watch longer, then call Tony to relieve me. Then I sit in the mud of the bank huddled in my overcoat. I have not eaten today or had a drink of water. Yesterday I had a handful of corn willie and no water, the day before a handful of corn willie and a box of hardtack. I have dozed a little in cat-naps for four days and no sleep at all during the days. I am cold, hungry, thirsty, dirty and exhausted. My spirit, what I have left, is at the bottom. Tony stands as long as he can and then I relieve him. Other men are doing the same thing, all as uncomfortable as I.

A German shell shrieks through the night and bursts back in the woods to the left. A man screams in pain somewhere in the blackness. It unnerves me. Now a bombardment will come in this black night and it will be terrible. I tremble and am afraid. But it is only one shell, the minutes pass slowly and no more come. Later two men stumble down the road carrying the man wounded by the shell. He is hit in the head but we dare not strike a light to help him. It would be impossible to take him anywhere in this blackness down over the cliffs. So they lay him down along the muddy sunken road. half conscious, cold and wounded and no chance of relief till daylight.

September 29. The rain lasts all night, slow, steady, cold and drenching. It seems that I have been doing this watch endlessly. Tony watches while I rest in the mud, then he calls me and I stand in the mud again, till I am ready to fall over and then I call him. Tony is a good partner and does not try and cheat me.

Sometime after midnight Tony called me and I stood up again. Pitch black in the woods, silent and still as a cave, except for the dripping water and the sighing of the wind in the trees. I push my chin as far as I can in my overcoat collar and my hands in the overcoat pocket. I am glad I found this overcoat, many do not have them. I wonder how I am going to stand up this time and wearily stick as long as possible to be fair to Tony. Someone grabs me by the arm, I come to with a jump, it is breaking day, my head is above the trench an excellent target for a sniper. I drop down in the road confused; surely if I had gone to sleep I would have dropped. But then the man wakened me standing up and if I had been down he would not have bothered me as there are many still asleep in the mud. I must have slept for hours standing up, for the last I remember it was pitch blackness and now I can see plainly. Scarcely a man had remained awake and one of them noticed me. Tony had also fallen asleep in a hole in the bank.

He and I look for "A" Company and locate them down the hill, about twenty men in all. I ask where the rest are and Sgt. Ross Fehlman said they were back in that field. Lieut. Randall Houghton, Arlo Warren, Hanes and Conyua were killed that I knew. Houghton and I had attended high school together. Stuart Houghton, Randall's brother, is there but has little to say. Many more are seriously wounded. "A" has few men left but just before the attack yesterday one platoon had been detailed as runners. Davie Lett has a small can of sardines that he divides among a dozen men and I receive a thumb nail amount for my share.

Orders are received to withdraw from the hill. We are perplexed by such orders and at first do not obey. It seems unreasonable to retreat when we are not chased back and we had a hard time taking this yesterday. Yet we obey and fall back wondering. At the foot of the slope the regiment assembles and lies down. Lieut. Colonel Bubb and Major Smathers, pipes in their mouths and canes in hands, walk up and down behind the line, whacking men with the canes for having their heels too high. Privates yell at them to get down themselves, both are popular, and if we have to be safe they should also. But it does not occur to them that they might be hit. They explain that the withdrawal was so the artillery could blow up the hilltop.

A German plane slides over the hill and dives like a landing bird gracefully over us not two hundred feet from the ground and circles. We do not look up, he will see our white faces. Major Smathers cautions repeatedly against that. We wait expecting to feel the sting of his bullets or hear his bombs but he must have been just a scouting plane for after a few circles he leaves.

Colonel Bubb moves the regiment back again until we are a good half mile from the hill. We will go back and occupy it after the artillery have blown it to bits but he wanted his men safe when they started; they have missed before. It's puzzling to know why they cannot shell ahead of us as that was where the Boche were.

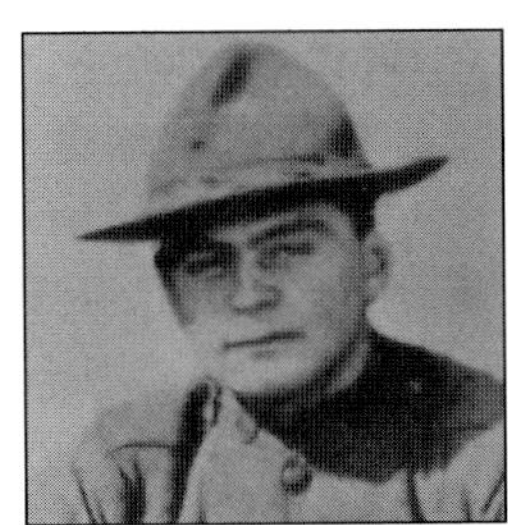

Pvt. Arlo Warren.

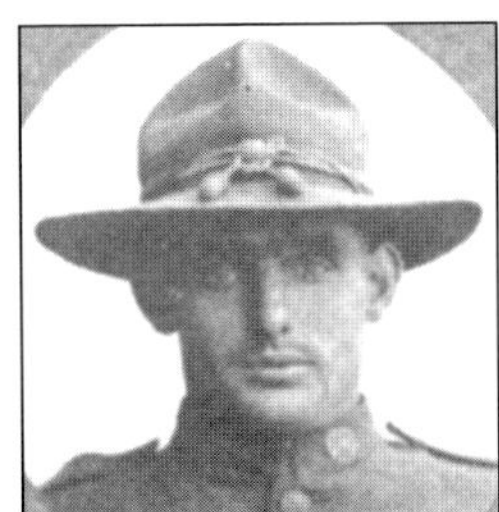

Pfc. Harry Hanes.

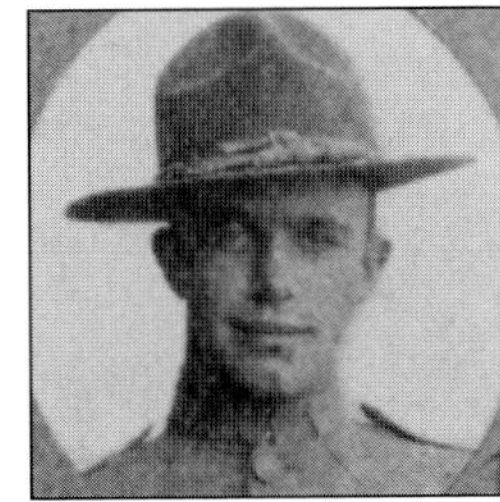
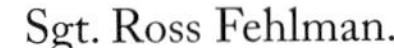

Sgt. Ross Fehlman.

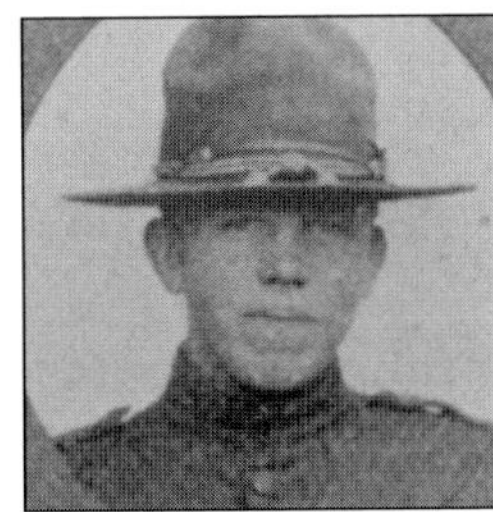

Pvt. David Lett.

Suddenly behind us a salvo from the field guns opens the chorus and shells rush over our heads and sure enough burst back of the positions we held last night. Other batteries join in the horrid chorus and Le Chene Tondu is in commotion with smoke, trees and dirt in the air from the explosions. The six-inch howitzers and naval guns join in. The air is filled again with those howling shrieks while ahead is a line of bursting shells that keeps a wall of smoke in front. Some shells, big ones too, barely miss our front as far back as we have been withdrawn and then we realize the wisdom of the Colonel in pulling us back. Le Chene Tondu is a hell now but as I see it most of the shelling is on the positions we held last night and very little on the Germans. The gunfire lasts for hours, we wait on the ground. expecting the order to attack.

Instead of us attacking, the 111th leap frogs us and when the shelling stops and the barrage is lifted they pass through our lines and attack the hill the same as we did yesterday. We watch them climb the cliff unharmed but they only push on a few feet farther than we did the night before for as I had noticed most of the barrage hit our old positions.

Rations are brought and dumped about four hundred yards away. I have not eaten for four days except a little willie and a bite of German bread from a dead German's pack today and still I will hardly walk that distance for I am beyond being hungry. The last real meal was supper of the 25th and this is the 29th. But I go and draw my share and eat a little bread. A sergeant and about fifteen men of the 109th come running through the grass from the direction of the front and stop, panting, to remain with us. They had attacked up the valley to the right of Le Chene Tondu and they said they were all that was left of their battalion but I think they will find more when they are all rounded up. Ahead our machine guns are keeping up a continual racket dispersing Germans in the valley in front.

After eating, the 112th Regiment climbs the hill and settles in the sunken road again. The 111th is ahead a couple hundred yards. Climbing the hill is much harder as the shells made regular cliffs in the steep hillsides. I rejoin Battalion Headquarters and remain with them in the road. The afternoon is fairly quiet, not much firing except for an occasional rifle shot or a short burst of machine gun fire.

At dusk all Scouts were ordered to occupy the old German horse stables, which was the building I had reconnoitered during the attack last night.

When I leave the sunken road I realize what a comfortable place it was. Bullets whizz as we run to the stable. I do not like the looks, the walls are sheet iron and perforated with jagged bullet holes. Another hole opens and we lie in the manure on the floor, agitated at being sent to this dangerous spot from the safe sunken road.

Outside a whistle and an explosion, then another and another close by. Startled we leap to our feet. It is the whistle of seventy-fives coming from our own lines. All crowd to the door and burst forth like water out of a sewer. It is our own shell fire again and just as we reach the outside a terrible curtain of fire drops on us. Everywhere in the woods men are retreating panic-stricken. "B" Company men are behind me and Lieut. Pond yells, "Don't run boys. Don't run," although he is running as fast as I am. I turn my head to him and run bang into a tree. The wind is nearly knocked out of me but I raise my gun to fire but I would only hit our men, another shell bursts close and I am off again with everyone else through the bushes. The German machine gunners alive to their opportunity blaze away at us. Back at our guns the artillerymen are firing on recoil and hitting us. Their barrage is terrible. I run in terror through the woods. Shells bursting around me filling the trees with smoke and whizzing pieces of steel. A man on my right grabs his throat and yells, "Oh, my God, this is awful," stumbles and goes down. Another man catapults through the air as though struck from behind and slides on the ground. I see a foxhole, dive like a diver does an air tumble and light on my stomach in the hole. I pray fervently to God, as others are doing, to help and save me, hugging the ground in terror. Outside the shells burst wickedly and all around and above me the air is filled with deadly pieces of steel. I am frantic with fear and helplessness in an inferno of hell.

I find a house that has part of a roof. Inside the door among the rocks and debris I find a water soaked shelter-half. I cannot find a place to lie down and start through a doorway. On the threshold though I stop and return to the first room. In the morning I see that if I had taken another stop I would have fallen fifteen feet as there was no floor in the next room. In the doorway at last I lie down and cover with the wet shelter-half. For over a week now I have not had a blanket and most of the time it has been raining.

September 30. The sleeping was not good. I doze, but the cold and the roughness of the floor will not let me sleep. Outside the rain falls and occasionally a shell bursts on the crossroads. At last I fall asleep to be awakened by men stumbling over me. They talk in German. I cannot conceive how they could have pushed back so far tonight. I decide to remain quiet and when they settle down I will leave. They mill around but one remains near me in the doorway. Finally he says "If you — — — Dutchmen don't lay down and go to sleep, I'll kill you all." I settle down to sleep again, they are prisoners.

At daybreak I am looking for food. A mile from the town I locate the Regimental cookers. On the way I pass batteries of seventy-fives along the road, the ones that hit us last night. They had driven hurriedly, wheeled into position and began firing with hardly enough time to get their right range. It was not altogether their fault, just another mistake. Some had cried broken-hearted when they realized what they had done. My brother is at "A" Company's kitchen as he was detailed with the baggage. It is over a week since we have seen each other and he had looked through the Field Hospitals for me. "A" Company serves a good breakfast, the first warm meal and practically the only real meal since the night of Sept. 25th but strange I am not hungry. The kitchens are in the same orchard that we passed and beyond which we had so much trouble. I fill my pack with "Bull Durham" for the boys. I have taken plenty of time, it is nearly noon, I have been in no hurry to return but at last I feel I must go. The "Bull Durham" makes me popular when I am back in the sunken road in Le Chene Tondu.

Captain Doane had been killed and buried back of the sunken road on the brow of the hill in a rapidly increasing graveyard. Goodling of "A" being one. In the afternoon the Germans use trench mortars on us. In their lines we hear a "Crump" and a few seconds later something drops through the branches. Some explode on contact and some lie on the ground and explode on a fuse. With the regular artillery there is a warning screech but none with the Trench Mortars.

Near the new graveyard I find a wet German blanket but

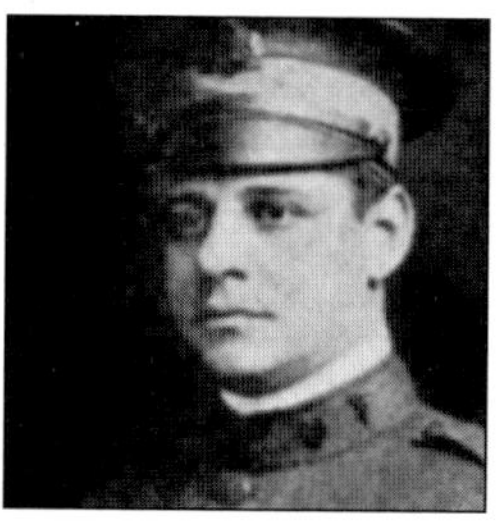

Capt. Hugh Doane.

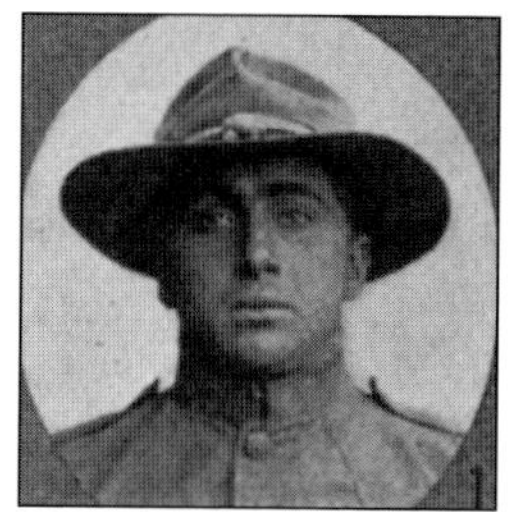

Pvt. Howard Goodling.

the sky is still overcast, by evening most of the water is out but still damp. I dig a hole in the bank of the sunken road and cover with the blanket. The night is cold, the wet blanket is little better than none. I sleep fitfully in dozes, my legs are cramped from wearing the uniform and leggings over a week, the ground cold and hard and the cooties bite. I wish, as I shiver, for a dry blanket and wonder why the officers sent us into this battle with only combat packs and no blankets in this fall weather.

October 1. Before daylight I waken from a doze and in the valley toward Apremont shells are falling. I pull my knees closer to my chin for a little more warmth. Sgt. O'Connor, Sgt. Denning and others run up the trench and said a shell hit a house they were sleeping in. I had looked at those houses but decided I would rather sleep in a hole in the ground as houses are such good targets. Outside a damp, cold fog that prohibits knowing what has happened in the valley. On top of the hill I can see Captain Graff, face white and set, with all available men lined up in the sunken road peering into the woods in front. It looks as if an attack is going to take place and I better stay in my hole till they are over or until some officer forces me out and into line. A man goes by and says the Germans tried a big counter attack on Apremont but thinks they were stopped as the machine guns from our brigade caught them from the flank. I wait a little longer, my curiosity is too much and I go up and join the line on top of the hill. We do not know what the outcome in the valley is, the fog is still too thick to see Apremont and no word has come through. Captain Graff expects them to come over Le Chene Tondu and he is very much worried. If they have run the 55th Brigade out of Apremont we are sticking out like a sore thumb on top of this hill. To our left is no troops at all except the later famous "Lost Battalion." Back of us to our left several miles intervene where the 77th Division has failed to keep up with us. As it is we take it from the left flank and the front and if they have Apremont we will take it from three sides and we can easily be surrounded on this hill. It may be the long expected counter-attack on the whole front that is to be expected. The 35th Division on the right of the 55th Brigade is crumbling and our outlook is bad right now. It all depends on how the 55th held at Apremont.

About nine a.m. the fog drifts away. I walk over the hill to look at Apremont through field glasses. The town is quiet but I cannot tell who holds it. I see five figures on a dog trot into Apremont: Germans and from their actions not much afraid of being shot at. Then the Germans won and we are in the soup. But a short distance behind them another figure appears, runs a short distance and turns as if someone had called him. He has the good old American gas mask on his chest and I recognize him as a Yank. Those Germans were prisoners, the 55th held and stopped the last big counterattack the Germans delivered. I send the news to Captain Graff.

It was hand to hand fighting in Apremont. I believe if our machine guns from the 56th had not caught them from the flank they would have made it. They attacked under cover of the fog, killed many and took several prisoners. Part of the ebb of the attack hit on the line of the 111th and men out of ammunition began throwing rocks.

The worst hit on the 112th and forced them back. Part of the 111th did attack ahead of the barrage and advanced some but had to retire without the support of the 112th. The part of the line I was on was completely disorganized and unable to get together that night.

I walk up the road a little distance and sense rather than see a man in the blackness. He is leading wounded men that can walk. When I speak to him he asks for assistance and I help him up the trench. With him is about thirty slightly wounded, the word slightly being far-fetched for if all these men were hurt back home they would be carried to a hospital and not have to walk three or four kilometers on their wounds. Joe Smith and Clay, both shot in the arm, are in the group. At the top of the hill I ask Captain Graff if I can show these men to the dressing station at Montblainville. I cannot see his face, his voice sounds reluctant to let me go as he probably thinks I am trying to get away from the front and he is about right. But I show him there are thirty that will be lost in the woods and at last he agrees to it. [*One of the wounded men is "Red" Mohnkern of "A" Company. He has a leg wound. His leg is not off but he has a big hole above the knee and can walk a little.*]

Three kilos to Montblainville, pitch dark and raining, no lights, woods and underbrush, thirty wounded men and I don't even know where Montblainville is but I am a Scout and I don't care how long it takes me to find it. Men with aching, smarting, sickening wounds, legs too stiff to walk, aching dizzy heads, weak from loss of blood, shell shocked and exhausted follow me by sound down over the steep cliffs behind the hill. I slide in the darkness over drops ten feet or more made by the shells, then warn the wounded back of me and assist those that lean as they tumble down. At last all are down at the foot. My sense of direction warns me to turn to the left and after wandering an hour through underbrush we are on a road. Red's wound is bothering him and he leans on me for support; the rest, mostly arm, shoulder or head wounds, are able to walk themselves.

The road is slippery and muddy and mud and water-filled shell holes trap the unsuspecting men. Two men from "G" Company carrying a badly wounded man on a stretcher inform us that it is a kilo to Montblainville. They were mad for they had been carrying a man on a stretcher nearly dead, a few shells burst and he ran out on them. Red's leg is worse but he still insists he can walk slow and the others go on as they will have no difficulty in finding the place now. But he cannot stand as much as he thought so he places an arm around my neck for support. We do not notice a mud-filled shell hole till he slips into it directly on his wounded leg. From then on I practically carry him.

At last at the Montblainville dressing station but men with only big holes in their legs are not allowed in. Inside is reserved for the dangerously wounded. Outside on the ground, men with just ordinary wounds like Red's are lying in the cold rain. The ambulances have just left on their trips to the Field Hospitals and it will be hours till they return. Red drops on the ground without blanket or anything to cover him. There are no complaints, many of these men outside are glad to be wounded no worse than they are. I tell them they should be happy as they know what they have gotten while I still am in doubt. Every few minutes Jerry drops a harassing shell on the cross roads and though it does not endanger the wounded, just a little change will drop them directly on the dressing station.

In the afternoon Sgt. O'Connor detailed me to the kitchens to bring rations up. They have been having so much trouble getting food to the line that Scouts are detailed to see they get up. Could anything be sweeter? It does not take long to leave that sunken road behind. Near the road to Montblainville shells fall to my right and men are yelling. "A" Company was serving dinner and I received a mess pan full of rice. I sit down for a good meal in peace but just then five seventy-seven shells arrive and burst in the orchard. Cooks and kitchen mechanics dropped everything and run for their lives. Not me, no shell will cheat me of that rice. Balancing the mess pans carefully I walk sedately to the ditch in the road and calmly sit down and eat even if they do shell the orchard.

After the shelling ceased, my brother and I lay around the kitchen. He suggests we better have a dugout if they are going to shell. Across the road is an old German gun emplacement that we could dig in. He starts for it but I have found a newspaper to read. When I finish I also go to help him dig. Reaching the road I hear a German 105 coming. I flatten in the road to watch it burst. The shell passes over, down close, and to my horror bursts directly in the center of the gun emplacement. My brother is there and surely he could not escape as it was a direct hit. I dread to go to that hole and see the work that shell made of my brother, yet I must, he may not be dead yet. I rise slowly and weakly, looking over my shoulder to get someone to go with me and there coming to me from the orchard he was, alive and as well as a man can be on the front. Someone had called him as he started for that hole and had not gone to the gun emplacement as I thought. I thank the Almighty for having that man call him and for having me read that newspaper story.

Instead of the emplacement we decide to dig a hole at the entrance to a concrete dugout the Germans left in the orchard. Sgt. Merton and Bartlett arrive with terrible news. The shells that I heard as I left Le Chene Tondu hit a "D" Company mess line and one shell killed eleven men and wounded over twenty. All the officers were taken and most of the non-commissioned officers including the first sergeant. Lieut. Ogram was badly wounded, but though he would probably die, had insisted they take care of the other men first. Several are dead that I know well. (*Lieut. Hoyt R. Ogram survived. In fact, he lived to age 100, dying in Chicago in 1988.*)

The Germans shell the orchard all night intermittently and sleep is impossible. Bartlett and Merton cannot sleep for the day's horror is still on them and they talk continually of the dead and wounded in "D". Others from the same company are there and they add to the terrible story. Seeing your friends dismembered and mangled is enough to keep anyone awake but I wish they would not talk about it so much. A shell bursts above our dugout and a man sleeping in a wagon is hit in the stomach. He should have known better than to sleep so high off the ground. His partner calls loudly for help; I should go but I am to afraid to go. I am ashamed for being so cowardly, the man groans and moans pitifully, his partner yells loudly for first aid till his cries almost drive one insane. At last his cries stop a minute. "No use he is dead." A salvo bursts in the orchard some distance from me. I am sure I hear a scream, then whimpering. Another one. I must go this time. But my hole is safe. My feet will not take me. Suppose another one is dying, needing just a little company and someone to pray for him. I crouch in my hole instead.

My nerves are too bad for sleep. We move back and forth into the concrete dugout. Inside the "D" Company men still talk as they have for hours and I cannot sleep listening to them. They cannot sleep either, shell shock prevents that. Outside the dugout I cannot hear them but it is more dangerous. If I could only run away from it all. The night is dark and fearful, there is no safety anywhere, nothing in life is safe but I do not want to die. But life like this is no pleasure dreading every day a horrible death or a mangling that will leave me a broken thing to live on in misery for years. I pray, as I often have on the front, to God for help and that this cruel war might end but there seems little use.

October 2. From midnight on we are kept awake by the shelling, sometimes a single shot and then a salvo. It is harassing fire, the kind that keeps one awake and anxious, much worse than the barrage that lasts a short time and then is finished. When they fire we go into the dugout where the men from "D" are still talking of yesterday's horror. I wish they would stop.

Daybreak at last and we look for a better place to stay. Back a mile we find a German dugout in the woods about thirty feet deep, much safer and we will stay here tonight. The orchard is shelled trying to hit the kitchens and the field artillery along the Montblainville road. The Boche have increased their artillery. The first few days we had little cannon to contend with but now the front and back areas are shelled continuously, as bad as the Fismes front. A man from the Supply Company had both legs blown off in the orchard and dies soon after. His comrades bury him near the road and erect a fine cross over his grave.

Late afternoon Hugh and I go to the dugout we had explored. There are a few bunks but they are taken. We crawl under a bunk and make a bed on the floor. One candle sheds a weird light. I am against the wall, the light is extinguished and we have the blackest darkness possible. The bunk above me is a few inches from my face; if I lay on my side my shoulders touch. Coffins, buried alive, I feel like screaming. My legs are cramped from wearing the uniform and leggings for over a week now and I stretch again and again to get circulation going, my shoulders touch the roof of my "coffin". I want to escape from this confinement and blackness but my brother is here and I am physically about done so at last I drop off to sleep.

October 3. I cannot remain in such a coffin-like place. It is broad daylight and I have slept the night through, the first all-night's sleep since Sept. 24. I also have a very bad cold from being in that damp dugout.

Outside the dugout a handsome German lay, without sign of injury, so concussion must have killed him. He lies there peacefully as though asleep. I wonder why he should be killed and why I should be, why his friends and my friends should be killed. This war will go on for years yet, the days are endless and without hope. I have been on the front since July 4th, three months, and most of the men are casualties already. How long will I go? Sometimes I am brave and reckless and at other times I am an abject coward, and strange I am not ashamed of my fear. At times in the crash of the battle I feel that my mother's prayers and faith will keep me and that Christ is there at my elbow watching and protecting me. There was the gun emplacement recently and the Forest de Fere by the beech tree to prove my faith is His protection and other cases. At other times I feel hopeless, realize my littleness as if God had abandoned me as in the night at Death Valley.

If I could only be wounded, just a good disabling wound, an honest one not a goldbrick wound. It would be heaven to lie in a bed with sheets, women nurses to look at, hear feminine voices and eat clean food. What if the wound did hurt a little? I understand why the slightly wounded run gayly off yelling happily "I've got my blighty" and us uninjured looking jealously at them. How many times since I came to the front would I have changed places with the sitting and walking wounded. I have read in magazines how the wounded showed such cheerfullness despite their wounds and I know the reason now.

It may be that dead German boy is the best after all. No more terror for him on this earth, the bullets and shells pass over and disturb him none. The worst that could be done to him on earth has been done already. Sometimes I wish it had been me and I would know now the "Great Mystery". Away back in the dim ages, before the age of shells, bullets, bayonets and gas, I can remember faintly an age of comparative safety that I am afraid I will never see again. The cold has me weak in the legs and chills in the back. My brother also is sick. But when I report to the kitchen, which has been moved from the orchard deeper into the woods, I am assigned to go with the ration card to the front. The 112th has been moved between Le Chene Tondu and Apremont in support. The 111th is still on top of the hill and neither have moved ahead. The mule and cart cannot be taken close to the front as a mule is too precious. We locate an old German narrow gauge railroad and cars and push the rations toward "A" Company. The company is near Apremont but when we find them they are ready to come back and we push the heavy cart another half mile back. A shell just lit in the Machine Gun Company and killed three men. Big 210 shells explode along the road near Apremont. "A" Company takes plenty of time getting back. Finally they do come and we feed them. I help dish out but only a few men are allowed up at a time, "D" Company's experience being too recent for that. I hate to have these men think I am in a hurry but the truth is I am. The company has dwindled until there is only a few squads left. At last they are fed, we load the pots and pans on the car. Burt Oudett is the brakeman. On the small hills we ride. We have trouble getting the car over a place where a shell burst and destroyed the alignment of the rails but at last back at the kitchen.

We sleep at night behind a bank in the woods, not as safe as the dugout last night but more freedom and not as oppressive. The grippe bothers, luckily we have found enough blankets and a shelter-half. (*What Pierce is calling the "grippe" was very likely influenza, which was ravaging the world at that time, claiming the lives of millions, including thousands of American doughboys.*)

October 4. Sick all day and about able to move. When I stand I am so dizzy I nearly fall, yet I make another trip with the ration cart. It is not as bad this time, back before evening without trouble and the only danger was when a 105 shell landed in a field beside the road. The road is so bad a truck or car can hardly move but our mule cart is O.K. but rough. I prefer to walk for if a shell comes I can hit the ground quicker. No horses or mules for me, they are too high. A shell has hit a horse-drawn battery on the road and several dead horses pollute the air.

At night my brother and I are both sick. We remain in our foxhole covered with blankets. The shelter half above us keeps out most of the rain. Still I shiver and at times I am too hot.

October 5. So sick with the grippe I cannot stand on my feet. I just make it over to the kitchen for coffee to warm me up. Luckily I do not have to go anywhere, dizzy as I am. No one pays any attention to me; if we are sick we make the most of it. If I was back home I would be in bed with doctors, medicine, loving care bestowed on me, but here I cannot even get C.C. pills.

October 6. My grippe is much better and outside of a little weakness I am alright, still a little shaky but not as dizzy as yesterday. I feel that I belong on the front, it is not right that I be here and my pals there and they may think I am yellow. Common sense reasons that I should hang onto a good thing.

After dark I leave with the cart. We find the outfit on a bank in Apremont. Sgt. O'Connor welcomes me and says stay with Battalion Headquarters as they need men. Major Smathers says stay also as they are attacking in the morning. What a fool to come up and volunteer just before an attack, I could kick myself. But I tell everyone I do not like the kitchens and would be glad for a little action. Then I feel ashamed for lying like that. We have a new Regimental Commander, Lieut. Colonel Shannon, not the Colonel of the 111th, but another West Pointer. Colonel Bubb is relieved for timidity but I could never see where they could find anything timid about that man. He was one of the bravest I ever saw. Colonel Rickards is injured, but then he was Brigade Commander most of the time. Major Smathers is acting Lieut. Colonel. Colonel Shannon had patrolled with a group of officers and the result is an attack on a town in front of us. Bartlett and I lie on the high hank near the top. I have hardtack and a can of apricot jam and we eat. Jerry drops large shells in the valley. They light in the swampy ground and explode deep with a muffled roar and splatter mud and sods all over the terrain. Major Smathers orders "stand by" and we will move soon and attack. The front is quiet. A cold fog rolls down and blots everything out.

October 7. About one a.m. we line up in the roads near Apremont, Colonel Shannon in command. He appears like a real man, not stuck up and seems to know his stuff. The line moves and the jerky movements begin, moving a few yards then halting and waiting. We go down a railroad track in the valley and follow it for a mile or so. We are in enemy country I believe but are not disturbed. By this time the fog is very thick and renders excellent concealment. There is no

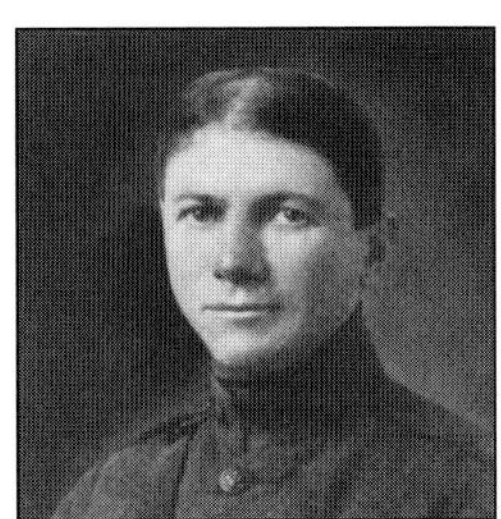

Lt. Col. James Shannon.

noise, moving very quietly in the foggy blackness. We rest on the tracks and then move into the wet fields. A shadowy band of men move in the fog, like ghosts ahead, and Captain Graff sends me to find out who they are. It is our own 3rd Battalion moving into the fields to deploy. About four a.m. deployed as skirmishers and in combat groups, we move forward, quietly and cautiously, across an open field. The grass is long and wet. The line halts frequently and lies down on the ground. The figures of the men float ghostly in the fog. At last we halt and wait for something we know not what. Somewhere in that ghostly blackness, not far, is the enemy but he has not discovered us.

Behind us about five a.m. the flashes of batteries of field artillery light the foggy sky, the reports of the guns, screaming shells pass over and burst in the fog and blackness in front. Our barrage is a perfect line, no short ones, except one that comes burning, end over end, lights but does not burst. The batteries play on this line a few minutes, then raise the range and we walk slowly forward and halt again while they shell about one hundred and fifty yards in front of us. Stray pieces sing back. On the German horizon, we see the flash as their guns waken, seventy-sevens scream at us but burst over and beyond us. They have underestimated, probably they do not think we will follow that close to the barrage. We are boxed in now by our own shells in front and the German shells in the rear. Our barrage lifts and we move forward, the fog and blackness still prohibiting seeing anything beyond the bursting shells.

We move again and almost suddenly it seems, a town we are to take appears three hundred yards ahead. An American officer, it's Colonel Shannon I believe, is standing a hundred yards ahead directing our battalions as if on a parade. Some men almost shoot at him for a German.

The barrage has lifted again and is playing on the hills behind the town. We break into a trot for a hundred yards, then about two hundred from the town we begin to charge, a regular old time infantry charge. The enemy machine guns and infantry, now awake to their danger, see us. Bullets whip by, hit the ground and stir up the dirt. The entire regiment is on the run forward, down a sunken road, climb the bank, running fast. Bartlett is in front of me, he is big and a good bullet shield. Bowers follows me and Gayvert behind him. A wide patch of barbed wire is ahead but we make a running broad jump and clear it as bullets spatter into the wire. For the first time I see ahead and behind the town a large cliff where the German guns are flashing. We run through an orchard as a shower of bullets hit the ground beside me and hand grenades from the cliff burst in front. A man to my front curls up and rolls over on his side, half sitting, with a pained look on his face. We pass him on the run, cross the main street and into the homes under the cliff. A quick search for Germans but they are on the cliff. The regiment is in a bad position, the Germans can drop hand grenades from the cliff and can look directly down at us from the bushes that fringe the cliff. The word is passed along the line to hold what we have and not try and go on. The 2nd Battalion is flanking them to the left of the cliff. Shortly after, their rifles begin to bang as they advance through the woods. Each minute the sounds of battle are a little farther and we know they are progressing. We peer through the holes in our roof for a sight of Germans on the cliff top but that is too dangerous as they may drop us a grenade to divide among ourselves.

Gayvert, Bowers and I remain in a room of the house we first entered. I have another can of apricot jam and a box of hardtack so we eat. Outside bullets snap and crackle. A few men are on the side of the house away from the cliff. They talk of one sniper on the cliff who seems to be a good shot as he has hit several already. Machine guns on the cliff spray the town continuously. The man that was shot ahead of me, Sgt. Van Dyke of "D" Company, is carried in and laid on a bunk in the other room. He is dangerously wounded in the abdomen. Men try and make him lie still as it is his only chance of living but he moves constantly. They beg and plead with him but the pain is too severe. Another man, shot through the shoulder, paces the floor, face set and white trying not to make a noise. A couple of men claimed they were hit with bullets that dropped off after stinging them severely.

The banging of the rifles of the 2nd Battalion is much further ahead and they will soon flank the cliff. But until then we must keep low. A man walks slowly out into the open on the other side of the street and stops, a beautiful target for the sniper. The men under cover on our side of the street frantically urge him to hurry across but he looks at them sarcastically and answers "Aw, go to hell". The sniper has been aiming, "plop", and the man howls with pain as a red hot steel jacket cuts through the calf of his leg. He dances on one leg across the street holding the burning leg, and into our house where he rolls on the floor. Everyone laughs, not a giggle, but a real hearty laugh, a little relieved too that he is only wounded and not killed as we expected. Laughing relieves the tension, even Sgt. Van Dyke and the other wounded men join, all but the wounded man, Lee Einsick of "A," and he can see no reason for mirth and emphatically says so. If I thought the sniper would hit me in the same place I would almost take a chance. I have no doubt he laughed from his post on the cliff top.

The 2nd Battalion has flanked the cliff and when their cross fire catches them the Germans hastily abandon the top in our front. One man observing dead Germans a few yards in front, crawls out to get their watches. But in searching the dead man, he suddenly jumped up and yelled "Kamerad", scaring the American so bad he ran. To our right, on the cliff the Boche still hold with machine guns and rifles so the town is still not safe. I receive word to report to Battalion Headquarters in a house near the center of town. Gayvert and I run as fast as we can still not confident the Dutch are off the cliff top. I stop back of a stone house as a hail of machine gun bullets rattle on the streets. Captain Smith, crossing the street, changes step as a bullet zips through his leg.

A shell is coming close and I run into a wine cellar. I wish I had stayed out. The room is filled with badly wounded men. Colonel Shannon is there, shot through the neck, mortally wounded, gasping for the breath that will soon leave his body. Sgt. Van Dyke lies there also very bad.

Another man is on his back, unconscious, with a big piece out of his head and his brain showing. I

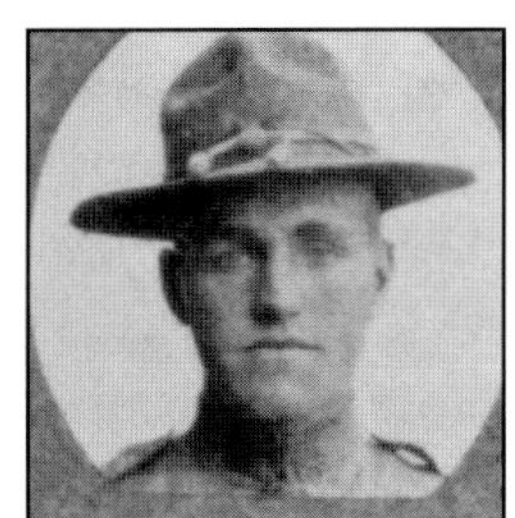

Sgt. Charles Van Dyke.

watch him fascinated, as his hands rise slowly toward the terrible hole in his head, then a first aid man grabs his arm and pulls it down. But the unconscious man repeats the movement. Groans, moans and gasps and I decide to leave this place. A weak voice calls me and there in the semi-darkness among the dying is Ray Wingard on his back on the floor. His face is white and I fear it is all up with him. "I guess they got me this time," he says in a whisper. He was shot in the abdomen at the same time Colonel Shannon was shot. I tell him to please lie still as that is the only chance he has of living. He promises and I can see he does not move a muscle and scarcely breathes. In a low whisper he tells me what to do for him at home if he does not pull through. I tell him to pray and trust in God and he says he has been.

Sgt. Denning and Angood are there. They try to help Colonel Shannon move his arms to get his breath but it is no use. I cannot stand the sights and I run into the open. It is not much better. Beside another building a group of German prisoners drag in an old German on a shelter-half, a machine gunner also shot through the neck. He lies there, calm and serene, apparently not afraid and dies smiling at the enemies that have killed him. An American first aid man tries to save him, even American wounded send the medical men over to do something for the old fellow, but it is too late. Two big, bearded Germans come down off the cliff carrying a wounded American boy. He has a bad wound in his head, conscious at times when he tries to walk, then his legs buckle and he falls over and the Germans support him till he comes to again. They leave him in the wine cellar and the Germans join the group of prisoners. It is so funny, shoot the old man then try and save his life, then the Germans shoot this American boy then carry him to safety.

The sights and sounds are unnerving. Captain Graff and Lieut. Murray with Bartlett in tow called me to join them. The Captain is looking for a suitable place for Regimental Headquarters as he is in command of the regiment since the colonel was shot. We four dash across the street before the machine gunner on the cliff can shoot and into a large house. A hall runs clear through the building. Reaching the rear door a shell bursts in front of me. I turn and run back to the other end and a shell bursts at that end. Bartlett laughs at me for being so jumpy. The house does not suit the captain so we dash across the street again. The machine gun fire from above slackens as the men to our right and left forge ahead but the shell fire is getting worse. German shells are blowing up the buildings. When we first came in this morning they hit in the fields behind us. I learn that this is Chatel-Chehery but outside of getting out alive I have no interest in it. Captain Graff finally located Regimental Headquarters and we stayed with him. Bartlett, Jack O'Day and I do not like the outlook with the shells blowing up buildings all around the town. It is nearly noon and all the Boche are supposed to be off the cliff. So we run up and climb to a ledge near the top. We have good grandstand seats. The day is clear and we watch the shells burst in the town and valley. They come over in salvos of threes and the runners are having a hard time getting through. Bursts of machine gun fire rattle harmlessly over our heads. We had cause for worry when the Germans dropped shrapnel over the edge of the cliffs but none were hit on the ledge. Later they dropped trench mortars to our right. Thoman from "A" was killed and Hull had his eye knocked out. Clayton Skiff of "A" was killed under the cliff in the morning when he and Tony Albina tried to bomb a machine gun. Tony went for more bombs but he was not permitted to return and the last seen of Skiff alive he was yelling "more bombs".

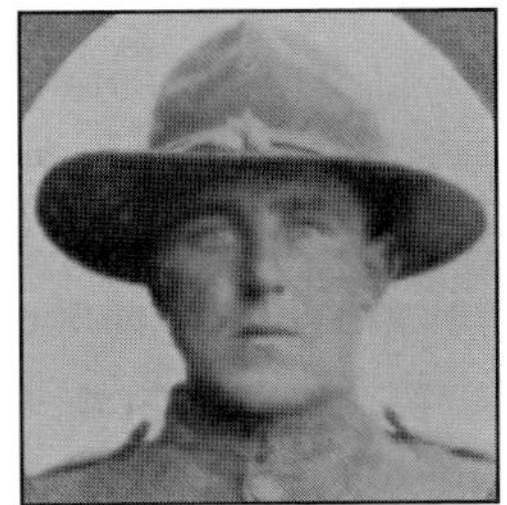

Pfc. Clayton Skiff.

About two p.m. a battalion of the 82nd Division, who are to our right, deploys in a field behind us and to the right of Chatel-Chehery. I pity these men for ahead of them is a two mile stretch of open country under observation. Officers new to the front making another mistake. I say a prayer for them and then watch through field glasses, fascinated to see the slaughter. I dread the sight, yet as a charmed bird watches a snake, I glue my eyes to the glasses for about two miles away some American lads have only a few minutes of life. The battalion starts in perfect alignment and reaches the middle of the first field. Over in the German horizon there is a "crunmph", the telltale whistles as a salvo speeds to them. Most of them take it standing up, another sign of green troops. The next salvo of seventy-sevens comes and before the shells burst the entire line disappears in the tall grass. They rise a little disorganized and press on. Another salvo and again they disappear, rise slowly after the bursts and again move forward. The shells come oftener, the battalion loses contact and bunches confused, but still moves on. Soon they are all running forward all formation gone as the shells search the ground and find many victims. About half make the stretch even with us. One group of men is nearly abreast of the town when a shell bursts beside them. A man grabs his head, spins around and falls. "There's a dead man," but he lies on the ground only a minute, jumps up and runs with the others, his helmet probably saving him. They could have filtered that battalion across and saved many lives. Back in the field men are moving slowly back, limping, carrying others while many more must be sprawled out dead.

Our ledge is safe from German fire just over the brim of the cliff. At three p.m. Bartlett and I are the only two remaining, the shelling having subsided and they went into the town. Suddenly a shriek as a shell from our own lines whizzes at us and bursts directly under us. Bartlett grabs his arm and yells "I'm hit" and falls onto the ledge. I hurry to him as fast as I can scramble. He is faint and weak and almost ready to roll off the ledge. I grab him with my right arm around him and stop him just in time and grab a root with my left hand. Thirty feet down is where he will hit and then roll a distance.

His body becomes a dead weight and half rolls over the rim. Two more of the same shells are coming. I may save myself if I let my friend fall. The shells burst again at the foot of the cliff sending the worst of their pieces straight up at us. My right arm is tiring fast and my left is giving from the root. Bartlett is out and I wonder if he is dead. Two more shells are coming. I pray for mercy for Bartlett and I. Evidently the prayer is answered for though the bursts are directly under again, the pieces whizz by into the cliff past our bodies sticking out over that ledge. My fingers are stretching and Bartlett will fall when my last ounce of strength gives out. He weighs about one hundred and eighty and I am one forty-five. But just as my fingers are loosening on the root, he recovers a little, just enough to pull himself back onto the ledge. I am exhausted from holding him. He is soon out of his faint and we examine his arm. He decides to run for the dressing station without being bandaged. He will not wait till I pick up my pack, jumps over the ledge, lands on his feet and slides down the incline. Even though I am unhurt, I cannot keep up with him and by the time I am at the foot of the cliff he is out of sight. I needed comfort of some kind and I found it in the New Testament.

The Scouts are in a house under the cliff. Lieut. Rhodes was now acting Battalion Commander. I was the Senior Corporal so I was Acting Battalion Scout Officer, as Sgt. Leinbach was Acting Regimental Scout Officer. Captain Graff is Acting Colonel. All three battalions are commanded by 2nd Lieutenants. Our battalion has about one hundred and fifty men present for duty. The regiment has less than five hundred men and a full strength regiment is nearly four thousand, three thousand of which are front line troops. The other regiments are about the same. The 109th and 110th are with us, the 111th still at Le Chene Tondu. A 2nd Lieutenant of the 110th walked by and our Acting Major recognized him. "What are you?" he asked. "I'm a Major," he answered proudly. "Well you don't have anything on me, I'm a Major too," and both laughed.

By now we can walk the streets as the Germans have been driven from the cliff and our men are up there. Gayvert and I move into a wine cellar, much safer, and with dry shavings on the floor. We lie down at dusk, fall asleep immediately and I dream I am home and in school again but still have my pack. The school teacher scolds me for throwing my pack on the floor.

October 8. A runner wakens me at five a.m. and I report to Regimental Headquarters. Major Smathers, now in command, hands me a message to deliver to Captain McLouth of the Supply Company to bring up rations. I hurried away, glad to leave for only a day. Two kilos from the town, I stopped and ate a box of hardtack on the railroad tracks. Finished, I hurried on and discovered my message gone. Frantic, I hurried back to where I ate and there beside the track was the message. I might have had a hard time explaining that one.

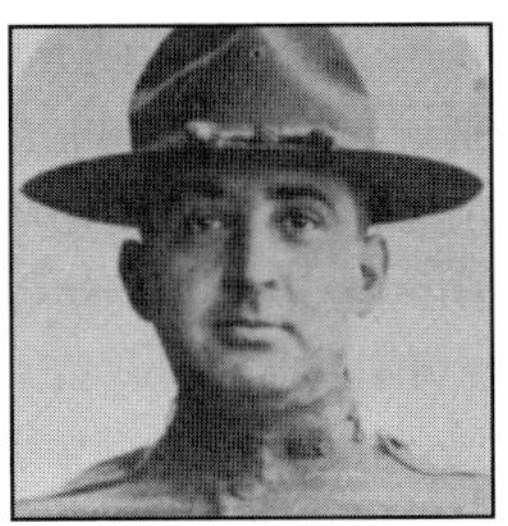
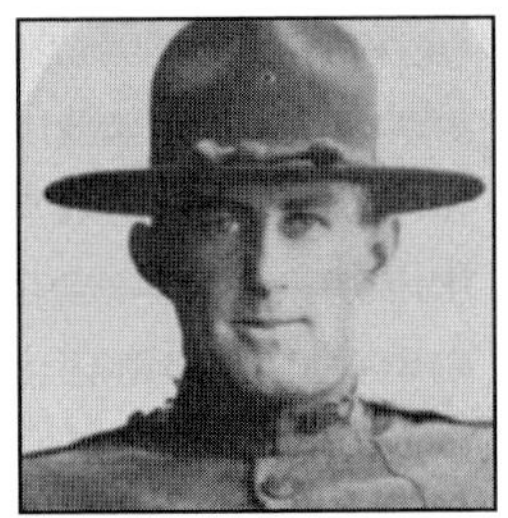

Capt. Ralph McLouth.   Lieut. Ignatius Meenan.

I pass through Apremont and Montblainville, locate Captain McLouth and Lieut. Meenan and gave them the message. Free then, I hurried to "A" Company kitchen for a meal. My brother is much better. Then I visit a Y.M.C.A. canteen in Montblainville, standing in a long line for hours to fill an order an officer gave me before I left Chatel Chehery. A Y.M.C.A.

man argues with his superior behind the counter. He wants to take a load of stuff to the men on the firing line. The senior "Y" man will not allow it as the men will form a line and the general will not have it. The argument helps pass the time and gives an insight into their difficulties. At last my pack is full of candy, cigarets and jam. Smith, Fry and Fish of "A" Company are going back with me.

We do not hurry, no one does in going back to the front. Beyond Apremont near the railroad tracks a Boche plane flies low, drops a few small bombs nearby but we are down before they explode. After he leaves we cross the field in safety and enter the orchard we charged through yesterday.

"Whizz bang" a shell bursts before we could get down. Another one closer but we were down. Another bursts. Smith, a few yards away, crawls close, and says, "I want to get close to you, I feel safer." One more bursts, we lie there a long time and then enter the town again.

My battalion was lost. At two p.m., under Lieut. Franks they had attacked and from that time regimental has no knowledge of them. The entire regiment had orders to attack but the orders were cancelled a few minutes before the zero hour. They did not reach the 1st Battalion in time and they had advanced not behind, but ahead of their barrage. Shells from our guns owing to an error hit behind them and they had to attack in front of their own shells. Since then they have not been seen or heard of. Regimental is looking for scouts to find them if they have not all been killed or captured. I keep shady till the scouts are picked, thankful I was given this morning's message and missed that attack. Smith and Jensen are picked. This patrol wandered around for hours that night until they finally found the lost men, not really lost but holding their objective and the Germans retreating in front, wagon trains and all. But they did not have enough men to take the trains.

I am in the same wine cellar tonight. Shelling begins again and one hits our house, knocking down rocks and rafters above us but does not come through to the cellar. The town is strafed till about dusk.

At dusk I am sent a mile on the road to Apremont to meet the ration detail and bring them into town. I sit in the ditch and wait. A few shells burst in the town and field and then quiet. The village is quiet and peaceful, cowbells should be tinkling. The rations are a long time coming. But a more welcome sight, the relief from the 82nd Division. Fighting for two weeks now in the Argonne we had despaired of relief. Other divisions on our right had been taken out after four days' fighting but they kept us in fourteen. There is nothing finer to a front line soldier than the relief coming up. They pass in single file, halting frequently. When they halt I advise them to get down in the ditch. They had enough men in that regiment to relieve our entire division. They have not been hit as hard as we. Fresh and confident they are, but they will soon learn.

On the heels of the relieving regiment the ration carts appear, Burt Oudett with them, and we take them to town. The companies are lost so the rations are put in houses. I eat with four men of "B" Company, guarding the stuff for the men if they ever come back.

The wine cellar is filled with men as it is recognized as the safest place. Sgt. Denning says he had a good bed next door but he had a feeling he better not stay. He tried to persuade Edgar and Whiteman to come with him but they laughed at his fears. Sleep is far away. My legs are numb and cramped from having the clothes on so long. I stretch to get the circulation back. Dull muffled explosions outside again, we cower in fear, one strikes our house above us, rocks fall and dust sieves through the ceiling. Another louder explosion nearby. A few minutes later Whiteman runs in begging for help in digging out two men buried by the explosion. No one volunteers at first. It may be the men from "B" Company that gave me supper so at last I borrow a cigaret lighter and go. It is the house next to us. A man is there already, one of the three sleeping there. Just before the shell struck he had wakened and stepped outside. Whiteman's relief at seeing him was great as he believed he was still inside. The shell had torn a big hole in the wall. The cigaret lighter blazed, I entered the hole and saw Edgar lying on top of a pile of rubbish, dead without a scratch, killed by concussion. Whiteman had also been inside. "One shall be taken the other left." A rock larger than a man lay on the bunk that Denning had been occupying so it was his hunch or an Act of God that brought him to our wine cellar. We leave Edgar there, he can be buried in the morning. But I cannot sleep for fear I had not made enough of an examination and Edgar may be only unconscious. At last I borrow the lighter again and examine him thoroughly but he is surely dead. I had known him well but we were not buddies. Back at the wine cellar I sleep without trouble. I dream again that I am home, riding on a truck leaning on my rifle and a boyhood girl friend waves at me.

October 9. Jensen is back before daybreak and has found the battalion. Now he is to take the relief of the 82nd Division up. As soon as we are relieved Denning, Hoke, Bowers, Smith and I start for the rear. Denning's feet are sore and holds us up a little till we run off from him begging us to wait for him. But it is our aim to put as much distance in as little time as possible between us and Chatel Chehery. A mile back we take it easier, then on through Apremont and Montblainville. The kitchens are safe from shell fire since we drove Jerry out of Apremont and Chatel Chehery.

Chapter 8

Thiaucourt

Editor's note

An exhausted and depleted 28th Division left the front line on October 9, but the Meuse-Argonne offensive continued. General Pershing was determined to meet the campaign's objectives. He ordered fresh divisions into the fight. Field commanders adjusted their tactics. Pershing relieved some commanders he judged ineffective. Both American and German casualties continued to mount, but while Americans could "afford" the casualties, the Germans could not. As pressure from the

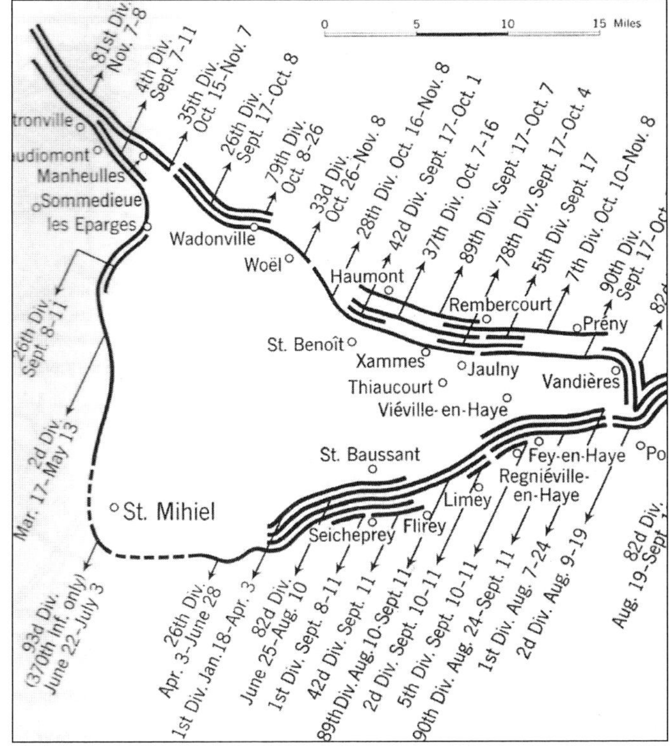

The Thiaucourt sector was the area occupied by the Allies after the St. Mihiel campaign eliminated the St. Mihiel Salient. The 28th Division took positions in the vicinity of St. Benoit beginning on October 16. (*American Battlefield Monuments Commission*)

Americans, the French and the British continued, Germany finally hit the breaking point and sued for an armistice.

The 28th Division, by now known to Germans as the Bloody Bucket Division for the red keystone patch its men wore, had moved to a quieter sector. For the men, this was a time to get some rest and to recover. Pierce needed to recover from digestive issues that hit him hard and left him weak. As he noted, A Company is down to 70 from its original 250.

The Allies looked to continue the pressure. The 28th Division was now part of the newly created Second Army in the former St. Mihiel Salient, now known as the Thiaucourt sector. The Americans undertook active patrolling, a task that often went to the scouts and which still had its perils. On every patrol, the soldiers stayed highly alert for the moment when German machine guns or artillery might open fire. Full-scale attacks could be ordered any day as far as the doughboys knew. And, in fact, the American command was in the process of beginning a new offensive in the Thiaucourt sector right up until the last moments before the Armistice took effect at 11 a.m. on November 11.

With the Armistice, the soldiers on each side undertook something new – walking over to the other side to take the measure of the men they had been fighting … and to get some souvenirs. Pierce was among them, regardless of orders against fraternizing with the enemy. What is notable is Pierce's observation of the difference between German officers and American officers. The Germans were aloof; the Americans more willing to fraternize with enlisted men.

Chapter 9

Relieved from the Argonne

Our Division has been fighting for fourteen days and glad to get away. The kitchens feed a welcome meal. Stragglers come in all day. Friends are re-united and as each man comes he is welcomed by men who did not know what had become of him. But many cannot be welcomed. They are in shallow graves in the Argonne with a rifle or a small cross stuck at their heads for a marker or lying in the hospital wounded. I sleep at night with my brother in a hole by a narrow gauge railroad, safe and warm, and thankful to that Supreme Being that has saved our lives.

October 10. Our Battalion prepares to go to the rear. All the stragglers are in. A sergeant of "C" Company commands "Call Off." They count over a hundred men. The sergeant becomes sarcastic. "One hundred men. Up there we could only count about thirty, where were all the rest of you fellows?" "A" numbers about seventy of one hundred and fifty. The Battalion marches away with about two hundred fifty of six hundred men that started the drive on Sept. 26th.

We had advanced more than ten miles of hard fighting and broken through on a hard sector. The outfit that relieved us should have it easier. But that has been the lot of the 28th Division, to hit the hard lines and then when the Germans are retreating, another outfit takes them and the glory. We hope we are going to a rest camp this time. But for the last few days it seemed as if the only rest camp was a few feet of dirt and a rifle and bayonet above us for a marker.

A.Y.M.C.A. outfit gives a little food on the march. We pass through Varrennes. Up front an excited yell, "Look, look, a woman." The cry is passed down the lines and everyone stares. I see only a flash of skirts as a nurse runs across the muddy streets. Yet she is a topic on the hike, a curiosity like a strange animal, the lucky ones who saw her describe her to the less fortunate. All this fuss over one little woman. But we have not seen them for months, except a few rough peasant women. I try and picture an American girl but it is impossible to form a real picture of one, my mind is too occupied. Again I envy the slightly wounded who can lay in a bed and be ministered to by this nurse and her sisters. Just to look at a woman would be something. I wonder what I would do. The hike drags on into the night. It seems we will never stop. Farther from the front and the strain and tension relaxes. With the relaxation comes weariness and fatigue. We actually have not hiked far or hard and the rests have been frequent. It is the strain of the last two weeks telling on us. Burt Oudett, walking silently beside me, suddenly starts, seems to waken suddenly and looks around surprised. He claims he has been walking asleep and evidently he has. I have been almost asleep myself. At last a line of trucks driven by the Indo-Chinese. It is just another hard jolting ride as tiresome and exhausting as the hike. It seems funny that they piled us into these trucks for an all-night ride when we could have slept so comfortably by the side of the road.

October 11. About midnight our truck breaks down in a small town. We jump off, glad for a little relief from the jolts. Howard Jordan faints as he alights from shrapnel cuts in the legs, fatigue and exhaustion. An M.P. takes us to his warm dry quarters and Jordan is placed on his bed. A wonderful home, a fire even. Jordan revives but he is weak and sick. The M.P. looks for another truck. We lay on the dry floor and sleep, hoping he will not find one till morning.

About daybreak one arrives, but we have had some sleep. Jordan is too sick to leave and the M.P. promises to take care of him. A few hours' ride and we are dumped in a small shell-wrecked town near the old Toul Sector we learn. We lay beside the road and rest till orders come for us.

A fine looking body of men march toward us, an entire Regiment on the hike. I am impressed by their cleanness and freshness, like we used to be. We are a bunch of tramps who are dirty, muddy. "What outfit, buddy?" we ask. "The 112th." We cannot believe our ears, this could not be our Regiment, they are too clean. We stare at them open mouthed, looking for familiar faces, wondering how they got so clean and healthy looking in such a short time. Then some man asks "112th what?" "112th Engineers." The mystery is explained — they never could be the 112th Infantry.

An officer hikes us a few miles to a small village where we are billeted. Mine is an old house with a fireplace and we can get plenty of wood. The outlook is pleasant even if the weather is bad.

October 12. We spend the day in cleaning and general fatigue. Rations are issued and we cook them ourselves. Given the time, we can make some very edible dishes.

There is a commotion in the village streets. A new batch of replacements arrive. A crowd of yelling men gather around. The nice clean equipment is the spoils. "I get his socks," "I get his underwear," "I get his shoes." The new men are the center of a milling mob, bewildered and dumbfounded by such a reception. The packs are quickly broken open and the contents spilled out. Extra blankets, extra socks and shoes, underwear and other equipment changes hands quickly. It is not larceny for these extras will all be thrown away on the first long hike the new man makes on the front so we may as well get some use of it. His personal articles are left to him but by the time they are finished his pack is much smaller. The newcomers gather what is left to them, wondering how they can explain their loss to a hard boiled quartermaster sergeant. The older men do not mean any offense and try and make the newcomer as much at home as possible after stealing all he has.

The evenings are spent around a cheery fire in the billet. We fight the war and make ourselves the hero of many an engagement. Poker and crap games start although the stakes are small for we have no money. Songs are sung, then later we roll into blankets and sleep.

October 13. Sgt. O'Connor details me to have the billet cleaned. The detail works until there can be no cause for complaint. Later Captain Graff has me on the carpet. Sgt. O'Connor says he had detailed me to clean up the back yard also but he had not. It does no good to say I had no orders to do it, the back yard is dirty, the sergeant says I was told to do it. The Captain agrees with the sergeant and I am confined to quarters. It was unjust for I was not told to clean up the yard but the Sergeant must protect his skirts and I am the goat. Like most of the army discipline it is unfair and the underdog takes the punishment, guilty or innocent. Yet the punishment rests lightly on me as I will not obey it anyhow.

A Salvation Army canteen is established in a town nearby and I walk over and buy a supply of candy and much more to show my defiance to military discipline than anything else. I know that we are on the front and there is dirty work to do. I will be a good soldier in their eyes again. I am quite a veteran now and have learned not to take these things too seriously and obey their foolish restrictions when the officers are around only.

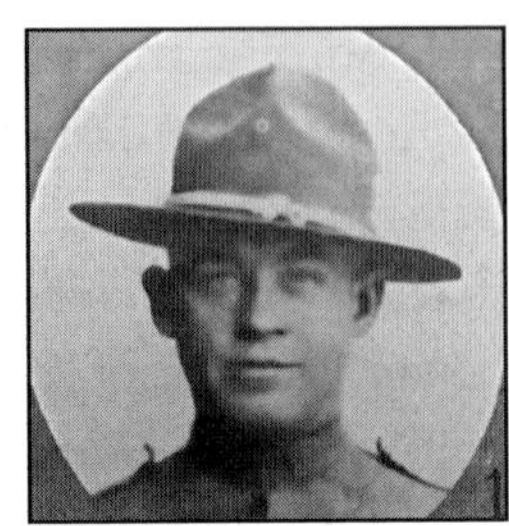

Sgt. Ernest Cridler.

We are paid and the crap and poker games are in full swing tonight. Reed, a runner, is drunk, a bad crying jag. All evening he mourns for Ernie Cridler, a sergeant of "I" Company killed by that shell that killed so many in the Argonne. "Poor Ernie Cridler," he moans. At first it is humorous and we sympathize with him but later it wears on jagged nerves. "Poor Ernie Gridler" over and over again. There is little sleep tonight, the gamblers are up till late and Reed cries hour after hour until at last he falls into a drunken sleep. I wish the Captain would come around and show some of his discipline so I could sleep.

October 14. Drill. Squads right and left and the manual of arms in the mud of the back yard. The drills are irksome and I tire easily. I have been suffering with stomach and bowel trouble for months caused by the bad food and water and the terrible living conditions so it is no wonder I am weak.

The rain is coming down but my brother and I hike to the Salvation Army canteen for a candy supply. Yesterday I was confined to quarters indefinitely but I take the chance.

On my return in the late afternoon the men are packing. It is a dismal, cold and foggy day. We line up and start a hike in the misty twilight. We do not go far till we halt beside the road. The cold rain beats on us and a chill wind blows. We remain in the ditch for hours wondering what is up but it is the front for us again. The outlook is black, I am wet, cold and discouraged all over again.

After hours of waiting in the dark, cold night, trucks appear and slide by and finally the train stops. We pile in, thirty to a truck. They are American ammunition trucks, larger but not covered. This is the worst ride I was ever on. The trucks slide all over the road, into shell holes and out onto the banks. We are first on one side and then the other banging into each other, squashed, tramped on, pushed and shoved. It is the grounds the St. Mihiel drive had gone over and no wonder the road is rough. The drivers have no lights and cannot see the holes till they are in them. The ride is as dangerous as an attack. At any minute I expect the truck to turn completely over and pinion us under it. The rain beats into our faces adding to the misery.

THE LAST FRONT

October 15. The ride ends in the early morning. We are dumped in a town named Pannes in the rain, tired, cramped, bruised, wet and hungry. Sore legs gradually lose their stiffness as we move around. We are all sleepy but the ditch is running water, the road is muddy and the fields worse yet. The fortunate men are those that can lay on the road on piles of loose stone. The prospect is as dismal as the weather, the front again.

About 2 a.m. we move forward three kilos to a town called Beney. The fog and mist hangs low so German observation is poor. An outfit plods slowly through the fields, a part of the 37th Division Ohio National Guard, who we are relieving. We slip and slide across this field then follow an old railroad track until we reach a dense woods. There we relieve the 37th. Our companies are only one third the size of theirs. They were in the Argonne four days, we were fourteen. They look much fresher than we do and it seems unreasonable that we should be relieving them as we needed the rest more than they did.

Battalion Headquarters is established in the woods a half mile from the edge. The 1st Battalion takes over the support line, the 2nd takes the front line. My brother, Forbes, Dechene and I locate some elephant iron and we drag in enough to cover a dugout. We dig down a couple of feet where the ground is not so soggy and cover the hole with the iron and have a nice comfortable home. There is little activity on this front. The Dutch were pushed back here

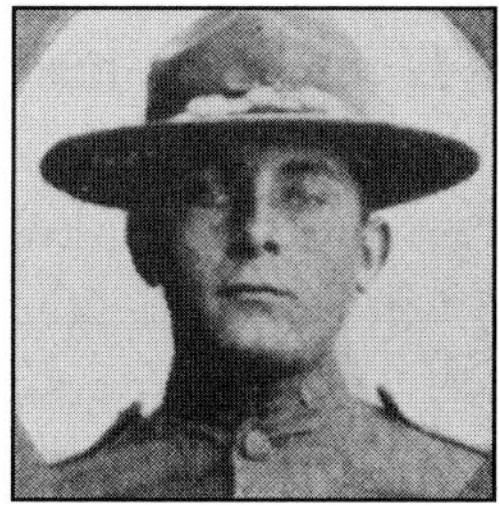

Pvt. Raymond Forbes.

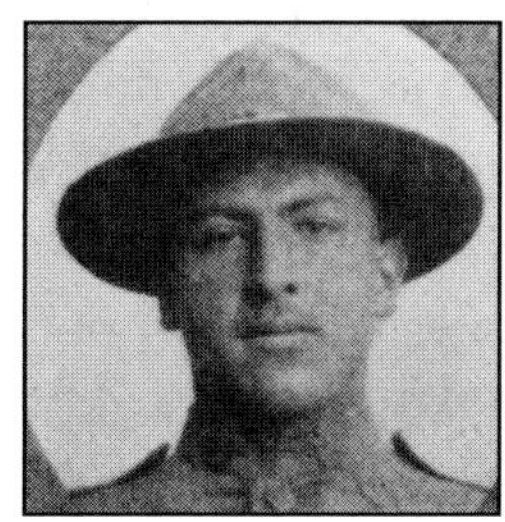

Pvt. James Dechene.

when the St. Mihiel salient was wiped out in September. Since then it has been quiet except for a few patrols, raids and a little artillery fire. The 37th reported it quiet and we have not heard a shell today. But the Argonne was the same, it is not likely to stay quiet now that we are here. At night the four of us sleep together. We have shelter-halfs and blankets under blankets, shelter-halfs and overcoats on top. It is dry and comfortable in our cozy dugout. A candle gives plenty of light. We talk of home, women, our experiences in the war until gradually we drift off to sleep not long after dark. In some of the other dugouts men are playing cards and shooting craps but most men are tired from that truck ride and go to sleep early. It does not seem like the front except for the mud and wet outside in the black woods.

October 16. The front is quiet except for a few shells traveling overhead. We dig the dugout deeper, then cover it again with the elephant iron and have a much more comfortable place. Now we can sit up and talk. We cook for ourselves and our group has doughballs. Captain Graff is Acting Major. I spend part of the day working on maps of the front with Sgt. O'Connor.

At night we sit in our dry, comfortable dugout by the candle light, tell stories and sing. We are not as tired tonight and stay up later. Outside the rain is dripping slowly, pitch dark, wet and cold but inside it is dry, light and cheerful. A few shells burst in the woods some distance away and we are hushed and fearful for a few minutes but they soon cease, it is quiet again and gradually we drop off to sleep.

October 17. At night I am in bed, comfortable with the other three men. It seems so nice and warm and cozy and I am thankful for a dry place to sleep in comfort. I roll over to enjoy it more and in the darkness outside I hear my name called. Davie Lett is calling me and it sounds bad, there is work in the cold and wet for me tonight. I do not answer at first, in the pitch blackness he cannot find me and I can easily say I was asleep and did not hear him. Yet Dave is a friend of mine, so at last rather than have him stumbling around in the black woods, I give in and answer, "here." I am to roll my pack and report to Captain Graff.

A dark and rainy night so black I can only guess directions. I hate to leave that cozy hole; maybe the Captain caught me going off to that Salvation

Army canteen. I report to the Captain's dugout and Sgt. Leinbach and I are detailed with the 2nd Battalion. Their Scout Section was badly used up in the Argonne and we are being loaned for the time being. A runner takes us through the black night, slipping, sliding, hit with wet bushes and trees, grumbling and wondering why we could not have waited till morning. We travel a mile or so in this fashion and report to Captain Miller about 10 p.m. He welcomes us with a friendly greeting but his dry, cozy dugout is not for us. He informs us that we are to work with the 2nd Battalion Scouts and help build up his Section, which was badly depleted in the Argonne. Also we can find a dugout to sleep in outside. The good holes are all taken and in the inky blackness it is like finding a rabbit hole. We finally locate one, covered with dirt but muddy on the bottom. The water drips through the dirt roof, the blankets get wetter and wetter but I may as well make the best of it till morning. The roof is only a few inches from my face and dirt falls onto me. And what a nice place I helped build back there and we could have come up in the morning just as well. But in the army a man's comfort means nothing. I sleep what I can, wet, itchy and miserable.

October 18. In the morning I went back to the 1st Battalion and brought up the rest of my equipment. I locate another dugout, a bit larger and drier. It had an entrance with one step leading down and easier to crawl into. The roof was about two and a half feet from the floor and two men could sleep there. I covered the top with a shelter-half and stopped the water dripping through. It was not much of a home but better than lying on top of the ground and a sure protection except for a direct hit. The front is quiet today, not a shell came close. "E" and "F" Companies, what was left of them, hold the front line a quarter mile ahead. The Scouts established a few Observation Posts but I am not detailed on any yet.

October 19. I escort a new detail of Scouts from "G" and "H" Companies to our Battalion Headquarters. Our meals are brought on the narrow gauge railroad before daylight and after dark. It is always cold by the time it arrives and poorly cooked. The coffee is black and tastes like iodine but we must drink something. My stomach revolts and I soon have dysentery again. Before a meal I can hardly stand, then as soon as I eat a little my stomach bloats with gas. Mornings, as soon as I am awake I must get out of the dugout in the wet, often in my bare feet. The cold, bad food makes it worse and I know I am losing weight fast. I cannot walk a mile without sitting down. It is caused from the gas, the shell hole water, rotten food, going without food for days and then having a big meal suddenly that my stomach cannot digest and all the other hardships of a soldier's life on the front. If I was home I would be attended by doctors, lots of medicine, watched over by mother and anxious and solicitous friends inquiring about me. Here nobody takes any notice at all, all are just as bad, there are even no C.C. pills. Nature may wear it off someday I hope.

October 20. At night about seven p.m. "E" and "F" Companies raid the German lines. I stayed at the Captain's dugout for orders. The Germans retaliated with shell fire and the fire was so close I took refuge in the dugout entrance. Big Mike, the Captain's dogrobber, was also there. There is a large can of molasses in a shed outside the dugout but I cannot steal it with Big Mike around. The shells drop closer and buzz a few pieces of steel close and Big Mike goes inside. Shells or no shells, now is my time for that molasses. I grab the can and carry it to my dugout and hide it quickly, then run back to the Captain's dugout entrance as a few more shells burst in the woods. When the fire stops I am standing there innocently enough. I do not feel guilty, the officers appropriated this whole can of molasses for themselves and it is really as much ours as theirs.

A half dozen prisoners come running down the path escorted by doughboys. They are laughing and joking. Captain Miller lines them up and talks to them like an old friend and they swap cigarets and souvenirs. It is more of a reunion than a war. We kid them and they kid back good-naturedly. These men did not fight, they surrendered peacefully and no one in the raiding party was hurt. Many Germans are ready to call the war off as they feel that with the Americans in it they cannot win. They were kept at Battalion Headquarters till the strafing is over and then taken through the woods to Regimental P.C., waving and yelling "Goodbye" to us.

October 21. Fitzgerald, another scout of the 2nd Battalion, and I locate a fifty pound sack of sugar on a car on the narrow gauge and we steal that also. Then I make fudge from the sugar and molasses but too much sweets is bad for my weak stomach and I suffer intensely from indigestion. For days I cannot look at sugar or sweets.

Nothing doing all day. Every opportunity I have I visit the 1st Battalion for mail and to find out how they are making out. Casualties were light as there is little shelling. Once two men left their dugout and when they came back a direct hit had been made on their hole during their absence. Two other men were not so fortunate: a shell landed squarely on them killing them instantly.

October 22. We start working on a spur of the narrow gauge railroad into Battalion Headquarters so we can run our rations without carrying them so far. Sgt. Leinbach is the Engineer. The rails were back at St. Benoit station, some that the Germans left. I had the detail bringing up the rails. The work made me feel better, even giving me an appetite for the food we have, bad as it is.

October 23. Completed the spur so now we do not have to send details for the rations. Very quiet.

October 24. Went for mail at the 1st Battalion. Mother's letters are always full of hope and good cheer with never a word of discouragement.

October 25. I am sent to escort "G" and "H" Companies to the line and relieve "E" and "F". They are in the woods back of St. Benoit. The day is dark and foggy and visibility is poor so the relief is made without excitement. The two companies had recently been filled with new replacements, drafted men with no experience on the line.

At night the Germans gassed them and many new men were casualties. They could not realize quickly the danger. Many had not received any instructions in gas or gas masks and when the gas shells exploded they did not know what to do. Many of the replacements do not know how to load a rifle to say nothing of other things. Some have only been in the army six weeks or two months and already across the ocean. It is a shame to throw their lives away when a few months' instruction could save many of them.

October 26. At night another raid. At dusk I was detailed to establish liaison posts with the raiding party using Scouts and Runners. I talked with a very nervous lieutenant in charge of the raiding party. His remarks were grunts between cigarets, which he smoked one after the other. I am glad I am not going even if the Dutch are not resisting. Sometime they may fool us. I walked back half the distance and lay down with Johnson, a Scout, in the middle of an open field. Behind us several batteries of seventy-fives open up, flashing in the darkness, and salvos of shells pass over our heads and burst on the German positions. The raiding party is over now. The German retaliation starts, shelling the woods on all four sides of me and I am glad I kept to the center of the field. I lie on top of the ground and hope for the best. Suddenly a seventy-seven bursts a few yards ahead of me. I jumped in its hole, still warm and smoking. I can curl up in it with my head below ground. A shell seldom bursts twice in the same spot. Other shells follow immediately and I have plenty of reasons to keep down in the next few minutes as they burst within a few yards. Then the Germans shift their fire to the edge of the woods again. Johnson had run to the woods but now he returns and we sit together in the hole waiting for news of the raiding party. The German fire slackened, then quit and we raised our heads above the hole's rim.

One man is talking loudly in broken English. A detail is returning with German prisoners. The loud talker is a German sergeant, from Mannheim, Germany, in charge of a machine gun that did not fire on our men as they came over. He had had his goods packed and preparations made to surrender on the next raid. Tonight was his chance and when they came over he yelled to the Americans to come and surrendered with all his gun crew. He had lived in New York, Chicago and London and spoke English well.

He had fought against the other Allies but Americans seemed like his own countrymen even though his wife was French. He said the Allied air raids on Mannheim were terrible. The people at home know that with America in the war they could not win. I followed them back to Battalion Headquarters and then my duty finished I went to bed in my hole in the ground thankful that I was not killed tonight.

October 27. At night another raid. We are making a live sector of this place. I was detailed on a liaison post the same as last night. Several more prisoners were taken but they did not come back in my direction. There was no interest for me but to sit at my post in the woods and wait.

October 28. In the afternoon our battalion raided in broad daylight without a barrage. They simply walked across "No Man's Land" and came back with twelve prisoners, scarcely any resistance and none killed. Captain Miller met the prisoners with a big smile, gave them cigarets and they held matches for him. Everyone was happy, no hard feelings, laughs, jokes and good natured kidding. It seemed impossible that these men ever could be our enemies. But those opposing us are largely Alsatians and never very loyal to Germany.

I was near the narrow gauge railway while the raid was in progress and a working party passed by. I recognized Rip Young, from my home, in the working party. He was with the last replacements and had only been drafted three months before. The Dutch were dropping high explosive shells in retaliation for the raid. It was Rip's first experience under shell fire and he did not like it. I followed him asking questions of home, but Rip is not interested in home, his interest is in those shells. I felt sorry for him for I know how they worried me at first, though by now I scarcely notice them unless they are real close.

October 29. I secure permission and go to Pannes and have a tooth fixed. The tooth is only an excuse to get away and this is more in the nature of a vacation. Pannes is five miles in the rear. After the tooth is fixed I loiter around "A" Company's kitchen waiting for a hot meal. In this place is comfort compared with my hole in the lines. I stay as long as I dare and late in the afternoon walk back to the front again. At Beney the Salvation Army have a fine canteen, ladies close to the front give me hot chocolate and I buy chocolate bars. Then on to my hole, hating to go.

October 30. I work the tooth racket again and have another day at Pannes. A detail of machine gunners pass me with a supply of doughnuts for their men on the front. They look good but I know it's useless for an infantryman to ask. One man has just taken a bite when a shell comes close. Now is my chance. He drops to the ground, his doughnut also falls and shell or no shell I have it before he can get his hooks on it and I am off down the track.

An Engineer Captain walks up the narrow gauge railroad toward me. I straighten up as though to salute and jerk my hand out of my pocket and then when he returns the half finished jerk with a snappy salute I laugh at him. He is a good sport, he grins also and I feel ashamed for not saluting him properly. It takes a long time to have that tooth fixed, then I loiter as much as possible till late in the afternoon I return to my hole in the lines.

October 31. At night I am detailed for a reconnaissance patrol. Our regiment has taken so many prisoners from the Dommartin Woods ahead of us that now they wonder if the woods are still occupied and our patrol is to try and find out if they are still held by the Dutch or not.

At the outposts I meet a sergeant of the 2nd Battalion and a few men who are going along. The night is dark with a heavy fog that conceals entirely the woods ahead. A railroad track runs from our lines to the German lines and then on to Metz. We start on this track, walking upright as there is little to fear with the enemy a half mile from us. The sergeant is ahead and I bring up the rear. Halfway across we all stop to listen. I look at my feet and I am standing over the skeleton of an American soldier whose white skull gleams between my feet. Startled, and it reminds me that this man was killed here doing the same as I am doing. The sergeant informs me in a low whisper it is a Lieutenant of the 37th Division killed on a patrol. We proceed a little more cautiously, jolted by that white gleaming skeleton. The patrol stops again and we all take cover in a shell hole to the right of the track. I estimate that we are a little more than half way across. We talk in whispers and decide to stay in the fields away from the track but to keep the track in sight. Then we move slowly and quietly to another shell hole and lie down again and listen. It is perfectly quiet except for the ghostly movement of the fog. Ahead is a slightly darker mass where the German woods are.

The sergeant remarks that we have gone far enough and we will wait in this shell hole a few hours, then go back and report there are Germans in the woods. It puzzles me to know how he is certain there are Germans in those woods. I remain a few minutes in the shell hole and not liking the idea of being still decide to go a little closer alone. He is glad for a volunteer to go farther as we may secure a little more information but as for the sergeant the shell hole is close enough.

I crawl over the shell hole rim and walk quietly. I can see only a few feet but that is my best protection as they cannot see me. The railroad is my guide. Halting every few feet to listen and observe, then on again. I raise my feet high, then slowly lower the toe first to the ground then the heel comes down noiselessly. A hundred yards of this slow walking and I drop to the ground on hands and knees. I reach forward with my hands to feel the ground and carefully bring my knee up to my hand. It is slow but safer. The woods to my front are a plainer blur through the fog. I lie on my stomach frequently and search the ground for signs of the enemy. All is quiet and still.

My gas mask is slung carelessly on my back while crawling, easier to carry and if I am compelled to hug the ground from machine gun fire it will let me down two inches lower. Suddenly while crawling it comes down with a thud on the ground, in the stillness like an explosion. I ease to the ground expecting a burst of machine gun bullets. Nothing happens, a long time quiet and certain it was not heard then forward again crawling. Again the gas mask is on my back but I will watch it closer. The woods are a dim outline still many yards away. Again, suddenly the gas mask slips with another loud thud to the ground. Thoroughly frightened now, I hug the ground expecting a real blast this time. Nothing happens, the stillness is horrible, gradually I raise my eyes forward. A sudden movement may be the end. To my left is a telephone pole beside the track and the next pole is in the woods in the German lines. The fog had deceived me and I have crawled within half the distance of two telephone poles from the enemy lines. The shock of being so close all alone makes me cold and shaky and my mind sees that skeleton on the railroad tracks. My muscles dare not move, but my heart is pounding, torturing me with its loudness. The fog is shifting ghostily, swirling vapors. Or is it Germans crawling to me? If my gas mask had not slipped I might have crawled right into the woods.

I am now thoroughly scared. Only a few yards from their woods and even now they may be sending men out to get me with the long knives. Why did I leave that shell hole with the sergeant; he will see his mother again. Is that a man or is it fog? Footsteps, no just my heart. A new dread, turning around and going back. I must not lose my head and run; my best chance is to turn slowly and crawl back as I came up. Quiet a long time again, trying to muster the courage to turn. Desperately at last I start to pivot myself on the ground. I know my life will depend on how quiet I am and a sudden move may bring down a searing blast of fire that will leave my skeleton like that poor man on the track. If I had only stayed in that nice big comfortable shell hole so far away from the Boche. The turning operation takes a long time, a few inches at a time like a turntable. Maybe I should yell "kamerad" and surrender, a machine gun might now be swinging, a finger may be squeezing. Comforting, but at last the turning operation is over and I am headed for home. My hands reach out on the ground cautiously, then pull my body to my hands and wait and listen. Then on another foot and listen, another foot and listen, another foot, another and another foot, feeling almost a big German dropping on me suddenly from the fog and blackness with a big knife to finish me. The fog swirls. Ghosts are moving, ghosts of dead soldiers or are they live ones. Only by a great effort can I keep from jumping up and running but that will surely discover me to them and will endanger the patrol. A few yards on my stomach, cautiously look around and already the woods are dimmer and I am safe so far. Then on hands and knees, still slow but faster than crawling on my stomach. At last I am two telephone poles away from the woods. Then I rise and walk still using all the precautions. My terror dies down when I am one hundred and fifty yards from them. Back that far is a great distance and the shell hole where the rest of the patrol are waiting is absolutely safe it is so far away.

As I near the hole I walk more boldly till a hiss from the sergeant brings me to them. Nonchalantly, I explain in a fairly loud voice. He bawls me out in a low whisper for talking so loud and taking so long but it sounds good to me and I laugh at him in relief. It is good to be with those that I know will not kill me. The patrol is ready to return and so am I. I set my prismatic compass and we start. Although still in "No Man's Land" the trip back is much easier. The skeleton glows whitely on the tracks, poor fellow. I know what his last few minutes were like and I was much closer than he was. We are challenged by our own men. I remain with the outposts and the sergeant reports. I still don't know for sure if there were Germans in those woods or not, but if imagination could tell, the woods were full.

November 1. I had little to do all day. There are rumors that the war will soon end. Papers say the Allies are driving on every front and the Germans are crumbling. I surely do hope and pray it will happen soon. But there is another big drive coming soon and it is right here. I dread that drive. My company has been on the front since July 4th and of the two hundred and fifty men that started we have about thirty left. "G" and "H" have less than ten original men. When I see my own company I cannot recognize it as I know so few. At this rate what chance do I have in another drive. I have already passed over onto borrowed time. Some expect the war to end in the spring. Bad weather may save the German army but the spring drive will end it we are certain. I still have a chance if I get wounded but the suspense of waiting for that is still very hard as it may be death just as well. The field mice remind me of the Bible, "the foxes have holes and the birds their nest but the Son of Man has nowhere to lay his head". In Romans I read, "Oh Death, where is thy sting, Oh grave where is thy victory" and it gives me strength and consolation. If it was not for the help from the New Testament I believe I would be a nervous wreck. There have been too many instances of God helping me, shifting me from the death spots and allowing me to go unscathed. If he will only continue his protection, but what if he decides not to any more? It is not the hereafter I dread, that would be sweet release, it is that awful sock you get when you are hit and the misery before you die.

The dysentery is worse and bothers me all the time. I am no worse than the rest. All have it but are expected to carry on. I know I am losing weight fast for I can see my cheeks sunken when I shave. My underwear and clothes are the same that I have worn for weeks and naturally filthy. They would itch even if they were not filled with cooties. Every day I try and have a cootie hunt but then the next day they are just as bad. I even have them in my overseas cap.

Nights I have been having nightmares. The first one terrified me as I thought I was dying. I became partly conscious but could not move, clamped in a vice. At last by a great effort I could move my fingers or toes, just a little, then a few more twitches and I could kick and at last roll over on my side. This seems to break the spell and at last I either waken or continue on in my sleep. If I waken it is almost as bad as my hole had every appearance of a grave. I have had three or four of them in one night and I dread to go to sleep at night. I realize there is no use going for medical attention, there is none and wounded men cannot he taken care of properly so they will think I am goldbricking if I complain of nightmares.

November 2. Raiding parties have been going over in broad daylight and capturing prisoners, usually without resistance. "No Man's Land" is our land. Today the infantry were to attack on our front with artillery preparation, but the infantry did not receive the attack orders till the artillery preparation was all over and so they did not go. Two artillerymen, thinking the infantry had attacked and advanced, brought telephone wire up and laid it over into the German lines. When they arrived there fourteen Germans surrendered. The bad features of the surrender was that one of the Scout Sergeants of the 1st Battalion had just reported that he had been in those same woods that very day and they were unoccupied by Germans. He will not tell his grandchildren about the next unhappy hours he spent with Captain Graff for he made his observation from our own lines. Sgt. Mars asks Fitzgerald, another Scout, and I to go with him and make a raid of our own on the Mirambeau Farm. There should be lots of souvenirs and perhaps some German prisoners. Fitzgerald and I, trying to call his bluff, agree to go along. But he is not bluffing and the minute we find that out we are sorry but we cannot back out now. The Runner Chief also wants to go. Captain Miller would block such a thing if he knew.

In the afternoon we decide to make the attempt. We walk through the bushes to the front line. Fitzgerald has been in an observation post there and he and I climb a tree and have a look around. A peaceful landscape, no signs of Germans anywhere. Descending, we hope that Mars has changed his mind, but he has not. Three artillerymen, A.W.O.L. from their guns, up to see the front, join us and wish to go also so we have seven. We decide to go over by twos but just at the edge of the woods, Sgt. Mars steps aside and leaves Fitz and I in front. Now more than ever, he and I are dubious of the propriety of the thing, especially since we are the lead team, but we will not back down now.

Daylight, Fitz and I are in "No Man's Land", and how big and wide it looks. The others back of us decide the interval will be a good hundred yards with the three artillerymen about three hundred yards back of us. Ahead is a line of bushes and we walk over to them unhindered. Fitz and I observe from the bushes, he says let's go and we are off on the last leg. If there are Germans in that Mirambeau Farm they are kind-hearted ones. We are now three hundred yards from them and more than halfway across. My enthusiasm, lagging terrible since we started, is at its lowest ebb. I am liable to be killed or captured just to call somebody's bluff and the nearer I get to the Boche the more foolish it seems. I am ready to bolt and run back. So is Fitz if he would admit it. It will be fine if the Germans will take this as a social call but we have been so very unsociable with them lately.

And now that I am already to show a yellow, or should I say, a sensible streak, a lucky break happens. A battery of seventy-fives decide to register for the day. A shot strikes two hundred yards to our right, then another closer and on a line with us. A third shot is closer, I am down in a shell hole but Fitz stays on top. The fourth shot skims over my shell hole, Fitz takes it standing and luckily is not killed. Then he jumps in the hole with me. No more come and we look over our hole to see what has become of the other five. The three artillerymen are just going into the brush of our own front line with Mars and the Runner not far behind. We are both well pleased even if they did leave us alone in "No Man's Land." Without any reluctance we give up our private raid although we both agreed to light into Mars for running out on us. We find him in the bushes of our front waiting on us, and as prearranged Fitz and I hop all over them, pretending great displeasure and disappointment at having to abandon our project. If they get me out in "No Man's Land" again it will be by sending me. We all decide not to mention it to Captain Miller and save us a good bawling out....

November 3. At night the 1st Battalion relieves the 2nd on the front line. The relief is made after darkness but I had no desire to hurry back in the night so I slept in my dugout, now quite comfortable, and did not leave with them.

November 4. In the morning I went to the rear to find the 2nd. The Scouts are in the railroad station at St. Benoit on the road to Beney, a whole building undamaged by shell fire, with several bunks the Germans left. It is within easy range of the front, about three kilos from the outpost line. I slept in an upper row of bunks but I was afraid. I like to be underground if they shell.

November 5. In Beney, the Salvation Army have the best canteen I have seen in France. The town is shelled every day but those three women stick. The seventy-fives are on a line with the town and some guns behind the town. I bought the first American candy, the favorite Hershey bars. They did not appear to be limited, a man could buy as much as he could pay for, much different than the Y.M.C.A. where usually a man was limited to one bar of candy, a few cookies and a pack of cigarets.

November 6. In Beney again at the Salvation Army canteen. For months I have craved candy. Those Hershey bars are especially good. While at the canteen Jerry dropped a few shells near the town. The women kept on serving quietly. I wondered if they had cooties. They looked tired but not cranky and their voices were American women's calm voices. The best of order prevailed in the line, as self-controlled as those noble Salvation Army women. There a Lieutenant did not run to the head of the line and buy out everything in front of the privates. The officers waited their turn. There was no cursing or dirty stories. If a man had the money he paid but if he had no money it made no difference. But if he had money and did not pay he would be given a good dressing down by the rest of the men. I noticed that nearly all men paid without squawking.

At night we sat in our station and talked. We build a little fire in the stove, singing and apparently cheerful. But back of the cheerfulness we listen for that dread shriek of the approaching shell or the whistle of the air bomb. In the bunk before sleeping I say a prayer and hope that I can sleep till morning. Strange that this station has not been shelled.

November 7. I belong to the 1st Battalion but am attached to the 2nd. The 2nd now hardly uses me and they are not sure but that I should be back with the 1st. But without orders I am staying with the 2nd as we are off the front and the 1st is on. If we go to the front again I will try and go back to the 1st.

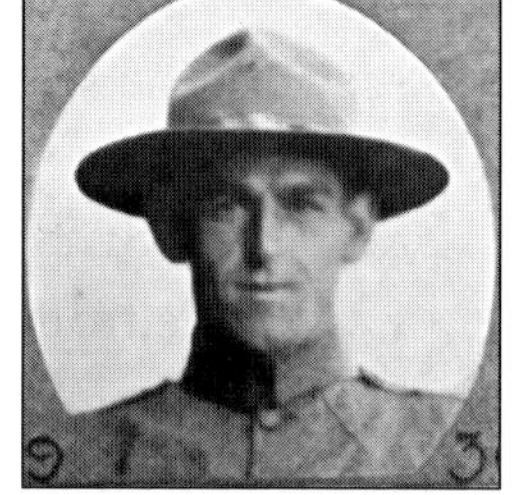

Pvt. Edward Sheldon.

So today, being a free lance, I walk to Pannes where rumor says there is a cootie bath and clean clothes. I am lucky, a bath and clean clothes though not new ones. Also two meals, hot from "A" Company's kitchen. Burt Oudett was there and late in the afternoon he left for the front again. Eddie Sheldon, a cook, said "Well goodbye Burt." Burt turned and said, "Don't ever say goodbye Eddie, always say, so long." I have a strange feeling it will be a long time till I see

Burt again, if ever, even though he does say "so long." I remain at Pannes at night, sleeping on the second floor of the building occupied by the kitchen. But I cannot sleep, even this far away, I wish I was in a hole in the ground.

November 8. Went back to the St. Benoit Station. More batteries of Field Artillery are coming up. The road from Beney to St. Benoit is lined with seventy-fives. Back of Beney several more batteries concealed with camouflage. In the woods near the St. Benoit station heavy eight-inch howitzers are setting up. I visit them to examine them. More 155 howitzers and the long range naval guns and long piles of shells covered with camouflage. The signs are the same as the Argonne. A few more days and we will be in another drive again. More dead, wounded, gassed and missing and it may be me this time. Rumors of an armistice vague and unreliable, but a ray of hope if only it will come before the drive begins.

German prisoners were loaded on a truck near us. One fine looking, blonde German, about forty, complained he could not get in alone. He looked O.K. and some Americans started to get rough with him. Then the old fellow explained that he had been shot in the shoulder and this was the first he had mentioned it. He had stood there stoically as if nothing was wrong and only mentioned it when absolutely necessary.

November 9. Visited the canteen at Beney, then explored beyond the town toward Thiaucourt. Rambled around the country seeing the new batteries in place and conjecturing on the new drive. More rumors of an armistice but they are the same as the rumors of the big rest camps we were always going to.

Back at the St. Benoit station the 2nd Battalion is making preparations to move to the front to attack. For the first time I ducked out. I inform the sergeant in charge of Scouts I would like to return to the 1st. But I have no intention of seeing the 1st if I can keep from it. After dark the men of the 2nd file off into the dark on the railroad to Metz and I am left at the station alone. A feeling of loneliness comes. I miss their company, their cheery talk that has helped put in the last, few evenings at the station. They will attack at dawn and some will be dead or terribly wounded. I feel like rushing into the blackness and be with them but better sense prevails. I may join the 1st in the morning and be with my brother in the last drive together.

November 10. The 2nd Battalion attacked the Dommartin woods early in the morning. The men are showing little enthusiasm for the attack. News that an armistice is coming has slowed them down and made them cautious. They can see no reason for fighting when in a few days the war may be over. Men are anxious now; what a shame to be killed or wounded with peace perhaps only a few hours away.

The regiment has casualties, a few dead and wounded. Captain Miller has fought bravely on the front since we started. Now a shell burst wounds him severely in the head and legs and he is not expected to live. (*Captain Miller did survive.*) Sgt. Mars is also badly wounded in the legs. Burt Oudett stops a piece of shell with his Adam's apple and the outcome is doubtful. (*Oudett survived, too.*) The 2nd returns during the day. It is only a gradual start of the drive on Metz and it is not to start suddenly like the Argonne. Secretly I am glad I ducked out last night. I will wait a few days and if the Armistice is a fake I have plenty of time to be a brave soldier. The news of Captain Miller, Mars and Oudett's wounds saddens me and it also convinces me that I was wise in staying. Bravery, if I ever had any, is ended for me. I have been brave at times and a coward at other times. Obeyed orders, yes, when I had to, but when there was a chance to duck danger, even though I disobeyed a few orders, I have taken the safest way. There is no justification for evading this last attack. The front line soldiers will not condemn me for they will do the same when they have the chance. Military discipline is supposed to be very strict, yet soldiers are human beings and human beings are hard to force into places where death is their reward. A soldier's business is to die for his country, so they say in the patriotic meetings. Artillery fire though takes the patriotism away and leaves only a human being whose big consideration is his own life. It is foolishness to die for one's country if the war is to end soon.

THE ARMISTICE

November 11. The Armistice is to go into effect at eleven a.m. today. Nobody takes it seriously, we do not believe it, just another rumor. McElroy, now with the Signal Corps, confirms the statement. We accept anything with reservations; we will see at eleven a.m.

Firing has been going since early morning, artillery much too heavy if they are going to stop the war. The heavies back of us fire, heavy rocking concussions, the Argonne all over again. Instead of the Armistice we are getting ready for the big push. The 109th does make an attack at nine a.m. on their front and more lives lost needlessly. As the morning passes the fire is heavier. A few German shells come over feebly, but still heavy enough to kill and wound men a few minutes before eleven.

If there is an Armistice at eleven it seems so foolish to keep up the killing till the last minute. But the killing is the artillery way. He does not see the tortured, horrible looks of the slaughtered or feel the remorse the doughboy feels when he sees a man he has shot. I stay close to a hole, filled with horror at the thought of being killed at the last minute. At nine a.m. the gunfire grows louder, the minutes drag on slowly, anxiously, at ten a barrage growing in intensity. Artillery, safer than the infantry, are firing the light guns on recoil. The howitzers seem also to be firing on recoil, so fast are their explosions, too fast for the safety of the gun crews. This cannot be an Armistice, this is a drive. Doughboys in the front line are anxiously watching their watches as each minute drags on to find if the reports are really true and not another rumor.

I have a German watch and it is in my hands every few minutes. We have decided to get a stove in St. Benoit for our billet but we are waiting till eleven. If the war ends then we can go in safety but if it does not end we are going anyhow. Near eleven the guns are crashing harder than ever. My watch passes eleven and no letup but the watch may be fast. Five after, ten after, fifteen after eleven and the guns still fire. The same horrid racket continues. It is enough, it was only another rumor. I am disheartened, discouraged, all hopes false, the war will go on forever, this is really the preparation for the big drive as we said. My heart sinks and the future is hopeless all over again. But at eleven twenty by my watch, a break, the roar dies down like machinery in a large factory suddenly being shut off, gradually, a few last scattering shots, a last shot, then a strange hushed stillness, a peculiar feeling too sudden to be real. The news must be true and my watch was twenty minutes fast. It is a tremendous relief although we cannot realize its full meaning yet.

There are no demonstrations, no cheering even. Men at the guns leave the pieces hot from the final barrage and sit down. Doughboys in dugouts and shell holes emerge cautiously, unbelievingly. Except for the noise the front is the same. A half dozen of us who had waited till the end to bring that stove now walk to St. Benoit and lug it back with us. Outside of saying we hope it is really true we talk little of the Armistice. It may be only for a few days anyhow and the war will be on again in all its cruelty. It is too unreal, a battery is likely to start at any time and wake us from this dream.

At night I sleep with Vogel in the upper bunk. But even if it is peace now I cannot control the reflexes of fear and I still listen for that shell. The bunk seems high. I would rather be in a hole under the ground. Foolish fears, the war is over but the taut nerves have not learned it yet. Sleep is distant. An airplane hums overhead, we left a light burning for the first time, he may see and bomb us. I can hardly stay in that upper bunk till he is over. The war will not leave me for many months, gradually it will wear away but it is too close now to be recovered from its influence. Relaxation does not bring the rest or the feeling of security I had thought it would.

November 12. Strict orders have been issued that there shall be no fraternization with the enemy. Nut McElroy and I feel different. We walk up the railroad tracks to the front line and then follow it across to the Dommartin woods where I was caught in the fog on the night patrol and close to the place Fitzgerald and I tried to raid the Mirambeau Farm. Our troops now hold the Dommartin woods. McElroy foolishly asks an officer if we can go over but he angrily orders us away. Everyone is wanting to go, he says, and orders are no one is to go. We do get out, away from his vision at least. A man on guard challenges with military precision and informs us we cannot go beyond him and then points out a clump of trees and informs us that he cannot see beyond that clump of trees. Once by those trees we make a beeline for the German wire, much faster and with more courage than I ever ran for the German wire before. McElroy stops at the wire, thinking he has found a German grave and wants me to dig him up, we may find a watch on him. But I have seen enough dead, and lucky for us as it was a German mine he was looking at.

We found a group of Germans and almost as many Americans, who also had not taken the "no fraternization" order seriously. Everyone was happy. The Americans were trading tobacco and candy for watches and other souvenirs. I traded my slicker for a watch and the German went away feeling he had the best of the bargain. I don't care if the watch ran or not, I can pick up another slicker on the way back. Without candy and tobacco I can do little trading. I can understand a little German and with that and a lot of movements I could make myself understood. One German said, "How long were you in the trenches?" "Five months." "Ah. I was in five years." "Yes," I said, "but five months was enough."

The Boche had schnapps and many of the boys had been treated. Everyone was merry, even the American officers who had also sneaked over. The German officers were aloof and stood aside saying little and watching the men enjoying themselves. German soldiers could not understand the American officers mingling with the men. The enemy was a pretty good fellow and both sides are glad we can be friends and not shoot at each other. The war does seem so silly now that it is over and I am glad these fellows were spared. Some told us sadly that shells killed many men in a dugout just a few minutes before eleven, some who had gone through the entire war.

The Germans, according to the terms of the Armistice, were exploding the mines in the wire and German Engineers were at that work. I saw them working near the place McElroy had selected for his grave opening and soon a mine went off.

I walked back into a town and into a house where four Germans were playing cards, picked up one of their rifles to examine it but four black looks from the card players decided me to go out and look for good natured Germans. These card players were different from the ones outside. No one mentioned the war or the fact that we had apparently won the argument.

A Y.M.C.A. outfit and a K. of C. outfit came up and gave out chocolate and cigarets to Germans and Americans alike. A moving picture camera also came and registered scenes, in one of which a solemn faced German officer was persuaded to be taken with a group of Americans.

McElroy and I remained till nearly dark and then returned to our lines. No questions asked on the return trip. We will go back tomorrow with all the raincoats, tobacco and candy we can find. But on returning to the station, the outfit was gone. Too late to look for them and too tired, so I sleep at the station. Tomorrow I will look for them and find my brother. The billet is lonesome tonight but I drop off to sleep a little better than last night.

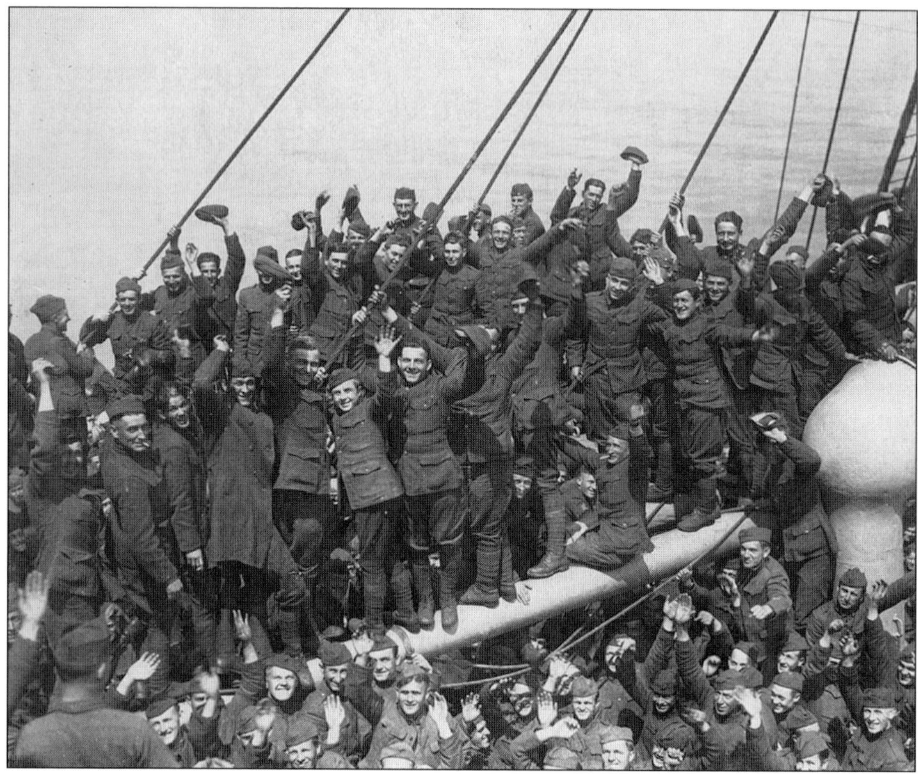

This photo from the National Archives is described as the 112th Regiment arriving at Philadelphia in May 1919. When it was published a week later in the Erie (Pennsylvania) Daily Times, the caption read that Company G of the 112th had arrived. Either way, the steamship *Pocahontas* had brought the men home.

Conclusion

So there it is. Harold Wayne Pierce survived the war. It seems like a miracle.

After the entry for November 12, 1918, he ended with that single word, "Conclusion," when he typed the diary decades later. For the reader there is a long exhale of sorts, knowing that Pierce will no longer have to endure the horrors he so vividly described.

We know that Harold and his brother Hugh arrived back in the United States in May 1919 with the rest of the 28th Division, making it to northwest Pennsylvania within a week. The time between Armistice and leaving France included more training, more drill, and three square meals a day. Harold Pierce's gastrointestinal issues likely subsided. They celebrated Thanksgiving, Christmas and New Year's in the same sector, headquartered at Buxieres. No longer did the troops have to carry gas masks wherever they went. On January 6, the regiment marched four days to Traveron near the home of Joan of Arc. The regiment trained there, but also granted leaves to some men to go sightseeing in France. Twice the full division passed in review, once to the Second Army command and then to the AEF command. In March, the division went to Le Mans and then on to the port city of St. Nazaire in April where they boarded the steamship *Pocahontas* to go home.

So what happened to Harold Pierce in the years that followed?

No one is ever the same after living through what he did. Yet somehow he managed to live a "normal" life, if not an extraordinary one. In many ways, H.W. Pierce was something of a Renaissance man. He was an artist, policeman, judo instructor, pistol marksman, trick horse rider, Sunday School teacher, Gettysburg battlefield guide, model railroad hobbyist, and an author on police procedures.

Daughter Brenda Pierce Simpson said her father went back to high school in Warren County, where he finished his studies to earn his diploma. How did this 21-year-old veteran of the Great War mix with teenagers whose life experiences paled next to his? Sometime after receiving that diploma, Pierce joined the Pennsylvania State Police. He served until 1938, leaving as a sergeant. While a state policeman, he occasionally worked undercover, arresting moonshiners, coal mine labor agitators (Molly McGuires) and even some members of the "Black Hand." He loved working with horses as a state policeman and became an accomplished trick rider. In fact, says Brenda, the switch from horses to motorcycles for routine police patrols was one of the main reasons he quit.

From the Pennsylvania State Police Pierce went to the city of Butler in southwest Pennsylvania where he became chief of police. That lasted three months until September 1, 1938, when he was named supervisor of the newly formed Public Service Institute in the Commonwealth of Pennsylvania's Department of Public Instruction. His duties there were, according to the state announcement, "to train local and city justices of the peace, aldermen, police officers and others in Public office." He also taught some FBI personnel how to make a sketch of a suspect from witness descriptions. During those years he wrote two textbooks on police procedures that still sit on the shelves at Penn State University's library. He retired in 1966.

On July 18, 1931, Harold married Martha Fern Lanning, who went by her middle name. They ultimately settled in Hershey Township outside Harrisburg. Brenda was born in 1940. Fern died June 8, 1974.

From his diary we know that Pierce was a religious person when he entered the Army and became more so as the war raged. The New Testament he kept in his pocket helped him endure those horrors. So it is no surprise that he became a Sunday School teacher for many years, teaching in the Evangelical United Brethren (EUB) Church until its merger with the Methodist Church, and later with the Presbyterian Church. "He had his own little twist on some views," Brenda said. They didn't always follow the standard lines of thought for the time, but would fit in better today, she said. The thing to know is that he was a gentle man. That gentleness extended to dogs. He loved dogs in general, and once rescued a seriously injured dog, giving it to his daughter.

Pierce had a lifelong love of history. While living in Hershey, Pennsylvania, he became a volunteer guide at the Gettysburg battlefield. His love of history passed along to Brenda and to her sons, David and J.P. Simpson, all of whom became educators.

That love of history did not mean he told war stories to his daughter, although he did tell stories about his days with the State Police. He and brother Hugh were active in veterans organizations throughout the years, including the Veterans of World War One. After reading his diary it is easy to understand why he had little to say about the war to his child.

Through all those years, he continued to paint and to draw, often depicting scenes from the war. Veterans of Foreign Wars Post 264 at Corry, Pennsylvania, about 20 miles from his hometown of Youngsville, had four of his paintings on its walls for decades. They were ultimately donated to the Erie County Historical Society and are included in this book. He donated paintings to VFW posts around Pennsylvania and to a church

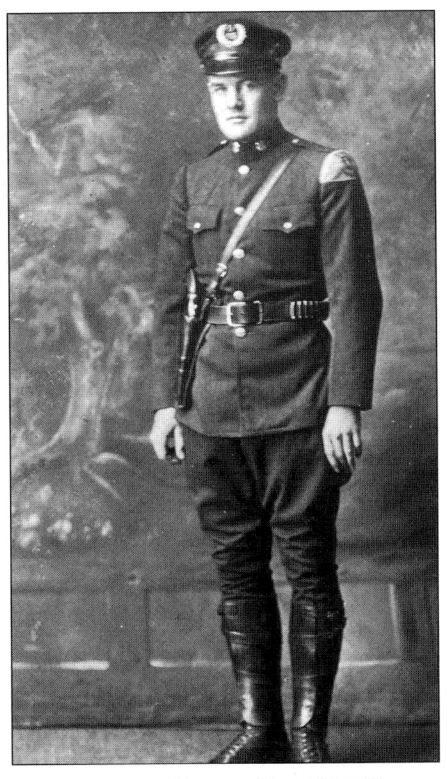

Newly sworn-in Trooper Harold W. Pierce is back in uniform, now as a Pennsylvania State Policeman. He successfully applied to the State Police when he turned 21. (*Photo courtesy of Brenda Pierce Simpson*)

in Youngsville. That painting showed a doughboy crouching in a foxhole. The title is "No Atheists in a Foxhole." Brenda said some of his World War I paintings are at the Pennsylvania museum in Harrisburg. He also made pen-and-ink drawings, including the one shown in the centre section of this book. That and another oil painting shown in this book were on the wall of his grandson, David.

Harold Pierce lived in Hershey until 1983 when he went to live with Brenda in New Jersey. He died there August 30, 1983, and was buried next to Fern in Newton Cemetery in Grand Valley, Warren County, Pennsylvania.

Acknowledgements

I want to thank a bunch of people who helped bring this project to fruition. Chronologically, it starts with the staff at the Erie (Pennsylvania) County Historical Society – now the Hagen History Center – where my friend, George Deutsch, then the executive director, showed me some interesting paintings from the First World War that Corry VFW Post 264 had donated. At the time we didn't know who the painter was. A year or so later, the volunteer staff at the Corry Area Historical Society allowed me to copy the Harold W. Pierce diary clippings. The idea was to have one more reference for the book then under production by the Erie County World War One Centennial Committee, of which I was a part. That book is *Answering the Call: Erie County in World War One*. So now we knew Harold Pierce. At the Hagen History Center months later to photograph one of the paintings for possible use on the book cover, we discovered the painter was H.W. Pierce. It had to be the same person. Later, HHC curator Becky Weiser made the rest of the paintings available for photographing – no easy task with canvas that had been behind the frame for decades.

Enormous thanks go to Brenda Pierce Simpson, the daughter of H.W. Pierce. She graciously filled in the details of his extraordinary life. Her son, David, patiently photographed the art work that hung in his house.

Thanks also go to Arthur H. Mills II, my friend and former Mercyhurst University colleague, who read over my portions of this book and made some very helpful suggestions.

I'll use this space to mention the World War One veterans I interviewed during my journalism career: Carlisle Green, Byron Mackintosh and Felix Kruszewski from Company G of the 112th Infantry Regiment, and Alex Zalewski from the 318th Infantry Regiment, 80th Division.

Deepest thanks go to Patty, my patient wife. She wasn't sure sometimes whether I had really retired because she never saw me while I was planted in front of the computer working on this.

Index of Soldiers' Photos